Think, Act & Be Happy

Chicken Soup for the Soul: Think, Act & Be Happy
How to Use Chicken Soup for the Soul Stories to Train Your Brain to Be Your Own Therapist
Amy Newmark & Dr. Mike Dow

Published by Chicken Soup for the Soul, LLC www.chickensoup.com
Copyright ©2018 by Chicken Soup for the Soul, LLC. All Rights Reserved.

The publisher gratefully acknowledges the many publishers and individuals who granted Chicken Soup for the Soul permission to reprint the cited material.

Front cover photo credit for Dr. Mike Dow: Courtesy of Erik Johnson for E-Studios Photography

Cover and Interior by Daniel Zaccari

Distributed to the booktrade by Simon & Schuster. SAN: 200-2442

Publisher's Cataloging-In-Publication Data
(Prepared by The Donohue Group, Inc.)

Names: Newmark, Amy. | Dow, Mike.
Title: Chicken soup for the soul : think, act & be happy : how to use
    Chicken Soup for the Soul stories to train your brain to be your own
    therapist / Amy Newmark [and] Dr. Mike Dow.
Other Titles: Think, act & be happy : how to use Chicken Soup for the Soul
    stories to train your brain to be your own therapist | Think, act and
    be happy
Description: Cos Cob, CT : Chicken Soup for the Soul, LLC, [2018] |
    Summary: "Book combines true, personal Chicken Soup for the Soul
    stories with advice from New York Times bestselling psychoanalyst Dr.
    Mike Dow, who shows readers how to use the lessons in the stories to
    practice Cognitive Behavioral Therapy on themselves - how to train
    their brains to use the steps of CBT to act as their own therapists.
    Easy to follow steps complete with guided journal entries."--Provided
    by publisher.
Identifiers: ISBN 9781611599794 (print) | ISBN 9781611592795 (ebook)
Subjects: LCSH: Chicken soup for the soul. Selections--Psychological
    aspects. | Cognitive therapy--Handbooks, manuals, etc. | Behavior
    therapy--Handbooks, manuals, etc. | Self-help techniques--Handbooks,
    manuals, etc. | Self-management (Psychology)--Handbooks, manuals, etc.
    | Conduct of life--Literary collections. | Conduct of life--Anecdotes.
    | Happiness--Literary collections. | Happiness--Anecdotes. | LCGFT:
    Anecdotes.
Classification: LCC BF632 .N49 2018 (print) | LCC BF632 (ebook) | DDC
    158.1--dc23-dc23

Library of Congress Control Number: 2018906946

PRINTED IN THE UNITED STATES OF AMERICA
on acid∞free paper

25 24 23 22 21 20 19 18   01 02 03 04 05 06 07 08 09 10 11

Think, Act & Be Happy

How to Use
Chicken Soup for the Soul Stories
to Train Your Brain
to Be Your Own Therapist

Amy Newmark
Dr. Mike Dow

Chicken Soup for the Soul, LLC
Cos Cob, CT

Changing your life one story at a time ®
www.chickensoup.com

Table of Contents

Chicken Soup for the Soul Stories Included in This Book

Introduction

How to Use This Book to Train Your Brain

You know what's truly incredible about your brain? Whether you know it or not, you have the power to make it better every day. You can change it by the way you *think* — like reframing the way you look at something. When you make a simple decision — like doing volunteer work, you're changing your brain by the way you *act*. And, these everyday choices have the power to make you *happy…* really, really happy.

We're sure this isn't your first time reading a *Chicken Soup for the Soul* book. Chances are you've read a story in one that has really touched you. You probably caught yourself thinking, *I feel that way, too!*

Like all the other *Chicken Soup for the Soul* books, this one also contains the real-life stories you've grown to love. What's different about this book: We'll be taking you by the hand on a journey to improve *your* life while you're being touched by the stories from our writers. You'll learn how to *train your brain* to become *your own* therapist. Of course, if you're in therapy or in a support group — that's wonderful. This book can serve as a companion to all the great work you're already doing.

Here's how to use this book:

Step 1: Read the Chicken Soup for the Soul story or stories found in each chapter. Each chapter focuses on a specific issue — things like anxiety or dealing with chronic illness or learning how to use the power of forgiveness. If there is a particular issue you are dealing with today, feel free to skip ahead to the chapter you need most. You can always come back to the other chapters later. We're sure you'll find inspiration in *all* the chapters — even in those that may be addressing an issue that's not as important to you. After all, we're all human beings on this journey called life. The stories may be different but the truths and the lessons in these stories apply to all of us, no matter our specific circumstances.

Reading a relevant Chicken Soup for the Soul story is a bit like being in a support group. It reminds you that you are not alone. It's so much easier to change when you realize there are other people in your shoes. Maybe the way someone else felt was similar to the way you feel, and maybe you'll find strength and hope in his or her journey. It's also so nice to be reminded that healing , hope, and happy endings are possible. If they're possible for the real people in this book, that means they're possible for you, too.

Step 2: Dr. Mike will put on his therapist hat and explain what he sees in the story or stories that you have just read. And then he'll help you apply those lessons to your own life.

Step 3: Dr. Mike will talk you through some helpful cognitive behavioral tools at the end of each chapter. For example, guided journal entries in each chapter will help you to apply CBT tools to your life. Cognitive behavioral therapy — or CBT — is an incredibly effective therapy because it taps into the resources you already have within you. And, it has the power to actually change your brain. By doing so, you're becoming your own therapist.

CBT is actually quite simple. It has two main targets: it changes the way you *think* (the cognitive) and the way you *act* (the behavioral). At the end of every chapter, you'll see a section called "change *how you think*" and "change *how you act*." Grab a pen or pencil, because there will be a few questions for you to consider and answer.

***

Before you begin this journey, we'd like to take you through a quick introduction to CBT. Consider this Cognitive Behavioral Therapy 101, taught by your professor — Dr. Mike Dow.

The first thing is to understand that the way you *think* affects your life. Throughout this book, we'll help you change the way you think by calling attention to **seven common pitfall thought patterns** when they show up in other people's stories. People who think in these seven ways are more likely to experience dips in mood, along with pessimism and anxiety.

Here are the **seven pitfall thought patterns** and an example of how each one might sound:

1. Paralysis-analysis: Getting stuck or stewing in your own thoughts.

I still can't believe Becky made that comment to John last Friday at dinner. She is so insensitive. I should be working, but I can't stop thinking about this. You know what… I just thought about this time five years ago. Peggy said she said something similar then, I think.

2. Permanence: Using the past or present to judge the future.

I feel sad today. I'm never going to get over this divorce. I'll probably always feel this way.

3. Personalization: Assuming that something is happening because of you.

I didn't get that job because I'm not smart enough.

4. Pervasiveness: Allowing a problem in one area of your life to invade other parts of your life.

I had a bad day at work. I'm going to cancel my dinner plans and skip my yoga class tonight.

5. Pessimism: Always believing the worst about everything.

If I keep feeling this way, I'll probably have a panic attack when I'm driving and then I'll hit someone. How could I ever live with that guilt?

6. Polarization: Seeing everything as either/or, black/white, yes/no.

I had a piece of candy after lunch today. I guess today's healthy eating plan is a complete failure.

7. Psychic: Feeling sure that you know what another person is thinking without that person telling you how he or she feels. Or, vice-versa.

I can't believe my husband just did that. He should know how I feel about this!

We're going to show you how our story writers fell victim to the **seven pitfall thought patterns**, and then we'll help you see how one or more of them may be showing up in yours — and get rid of them.

To do this, you'll need to talk back to those negative thoughts! We'll help you do that with the guided journal entries at the end of each chapter. They're fun to fill out and they'll help you to find the **contrary evidence** in your life: all the times this naysaying pitfall thought pattern *wasn't* true. You've accomplished *so much* in your life. Isn't it about time you gave more space in your brain to what you've done *right* rather than dwelling on what's *wrong*?

The other half of CBT is changing your *behavior*. If you were talking to a therapist and you were afraid of a cat, your therapist would help you face your fear — one baby step at a time.

Step by step, you would actually teach your brain that you're no longer afraid of cats. You can do this with all sorts of fears and situations that may be holding you back — just by changing what you do in your everyday life. This book will teach you how to dream up those baby steps yourself so that you can use CBT to solve your own problems. You really do have the tools you need already, right inside your own brain.

By the time you finish reading this book and completing all the guided journal entries, you'll be holding something in your hands that will make you proud. This book will be like a badge of honor and your journal entries will be a record of your hard work.

There will be plentiful rewards for you to reap. When it comes to the way you **think**, you'll be more optimistic. When it comes to the way you **act**, you'll make healthier choices every day. When it comes to the way you *feel*, you'll **be happy**… and you'll know how to use your brain to stay that way! We'll show you how to **train your brain** to use these techniques no matter what issues come up in your life, because you really do have the right, the power, and the ability to act as your own therapist as you navigate the ups and downs of your life!

Chapter 1

Think, Act & Be Happy

Tips for Overcoming Depression

Freshman Orientation

Many of our fears are tissue-paper-thin, and a single
courageous step would carry us clear through them.
~Brendan Francis

"At this time, we ask that parents and students separate into two groups for the remainder of the day. Parents and students will be reunited at the conclusion of the campus tour."

Flocks of incoming freshmen happily abandon their parents upon hearing this announcement. I am less than thrilled at the prospect of starting college, let alone leaving my mother's side to tour the campus with the rest of the wide-eyed incoming freshmen.

"Okay Laur, I'll see you in a few hours, and remember, this is going to be a great experience for you!" Mom says, her big brown eyes alive with enthusiasm. I am amazed by my mother's resilience, considering what my family and I have been through during the past four years.

My mother disappears into a sea of overzealous parents who look as if they have ransacked the campus bookstore; many of the parents, to the embarrassment of their teenagers, are proudly sporting university attire with slogans like, "I'm a Sunny Brook University Dad."

We follow our senior tour guide. The other incoming students chatter and make casual introductions. I drag behind. How could I have believed I was ready for this? After all, it has only been a few months since I was discharged from the hospital. I am feeling better for the first time in years... but college?

My brooding is interrupted by a peppy voice. "Hi, I'm Jennifer."

The voice is attached to a freckle-faced blond girl dressed in what can only be described as hippy-like sports attire. For some strange reason, I like her immediately.

"I'm Lauren," I reply.

"Commuting or dorming?"

I fumble for my words, still caught up in my own thoughts. I would dorm, but I have spent the last four years overcoming a major depressive disorder that nearly claimed my life. I am still readjusting to living back home, in a place where I can come and go without asking for a "pass" or for a staff member to unlock the door to let me outside. I'm not quite sure I'm ready for this right now.

"I, uh, I don't know yet. My parents think I should dorm, but I don't really want to," I say in my most confident voice.

"You should definitely dorm! I'm going to, and I think it will be a lot of fun!"

I can't decide if Jennifer's enthusiasm is annoying or refreshing, but I decide to give her the benefit of the doubt. Before I can utter my less than enthusiastic reply, the tour guide announces that it is time to create our schedules.

We crowd into the Student Activity Center, or as the true, full-blown university students call it, the Sac, a nickname that immediately reminds me of the warm, safe bed at home I wish I were nestled in. We are ushered towards stiff, metal-backed chairs that hungrily await our freshman flesh. Three seniors hand out course bulletins as thick as textbooks, and slap registration forms down on the tables in front of us. All around me, papers crinkle and pencils scribble furiously. These sounds blare like an alarm clock, screaming "Wake up, Lauren!" Students seem to be moving through the process at rapid speed and I have not even opened my course catalog.

Focus, I tell myself. You can do this. Just read through the catalog and find the courses you like and a schedule that works. No big deal.

Intro to Psychology A or B, Foundations of Biology 2, Calculus, Geology 101, English, History, sections 1, 2, 3, 4, 5, 6, 7… the list goes on, and on, and on.

I begin to panic. How am I supposed to know what to do? I'm just relearning how to live in the real world again, and they want me to make a schedule?!

Other freshmen are handing in their materials, grinning as they rush out to meet their parents.

I cannot breathe, anxiety is coursing through my veins, and my head is pounding.

In moments, I am sobbing.

Other students abandon their tasks to stare at me, making me wish that the earth would open up and swallow me whole. One of the seniors in charge walks over to my table.

"What's the matter?" she asks gruffly.

"I... I can't do this!" I cry.

"All you have to do is make your schedule, just like everybody else," she says, clearly annoyed.

I cry harder. Then, a warm hand on my shoulder... Jennifer.

"Everything is alright," she tells the senior. "I'll help her."

The insensitive upperclassman walks away, and I feel the weight of the dozens of staring eyes lift. The other students quickly lose interest in the spectacle I've created and I can breathe again.

"What's wrong, sweetie?" Jennifer asks.

I am touched by this near stranger's concern. She hardly knows me, but seems to genuinely care.

Jennifer's kindness gives way to new tears. If crying were a major, I would have earned my doctorate in it by now.

"It is just too much; it is just too overwhelming," I say. "I… I have depression and I take medication."

Why did I say that? She probably thinks I am a freak now. But Jennifer puts her arm around me and her words reach out and wrap warmly around my soul.

"I know all about that sort of thing," she says. "My mother has depression. Besides, I think it's pretty normal to feel overwhelmed right now."

And with these words, just like that, the stigma of my mental illness is lifted for a moment and I am just a normal teenage girl with real fears about this exciting but frightening new adventure called "College."

The room is nearly empty now, and I still have no schedule. The pages before me are watermarked with tears.

Jennifer reaches out and gently places her hand on my arm. "Okay, so you said earlier you wanted to be a Psych major, right?"

And with that, this girl who was a stranger to me before this day guides me through the process, step-by-step, until I have everything in place and my schedule is complete. I am amazed at how much more clearly I can see now that the veil of anxiety and tears has lifted. "See," Jennifer tells me softly, "you knew exactly what to do—you just needed to believe in yourself."

That was the beginning of what would blossom into a powerful friendship. With a hug goodbye and a promise to keep in touch, we left Freshman Orientation with much more than our schedules. As I went to meet my mother, I decided that I would give living on campus a try... after all, I had come this far, and with a little help from a new friend, I had been reminded of the strength that existed in me. Four years later, as I graduated from the university with the distinction of magna cum laude, I looked back on Freshman Orientation, on all of my fears and insecurities, and smiled.

—Lauren Nevins—

Dr. Mike...

What emotions came up for you while reading Lauren's story? Maybe there was a sense of sadness at the story's beginning… because you knew this young lady was capable of so much more. Maybe you wanted to give Lauren a hug or tell her she was going to be alright.

Here's a mini-exercise to help you start training your brain: take all the faith you had in Lauren or the love you wanted to show toward her. Now, imagine you're giving some of that positive energy to yourself.

Remember when Lauren's new friend Jennifer was there to comfort her and make Lauren's experience feel normal? I wonder if this was a reminder: There are so many kind and loving people in this world, aren't there? And yes, it is normal to feel scared and overwhelmed when you're in a new situation. It's true for Lauren, and it's true for you. It's okay to feel these feelings.

They say you're as sick as your secrets, and it was just so incredible that Lauren was able to talk about her depression so openly. Isn't it incredible that Lauren's words *I… I have depression and I take medication* were met with *My mother has depression. Besides, I think it's pretty normal to feel overwhelmed right now.*

In many ways, it was Lauren's willingness to talk about her mental illness that allowed these two young ladies to connect. Isn't that so true for all of us? It's hard to connect with people who pretend to be perfect. Aren't our truest, deepest connections with the people who *aren't* perfect? Don't we all crave vulnerability in our relationships?

Lauren's words were also so empowering. Depression was no longer a dirty little secret, because she was saying it out loud. Speak your truth. By doing so, you're training your brain.

Maybe you've struggled with depression in your life. Maybe it was severe depression that required hospitalization and medication — as in Lauren's case. Or maybe it was just a passing case of the blues that just required a chat with a close friend.

Wherever you are on that spectrum, there are some cognitive behavioral tools that work wonders for all of us when depression rears its ugly head. Let's start with changing the way you *think*, move on to the way you *act*, and get you on your way to making yourself a bit more *happy*.

1. Change how you **THINK**

One pitfall thought pattern that often holds people with depression back is **permanence**. It creates the illusion that the way you feel now is the way you will always feel. And if you're having a bad day, **permanence** can also rob you of hope.

Let's look at the way **permanence** could have held Lauren back as she sobbed in the Student Activity Center when she started college. Lauren felt panicked. She felt overwhelmed. It clearly wasn't the way she wanted this day to go.

The problem with **permanence** is that when we're feeling sad, our brains actually light up all the other sad memories from our past. This creates the illusion that our life has always been sad. It also creates the false feeling that our life will always be sad.

If you're depressed, this takes away your hope... and your light. If you're going through a divorce or grieving a loss, it may even feel like you will never be happy again. Don't believe that feeling. Feelings aren't facts. They change. The proof? Well... Let's get the evidence we need from *your* brain.

What's an experience in my life that I thought I would never recover from... but did?

_____

_____

_____

Does reflecting on this help me remember that gray skies pass... even when it feels like it will stay cloudy forever? If so, how?

_____

_____

_____

If I remembered this, I think depression or "blue moments" would be different because...

_____

_____

_____

Thank goodness Lauren didn't let **permanence** hold her back in her life. If she gave into the pitfall thought pattern **permanence**, she would have given up... and never graduated *magna cum laude*. Well done, Lauren!

2. Change how you ACT

Here's where the *behavioral* part of cognitive behavioral therapy comes in. This is all about changing what you do (AKA how you *act*).

When you're sad or blue, it often feels really difficult to do all the tasks you need to do. It may feel easier to just stay in bed watching TV all day. And, you may isolate yourself. By doing so, you probably aren't doing all the things that used to bring you joy or pleasure.

While this is what most of us *want* to do when we feel low, this also can create a downward spiral. One blue morning turns into a whole day on the couch. You don't get anything done, and you cancel all your fun evening plans that you used to love to do.

As counterintuitive as it feels, we're going to use a behavioral strategy to help shake you from the depression as quickly as possible. You're going to do the *opposite* of what you *want* to do.

Instead of sitting on the couch when you feel blue, you are going to do one thing every day that is either **productive** or **pleasurable**.

A **productive** task could be something as simple as emptying the dishwasher or going to the grocery store. It could be a bigger task like finishing that big project from work.

A **pleasurable** activity is something that you enjoy. It could be something just for you… like a warm bath. Or, it could be a dinner at your favorite restaurant with friends. Activities that connect you with people you love are the best **pleasurable** activities to choose, because you're building relationships while finding enjoyment.

And connection is an antidote to the isolation that goes hand in hand with depression. Even if it feels like you're forcing yourself at first, I bet you'll probably crack at least *one* real smile at that dinner with your best friend. (Did you ever hear of the Botox happiness study? People who couldn't frown were happier, because when your face is happy… you're happy. All you need to do is go to dinner… not the dermatologist!)

In part of her efforts to overcome depression, Lauren filled her days with all those Calculus, Foundations of Biology 2, and History classes. Some challenging stuff. But her college days were chock-full of **productivity**. Talk about brain training!

I'm going to go out on a limb here, but I'd imagine her four years in college were filled with a **pleasurable** moment or two. I'd guess Jennifer was the first of many friends Lauren made.

We all know how Lauren filling her days with **productivity** and **pleasurable** turned out for her. She's an inspiration to us all. Despite a serious case of depression, she filled her days with the stuff of life. What will *you* fill *yours* with?

Here are 5 **productive** go-to tasks I can choose to fill my day with the next time I feel blue:

1. _____

2. _____

3. _____

4. _____

5. _____

Circle one task you will do today… Now, *train your brain* by going out and *doing it!*

Here are 5 **pleasurable** activities I enjoy that I will choose from the next time I feel low:

1. _____

2. _____

3. _____

4. _____

5. _____

Circle the one activity you will do today… Now, feel better *and* train your brain by doing this activity!

3. BE HAPPY

Chapter 2

Think, Act & Be Happy

Use Gratitude to Become an Optimist

Sometimes It Takes a Child

If we experienced life through the eyes of a child
everything would be magical and extraordinary.
~Akiane Kramarik

Our savings were wiped out and there was nothing we could do. We were going to lose our house. Joe wouldn't even look at me. "I guess we'll have to move into Grandpa's old house."

Grandpa Mac's little house had been old and in disrepair when he was living. Now that the place had been empty for more than five years I shuddered to think how much worse it would be. But the construction firm Joe had worked at as a foreman had gone bankrupt a year ago and he had not found a new job.

We had managed to scrape by for a while with Joe's unemployment benefits and our savings. But those days were over. I had given up the privilege of being a stay-at-home mom and found a job in retail that barely paid for groceries and daycare for our daughter, Kelly.

I couldn't bear the pain in Joe's eyes now. He has always taken pride in being able to take care of Kelly and me. He loved coming home from work to Kelly flinging herself into his arms and me in the kitchen making dinner. Now Kelly was running to me when I came home from work while Joe watched with his head hanging low. He thought it was his fault that my feet hurt and my back ached from standing for hours at the cash register. He served us simple suppers while Kelly whined, "When is Mama going to make lasagna again?"

We both tried to be cheerful around Kelly as we packed to move. She was only three. As long as we didn't send her the wrong cues she wouldn't notice the poor condition of her new home.

We splurged with the last of our savings and bought paint for Grandpa Mac's house. He had been a widower for many years before he died and he had done nothing to keep the house up. I suppose without Grandma he just didn't have the will or the energy. It might have been foolish to use the last of our money in this way, but after inspecting the old house we just couldn't bear to move in to it without at least trying to make it look a bit more cheerful.

We let Kelly choose the color for her new room, knowing that it would be some shade of pink. When we showed her the color chart I held my breath, hoping she would pick one of the lighter shades. Of course she wanted the gaudiest shade of pink available. "She likes the Pepto-Bismol pink." Joe said, grinning as he shook his head.

"What's Pepto-Bismol?" Kelly asked, not knowing what to make of our rueful smiles.

"Oh, it's pretty girl pink," the salesman said, giving Kelly a warm smile. "That's what I'd call it." So Kelly got her "pretty girl pink" room and she thought it was absolutely lovely. At least one person was happy in Grandpa Mac's house.

The shingles on the roof were dry and curled at the edges and threatened to leak at any moment. Hundreds of thousands of footsteps had worn the finish off the hardwood floors and they squeaked as if in protest that they were being trod on again after all these years. The countertops were scarred and stained and one of the doors on the kitchen cabinets was warped and would not close so it stood perpetually ajar. Worst of all, the white paint on the house's exterior was brittle and cracked but there was nothing we could do about that.

One evening, as I stood at the kitchen window looking out at the back yard, Joe came up behind me and put his arms around me. "It isn't that bad, is it?"

I frowned at the unkempt flowerbeds that had gone to seed years ago, at the bare spots in the lawn that became mud puddles when it rained, and at the sagging corner of the back porch. "It is, actually," I said as I slipped out of his embrace.

One evening, I walked out into the back yard to escape the heavy heat in the house. Naturally there wasn't any air conditioning — not even a window unit. The one redeeming feature of the house was the leaning wooden fence that allowed Kelly to play outside safely.

Kelly was busy picking the dandelions that grew profusely in the yard. She grinned when she saw me and ran over to give me a bright yellow bouquet. She plopped down beside me on the bottom step and said, "I like our new house, Mommy. We have pretty yellow flowers in the yard. Most people just have grass."

She looked around the yard, beaming. "We have an apple tree and I can get one whenever I want. There are baby birds in one of the trees. And I hear the birds singing every morning when I wake up." Her eyes shifted to the lantana bush in the corner that was filled with butterflies of different colors. "We have a lot of pretty butterflies."

Just then we heard a loud rapping sound and Kelly squealed with delight. "And we have a woodpecker in that tall tree over there. I'll bet nobody else has a woodpecker living in their yard." She hugged her knees. "We even have a fence so I can play outside whenever I want." She wound her little arms around my waist. "I think this must be the best place in the whole world to live."

Later, when Joe came in from job hunting, he looked more relaxed than I had seen him in a long time. "I don't want to get your hopes up only to disappoint you," he said. "But I think I will be hearing back from Jones Construction. My interview went well and I have a good feeling about this one. Maybe we won't be stuck in Grandpa's old house much longer."

"It's not that bad." I said. "There's no rush. We should probably stay here at least until we have replaced our savings."

Joe looked incredulous. "Did you say it's not that bad?"

"It isn't," I said, laughing. Relief swept over his face when he saw that I meant it. It took a three-year-old to teach me how to see the blessings in our new home. There's always something to be grateful for no matter what situation you are in. You just have to look.

— Elizabeth Atwater —

Waiting for Kira

*Hope is the companion of power, and the mother of
success; for who so hopes strongly has within
him the gift of miracles.*
~Samuel Smiles

"I dreamt of the baby again," I told Mike, my husband. "She was beautiful." It was a muggy day, and we were outside on the stone patio of our cozy home in Atlanta. It looked like it might rain. We were enjoying the last drops of our morning tea (and possibly the last of the day's dry weather) when I remembered a detail. "She had your green eyes. Oh Mike, she looked just like you!" Mike looked at me for a moment, uncharacteristically at a loss for words, and then rolled away in his wheelchair. I rolled inside after him.

Mike's accident left him a paraplegic, but he has use of his strong upper body. I was not as lucky when I fell off a horse in my twenties. Most people think of Christopher Reeve when they hear the words quadriplegic, but my injury is known as a C-567 injury. I have limited mobility in my hands and arms and some feelings below my waist. Like Mike, I am able to get around in a wheelchair. A retrofitted steering wheel allows me to drive a van. For the most part, we lead fairly normal lives.

That didn't mean we could easily get pregnant. We would need to go through in vitro fertilization. We would also need a gestational surrogate…. and perhaps, a miracle.

Our lives up to that point were peppered with miracles, so Mike worried that it was a little greedy to ask for yet another one. It was miracle enough we were at this point: married and living together.

When Mike and I met at a wheelchair race in Florida, we had been living on different continents: He lived in England; I lived in South Carolina. Somehow, we persevered beyond our injuries and beyond our long-distance relationship. Years later, here we were, married and not afraid of a challenge. Which was what I told Mike on that warm July day. "Why not try for another miracle?"

Mike did not need convincing. "You are right. Why don't we call that doctor you read about?" he said.

I had read about a doctor who had helped other women with spinal cord injuries. I had studied his picture on the website. Dr. Toledo had salt-and-pepper hair and kind looking blue eyes. Before I could change my mind, I dialed the number and made an appointment.

In person, Dr. Toledo did not disappoint. Where other doctors had been discouraging, he offered us hope. "Shannon, I would not advise you to try and carry the pregnancy. There are wonderful options available for surrogacy should you…" We interrupted him. "Don't worry, Dr. Toledo," we told him. "We have a surrogate in mind."

Mike's sister Julie had offered to carry the baby — a generous offer considering she lived in England. Plans fell into place.

We started the process in high spirits, but over time, our hopes and dreams began to evaporate, one failed IVF after the other. Eventually we ran out of time. Julie returned to England, dejected. We were back in limbo.

Only this time limbo felt more like an abyss. For the first time in my life, I fell into a deep depression, unlike anything I experienced when I was first injured. That had been devastating, but this felt all together more primal: utter desolation.

I had always imagined myself as a mother. Beyond my own worries, I felt awful for Mike. This had been his biggest fear. "Shannon, the only time I cried after my accident was when the doctor told me I would never be a father," he had told me when we met. I talked to God: Lord, he is such a loving man. Why would You deny him the opportunity to be a dad?

For months, I fell asleep praying. I turned over the details like a puzzle to be solved, hitting the same walls and obstacles every time.

Our biggest concern at that point was the toll on Julie, who had left her life in England, camped out at our home for months and allowed herself to be subjected to more needles than a pincushion. How could we ask her to do that again?

One night, an idea germinated. The doctor never said I was unable to carry a baby. They only advised against it. What if, instead of Julie, I was the one to carry the embryos?

I prayed. "All you have to conquer is your fear," I heard in my head. That morning, I woke up and started researching. I spent the day on Google. The more I read about the success rate for other women with similar injuries, the more I believed it might be okay.

Dr. Toledo, by this point, had become a trusted friend. He was at a Falcons game when I reached him. "Can I carry our baby?" I yelled over the din, not thinking as to how that might have sounded on the other end. Over the noise of the crowd, I heard him hesitate, only for a second, before he answered. "Of course, but let's give some consideration to the risks — come in and see me."

Having been given a cautionary yellow light by Dr. Toledo, I moved forward with green light determination. "I'm going to carry our baby," I announced to Mike. Used to my occasional flair for the dramatic, Mike looked at me a second before responding. "Are you serious?" I excitedly told him what I had been thinking, the research I had done. We discussed the pros and cons, and in the end, we both decided to try it at least once.

"All you have to do is conquer your fears."

Weeks later, the phone rang. The caller ID indicated it was the clinic. "Shannon?" "Yes?" I answered breathlessly and put the phone on speaker so Mike could hear. "Mike is here too," I said to Dr. Toledo. I could tell by his tone the news was going to be good. His happiness radiated over the phone. "You are going to be parents!" he said. The tears streamed down our faces.

The pregnancy went forth without any complications and the months went by quickly. The delivery room was like a party — my family was there. Mike's family had flown in from England. There was a team of doctors on hand. All around the room, I saw smiling faces. Our child would be welcomed into this world with an overabundance of love.

At 11:30 p.m., Kira Francklin came into this world. I examined my newborn baby from head to toe and all I saw was her uncanny resemblance to her dad. I thought back to that dream, the sleepless nights and that moment when peace had come over me, telling me not to be afraid.

God had provided His best miracle yet.

— Shannon Francklin —

Dr. Mike...

think Kelly reminded her mom of a simple and important lesson we all tend to forget when she said: *We even have a fence so I can play outside whenever I want… I think this must be the best place in the whole world to live.* Oh, how wise kids can be!

It seems that to learn the most important lessons in this world, we have to *unlearn* some of the lessons we're taught in grown-up land. Every day, ads tell us to buy *this* new car and *that* expensive watch if we want to be happy.

Luckily, Elizabeth's daughter Kelly was too busy enjoying life's simple pleasures to buy into those messages. The dandelions, baby birds, and apple tree found in her new back yard reminded her: the best things in life really are free.

Shannon and Mike are teachers as well. I'm not making light of their tragic accidents. But their happiness together is a real-life testament to something found in research: your life situation doesn't matter as much as you think it does. Your *outlook* does.

As much as most of us have dreamed of what we'd buy or do if we became ridiculously rich one day, winning the lottery doesn't make an unhappy person happy. After a short-term bump in happiness, an unhappy *poor* person who wins the lottery eventually just becomes an unhappy *rich* person.

Maybe you've experienced this "short-term" bump yourself. Do you remember the first time you had a new car or sweater? Remember how special it felt for a few months? When you get in that car now, does it feel any different than your last new car? Did it change your life? How long did it take for it to feel just like any other car or sweater?

Here's a way you can win the "happiness lottery" today… and keep on winning it each and every day. By using this little exercise, you can train your brain.

Maybe you're living in a rundown house. Or maybe you're sitting in a living room that really needs one of those HGTV-style makeovers. Make your house or living room "the best place in the whole world to live" simply by shifting your perspective.

Imagine you're putting on a pair of glasses that only allows you to see "what's right" in *your* life. Kelly wore these glasses to see those baby birds… not the rundown yard her mom saw at first. Mike and Shannon wore these glasses as they saw the possibility of what was possible for two people in love who wanted to start a family… when they could have seen themselves as two accident victims held back by paralysis.

So, what do you see? What did your magic glasses show you about what's right in your life?

Now, imagine what would change in your life if you kept these glasses on for an entire day… or a year. Maybe they'll allow you to create possibilities that other people would scoff at. Elizabeth used her own mind to do an "internal makeover" of that house without any contractor, and just look at the life Mike and Shannon created for themselves!

If you keep these magic glasses on, they may end up saving your life.

One study followed people with cancer. After one year, the "optimists" were more likely to be alive than people considered to be "pessimists." The way we see the world has a real and profound effect inside our bodies, our brains, and in our everyday lives.

1. Change how you THINK

One pitfall thought pattern we need to banish is **pessimism**. When **pessimism** rears its ugly head, you may be tempted to put those "what's wrong" glasses back on.

You may even take the "what's wrong" and run with it. In these cases, **pessimism** gives way to its cousins: worst-case-scenario and catastrophic thinking.

In this case, Elizabeth may have even started thinking that her grandfather's house wasn't just run down. Maybe it would collapse on her and her whole family!

A wonderful antidote to **pessimism** is gratitude.

Now, I'm going to teach you a scientifically proven way to boost gratitude.

First, get specific about your gratitude. *I'm so grateful for all my friends* becomes *I'm so grateful for my two best friends Carol and Kathy, because they really were there for me when my mom passed away. They really bring so much light into my life every single week!*

Using that simple word *because* in your reflections on gratitude can be helpful.

Transform **pessimism** into optimism through the power of specific gratitude.

What three things are you really grateful for today?

1. I'm grateful for: _____

because: _____

2. I'm grateful for: _____

because: _____

3. I'm grateful for: _____

because: _____

2. Change how you ACT

The incredible thing about gratitude is that it actually shifts you into an abundance mentality. I've found that the more you're grateful for, the more good things you tend to create and attract in your life.

Gratitude is a Jedi mind trick, because it helps you to be happy *now* and happy *later*. Remember when Joe was about to get that great new job? They could have moved right away, but Elizabeth surprised him when she said, *There's no rush. We should probably stay here at least until we have replaced our savings.*

Elizabeth was happy with the house they were in then, and she'd be happy with a nicer house later. Talk about a win-win situation.

Her mindset shift allowed them to make more responsible choices.

Imagine what a fantastic house they'll have one day… and how much happier she'll be with it. The alternative: an always-needing-to-keep-up-with-the-Joneses and never-happy-with-what-you-have mentality. You become a rabbit running on a treadmill with a carrot attached to a string. That carrot is always just out of reach.

And Mike and Shannon's mindset shift helped them to be grateful and have faith. They found each other. And now, they're parents.

What will *you* create with your attitude of gratitude? What's a goal you have for yourself?

And what will change in the way you approach your day? Will these optimistic thoughts lead to a visible change in your **actions**? Is there a change in mindset or attitude that will make this goal easier to attain?

Will you wake up easily tomorrow morning with gratitude for the job you have instead of pressing snooze three times… dreading the day ahead of you? Will you have a little more pep in your step as you see all the great blessings you already have? Will all this positivity help you smile just a little more today?

What are your goals? Think about one of them and imagine one visible **action** that an attitude shift would enable you to take.

One goal I have for myself is:

_____

and a visible **action** or attitude shift I will make in my daily life is to:

_____

_____

_____

3. BE HAPPY

Chapter 3

Stress Less and Embrace Your Calm

It's Not the End of the World

*The greatest weapon against stress is our ability
to choose one thought over another.*
~Author Unknown

People say I was born standing up and haven't relaxed since. I was a nervous, worried child who often broke out in hives over things other children seemed to take in stride. I was desperately anxious to please people and failure resulted in crushing self-recrimination. When I was five years old and forced to play a difficult piece of music in a piano recital, I was terrified of not playing it well enough. I walked across the stage and became violently ill, putting an end to the recital before I'd played one note. A few years later I was in a school play and the bright footlights blinded me — I walked off the stage and took a nosedive into the audience.

I became so afraid of failing and humiliating myself in front of people that I started avoiding social events. What if I said the wrong thing, spilled something, or made a fool of myself? Something as simple as going to a birthday party would cause me so much stress that I'd hide in my bedroom to keep from going.

Early in my childhood I had decided the universe was an unfriendly place and was out to get me. I exaggerated my problems. I felt overwhelmed and unable to cope. The smallest thing could almost paralyze me.

I avoided people as much as possible because I believed people were the cause of my stress. Of course, that didn't work. I still had stress in my life but now I was lonely as well.

One day when I was walking to the store, I tripped on the curb and fell onto my knees. An elderly man came to my aid, helped me to my feet and asked if I was hurt.

"No, I think I'm alright. I'm just shaken up and a little embarrassed," I said.

"Well, if you didn't break your knees, then it isn't the end of the world, is it? There's no reason to be embarrassed. We all fall down sometimes. You're okay now," he said, and walked away.

His words rang in my head like a big bell. I'd had a little fall, and yes, I did feel foolish, but I didn't break my knees and it wasn't the end of the world. I realized I didn't have a single problem in my life that would either break my knees or cause the world to come to an end.

Suddenly everything was put into perspective and none of my problems seemed that big anymore. Most of my problems were in the future — very few had to be faced that day or even that week.

I began writing down the things that were troubling me the most: debts, money, family problems, the funny noise under the hood of my car. No matter how big or how small the problem was, I'd write it on a piece of paper and I'd put the piece of paper into a box. On the last day of the month I'd open the box and read the list of my "terrible" problems. I found that almost all of my troubles never happened at all. Or if they had happened, they weren't as bad as I thought they would be or the situation had solved itself without any action from me. The universe didn't need my help. It was a huge relief not to be in charge of the universe anymore. I didn't have to be perfect. It's okay to make mistakes; it's okay to be wrong; it's okay not to have all the answers. It's okay to fail; in fact, it's okay to fail magnificently, gloriously and spectacularly.

Over time, I've put fewer and fewer notes into the box, and some months the box stays empty. It isn't that I don't have problems or that I don't worry or get upset. I still get stressed over things. But I've come to realize that very few things are worth getting upset over, and nothing is ever as bad as I thought it was going to be.

When a new problem comes into my life, I ask myself if it is the end of the world or if it is going to break my knees. If the answer is "no," I write it down and put it in the box.

I'm grateful to that old man; he was only in my life for a minute or two but he changed my life forever. I feel I have cut the stress in my life by eighty percent. I've started going out more, I've made some new friends, and I feel like a new person. I recently played the piano at a party and discovered I'm really bad at it. It's okay — I made everyone laugh and I laughed with them. I'm not afraid of social events or being with people anymore. If I make a mistake or spill something or even fall flat on my face, well, we all fall down sometimes and it's NOT the end of the world!

—April Knight—

Bite by Bite

*Remember that stress doesn't come from what's going
on in your life. It comes from your thoughts about
what's going on in your life.*
~Andrew J. Bernstein

"Mom, I can't do this." My teenage son Bret stood in front
of me with his hands outstretched, full of papers.

"Can't do what?" I half-looked at him while preparing supper.

"All this!" He waved his hands up and down to show me. "There's
no way I can do everything my teachers are asking me to do!"

I stopped what I was doing and turned to face him. I had never seen
him so upset. He was my jovial, carefree son. He made good grades in
school and nothing ever seemed to bother him. As I studied his face, I
could see tears brimming in his eyes accompanying the look of panic.

Walking over to the kitchen table, I sat down and motioned him
to join me.

"Show me what you have to do."

Bret plopped down in a chair and dropped the papers in a stack
in front of him.

"Ms. Jones, my chemistry teacher, wants me to make a project
for the Science Fair."

"Okay. And what else?"

"I have an algebra test next week that will be one-third of our
semester grade!"

I knew how Bret hated algebra, which always gave him trouble.

"And I have to write an essay for English composition. And mid-
terms are the next week! I need to study for them and I have to get
help with Spanish. There's no way I can do everything!"

His hands shook as he picked up each assignment. It broke my heart to see him so stressed out. I wanted to help him, yet I couldn't do the work for him. I could relate to his dilemma though.

In my job as a sales manager, there had been many stressful times. Caught in the middle, I had to please upper management by producing results from my sales team as well as deal with ten individuals who each had concerns with making their quotas, taking care of their customers and personal issues.

I was particularly stressed out when I had to plan a sales meeting for the company. At that time, I was in charge of the agenda, setting up the presentations, arranging the people who would participate, ordering supplies, and so on. My performance was on the line and under the closest scrutiny at these times.

As much as I wanted to run away and hide from the responsibility, I knew I had to handle it. And even though I had my doubts about the outcome, I wanted things to run well. How did I handle it and not implode? I made a list. I listed everything that had to be done, then I put a deadline on each item and organized the list according to what had to be done first, second, and so on.

Back in the kitchen, I looked at Bret and said, "You don't have to do everything at once. You can do one at a time. Let's make a list of what you need to do."

So, one by one, we listed each item. Then we put the due date next to the item. Next we separated the items into parts; for instance, the chemistry project needed supplies. So we put a deadline on getting the supplies. He had a friend who could help him with Spanish, so we had to factor that time in. As we worked on prioritizing the tasks, I saw my son visibly relax.

When we finished with the list, I asked, "Do you think you can do this now?"

He smiled and I saw his confidence return. "Sure! Thanks, Mom!"

From that day on, Bret made lists for everything he had to do. I had to laugh when I saw lists on pieces of paper lying around, but I knew the process worked for him, as it did for me. Bret completed all his assignments and kept his good grades.

There's an adage that asks, "How do you eat an elephant?" The answer is, "One bite at a time."

— Marilyn Turk —

Dr. Mike...

Research shows that we have become more stressed than ever before. Anxiety disorders are the most commonly diagnosed mental illness in the U.S.—and around the world. How do we stress less and embrace our inner calm?

For April, the antidote to stress was all about *perspective*.

That nice man's comment changed the way April saw the world.

Well, if you didn't break your knees, then it isn't the end of the world, is it?

What a great brain-training reframe! For April, that helped to loosen her from the need to be perfect and to control everything in her life.

Did you know you can train your brain to release a lesser amount of stress hormones? You see, the way you *interpret* your experiences determines the amount of brain-draining stress hormones your body will release. If something *is* the end of the world, it's going to release *a lot* of adrenaline and cortisol—in an effort to help get you through a stressor.

But if you have trained your brain to perceive something as *not a huge deal* or *I'll get through this*, then you can actually prevent a tidal-wave surge of stress hormones.

When April revisited all those things that had been troubling her the most, she realized that one of three things happened:

(a) most of her troubles never happened at all

(b) the ones that had happened weren't as bad as she thought they'd be

(c) many situations solved themselves without any action on her part

April realized: *The universe didn't need my help. It was a huge relief not to be in charge of the universe anymore. I didn't have to be perfect.*

Kids are under more and more pressure to be "perfect" these days, too. Whether it's the scrutiny of social media or the increasing competition to get into college, stress levels run high. Even seven-, eight-, and nine-year-olds need to learn how to take a breath.

Marilyn knew she was going to have to help her son Bret find his inner calm.

And so, she taught her son a few valuable lessons that helped him manage his stress.

The first was to *lean into stress — don't run away from it.* Remember that a little stress can actually sharpen the brain. And every time you lean into it, you're actually making your brain bigger, better, and more resilient.

This was a lesson Marilyn had learned in her own career: *As much as I wanted to run away and hide from the responsibility, I knew I had to handle it.*

By *handling it,* she was training her brain. Marilyn became even better at her job, and she probably realized just how competent she was. In the future, she'd probably have *less* stress. After all, tolerating a small amount of stress in the short-term meant that stress would affect her less in the long run.

I loved when she helped her son break down his unclimbable mountain into a bunch of small molehills. The big task was now just a series of microtasks with specific, measurable, achievable, relevant, and time-sensitive (SMART) goals.

Chemistry project is due next Friday. Check. That means I'll need to get the supplies for that project Monday after school, and I'll have that week to finish it. *Check.*

Whether it's you or your child, leaning into those micro-chunks of stress may help you work in an easy and effortless way. You may not even notice the moment when your stress about a particular project has completely melted away.

1. Change how you THINK

A pitfall thought pattern that can make stress levels skyrocket is **polarization**. This all-or-nothing, black-or-white, perfectionistic way of thinking sets a very high bar. Anything less than *Guinness Book of Records*–performance becomes a failure.

In fact, that's the way it often sounds in our heads:

If I'm not a complete success, I'm a complete failure.
or
If it's not perfect, it's worthless.

or

The best or nothing.

Now, imagine that you have a little box — just like April did. In this box, I want you to write five things that you *used* to worry about. These are worries that have since resolved themselves in one way or another. For April, those stressors included debts, money, family problems, and the funny noise her car was making.

List five of your old worries that have now been resolved:

1. _____

2. _____

3. _____

4. _____

5. _____

Now, consider *how* those five worries got resolved. Was it because:
a) it never happened at all
b) it wasn't as bad as I thought it would be
c) it solved itself without any action on my part

Put an a, b, or c next to each of the five old worries above.

Now, consider a current worry of yours that involves some sort of polarized thinking. Is it work-related? Or is it family-related? Write it down here:

_____

How do you imagine this worry will get solved? Look at a, b, and c on the prior page. Which of those resolutions is the most likely outcome for your current worry?

_____

2. Change how you ACT

When Marilyn helped Bret separate his assignment into small, achievable tasks, she was also helping him use an incredible, brain-training tool: *mindfulness.*

Mindfulness is simply the act of paying attention to the one thing you're doing in the present moment. When Bret focused his attention on the *one* thing he needed to do next, Marilyn noticed that he became visibly relaxed.

With small tasks, your brain can simply stay focused on the *one thing* you are doing *right now.* After all, *this moment* is the *only moment your life is unfolding,* isn't it?

Did you know that brain scans show that when you think you're *multitasking,* what you're really doing is rapidly single-tasking and switching rapidly. And, you lose time, productivity, and brain power switching back and forth.

Here's a little exercise I call *the mindful way to work.* Consider all the things you need to do tomorrow. Write ten of those tasks in order of importance. The most important thing that *needs to get done* will be #1. Less important tasks will be at the bottom of the list.

1. _____

2. _____

3. _____

4. _____

5. _____

6. _____

7. _____

8. _____

9. _____

10. _____

When you wake up tomorrow, all you need to do is give *all your attention* to #1. Be mindful. Focus on that task—and only that. Finish it. Then, cross it off your list.

Then, mindfully focus your attention on #2. And so on and so forth.

Anything that doesn't get done tomorrow can simply become part of the next day's list. And if new tasks come up, you can also decide where they fit in terms of priority. It's okay to let them "cut the line" and go before one of your planned tasks. There's always the next day.

One bite, one task, and one day at a time.

3. BE HAPPY

Chapter 4

Think, Act & Be Happy

Weight Loss that Works

Overcoming Obesity

*The power to achieve the extraordinary is within each
and every one of us. Believe that you can, work harder
than everyone else, and never, ever give up!*
~Heidi Powell

I remember the moment I realized I was an emotional eater. I was angry with my husband about one thing or another, and I found myself in the kitchen stuffing my face with chocolate chip cookies. It was like I was having an out-of-body experience. I saw myself... and it wasn't pretty.

I realized at that moment that I was destroying myself because I was angry with someone else. Whenever I was happy, sad, or angry I would eat. I ate myself to more than 300 pounds.

That day I saw what I was doing to myself, but it felt so overwhelming, so impossible to change. I did not change that day. In fact, I continued the cycle for three more years.

Then, a couple of things happened. The first was when I was eight months pregnant with my third child. At my prenatal checkup my doctor said, "You cannot gain any more weight!" I was 328 pounds. She gave me some suggestions. "Cut back on white carbohydrates and sugar." That is what I did... after shedding some tears and wondering how I was going to do it. In the last few weeks of my pregnancy I lost twelve pounds.

But then after having the baby, and all that comes with recovering from a C-section, I started eating again. My husband was taking care of meals and I just ate what he made.

The second thing that happened finally got me to change.

My new baby boy was three months old and some of the older ladies at church were admiring him. "He's gonna be a big boy like his mama!" one lady said.

"I wasn't always big," I said.

"Oh really?" she said, and she sounded so surprised.

At that moment, I had my "aha" moment. You see, my mom is obese, and her mom before her was obese, and I don't know for sure, but I could imagine that her mom before her was obese, and so on. It infuriated me that someone just assumed that I was always fat, and that this boy was going to take after me and be fat, too. Nope. Not going to happen. I would not do that to my children! I decided at that moment that I was going to break the cycle of obesity in my family.

That Monday I began a journey. I cut out carbohydrates and sugar. It wasn't easy. I'm an Italian girl. We eat pasta and bread at every meal, pizza every Friday! But, I had to do this. I made up my mind. I told myself that I had eaten enough of those things in my thirty-five years of living that if I never ate them again I still had eaten a lifetime's worth of them!

I wanted to put things in perspective. I told myself that even if I only lost one pound a week, I would be down fifty-two pounds in a year! But, if I gave up, I would be once again saying "I should've" and "I wish I had..." at the end of the year.

You can't start a journey like this and say, "I'm going to lose 150 pounds." You will fail. Who can lose 150 pounds? That is too overwhelming! My goals were to be a better "me" each day. I told myself, "I am going to put healthy food into my body *today*. I am going to move more than I sit *today*." I started by asking my husband if I could mow the grass instead of him. Baby steps.

There is a big picture. We tend to see only what's right in front of us. I didn't set out two decades ago and say, "Hmm, I think I'd like to be over 300 pounds one day. I am going to eat without restraint and become totally inactive." It took me years to put on that weight, and even if it took a few years to take it off, that was okay. I was still improving, still bettering myself. Still becoming a healthier version of myself.

I wanted to be a better example for my three kids. I wanted to be someone they could emulate, someone they would be proud to call "Mommy." Now, kids don't really know the difference when they are young. And I know my mom has always been the most beautiful woman to me; her weight never mattered. But for me, and for the sake of my family, I needed to press on.

I set small, reasonable, attainable goals for myself and celebrated every one of them! But not with food! Every time I refused cake or cookies or chips, I felt stronger! I could do this! It was possible! I could envision my future self, and that was the image that I pictured in my mind as I was exercising.

It has been two and a half years since I started my journey and I have lost 150 pounds! I did it one decision at a time. Not one day, not one week… solely one decision at a time. I learned to say "no thank you" one decision at a time.

This is my body; I control what goes in it! I am thrilled to say that at age thirty-seven I feel healthier than I did at seventeen! I can say things to my kids like "race you to the car!" I take them for walks and bike rides, and I can go down the slide with them at the playground! My life isn't limited anymore. My daughter, who is five, said to me the other day, "Mommy, I didn't know you could run that fast!" Baby, I didn't either! I am still discovering my strength and all my body can do!

In the words of A. A. Milne, "You are braver than you believe, stronger than you seem, and smarter than you think."

— Gina Tate —

Dr. Mike...

I don't know about you, but if you're like most of us — your emotions sometimes affect the way you eat. Gina said she ate when she was happy *or* sad, so her emotional eating was sometimes tied to both good and bad moods. Culturally, so many of us have learned to use food to celebrate life's highs (e.g., wedding cake) as well as life's lows (e.g., ice cream on the couch after a bad day). Has this ever been true for you?

One helpful exercise is to stop and ask yourself if your hunger is "above the neck" or "below the neck" hunger. Hunger that is "above the neck" is coming from your *brain* or your emotional state. You may have just eaten a large meal an hour ago. Yet, sadness, disappointment, or boredom leads you to the kitchen. This kind of hunger tends to come on suddenly.

On the other hand, "below the neck" hunger originates in your *stomach*. It tends to come on more slowly and builds hours after your last meal. One of the things that helped Gina was learning to identify when she was eating based on emotional/above the neck hunger versus physical/below the neck hunger.

Use this as a tool to stop for a moment the next time you get the urge to eat. Ask yourself: Where is my hunger coming from? By doing so, you are training your brain.

If it's emotional/above the neck hunger, then choose an *activity* that will help you resolve this feeling. After all, a pizza doesn't solve the problem of loneliness. See who is free tonight for a nice healthy dinner so you can connect with your friends. It's a more direct way of dealing with what ails you (e.g., connection as the antidote to loneliness) as opposed to self-medicating with something that is probably going to lead to more negative feelings (e.g., eating a whole pizza which leads to guilt... and still leaves you feeling lonely).

When Gina heard some comments about her weight from women at church, she had what she called her "aha" moment. Have you ever had a moment of truth when it came to your weight, food choices, or health in general? Have you ever seen a picture of yourself and been shocked at what you've seen? Has someone's comment caught you off guard?

There are a few ways to deal with moments like these. Gina could have used denial. She could have said to herself, "I'm not *really* that overweight." She could have rationalized her weight gain. "All women gain weight when they're pregnant. This weight gain is normal."

Gina could have gone home steaming angry at the women for making a comment like that, and then, she could have eaten a whole pizza when she got home to self-medicate her feelings. Of course, overeating would have only hurt Gina's health even more.

But do you see what Gina did with this difficult, rock-bottom moment? She used it as a wake-up call that helped her to make a positive change in her life. Maybe there is something that *you* want to change. For Gina, she was thinking of her own health as well as her child's. Who are *you* thinking of when you make healthier choices? What's your *why*?

I love when Gina talked about celebrating her success. That's so important! She said that she felt stronger every time she turned down cookies or chips. Remember to do this for yourself.

1. Change how you THINK

Focusing on success is the opposite of obsessing about tiny failures. In fact, a pitfall thought pattern common in people struggling with their weight and food issues is **polarization**. Remember, this is a type of binary, black-or-white way of seeing the world and your choices as they're related to your eating patterns.

Imagine what would happen to Gina if she allowed polarized thinking to destroy all of that progress she had made in a day. She woke up and had a healthy breakfast and lunch. But then she had one cookie in the afternoon.

If Gina was using polarized thinking, she might think to herself, "Well, today's healthy eating plan is a complete failure!" If Gina's breakfast were fresh fruit over yogurt and her lunch was a healthy salad with olive oil and vinegar, it seems unfair to negate all the successes of the day because of one unhealthy food. Yet, that's how people who use polarized thinking view themselves.

They tend to think: *if I'm not a complete success, I'm a complete failure or if today's meal isn't absolutely perfect, then it's a complete disaster.* Have you ever had a thought pattern that was so rigid and perfectionistic that it blocked all the success and positivity you had created?

People who use polarized thinking tend to throw the baby out with the bath water. Of course, this pitfall thought pattern can make you feel bad about yourself. It can spiral into a bad mood, leading you to cancel your plans, sit on the couch, and eat a pint of ice cream while binge watching TV. The whole day is ruined because of that one cookie you ate.

But what if you could prevent polarized thinking from robbing you of all your success? Instead of that one cookie ruining your whole day, you consider your day through a balanced, gray-area lens.

If you had a healthy breakfast, lunch, and then one piece of candy, you still had far more healthy foods. Of course, this often helps us to feel better about ourselves. You'd probably leave work feeling energized, go to the gym, and have dinner with your friends. Oh, and you'd probably have a nice healthy dinner, too! You'd get right back up on that horse without beating yourself up. Imagine what this sort of energy could do for *you* in *your* daily life.

Isn't it so nice that this gray-area type of thinking actually puts more emphasis on what we do *right* instead of obsessing over what we do *wrong?* Now, it's time to train your brain by looking at where this pitfall thought pattern may be showing up in your life. By doing so, you'll find your own new way of thinking.

What's one area of my life where polarized thinking shows up?

_____

_____

_____

If I were to let polarized thinking go, how would my life improve?

_____

_____

_____

What's a better, more balanced, and gray-area way to think about my life?

_____

_____

_____

2. Change how you ACT

Gina's story also reminds us of the power of baby steps, a powerful **behavioral** strategy when it comes to overcoming being overweight. This strategy prevents us from becoming anxious or overwhelmed when it feels like we have a mountain to climb. As Gina said, *Who can lose 150 pounds? That is too overwhelming!*

The solution: take that mountain and break it up into small mounds. And then climb just *one* of those small mounds today. Take a lofty weight loss goal — or any other important goal you may have for yourself in your life — and break it into a SMART goal.

A SMART goal is Specific, Measurable, Achievable, Relevant, and Time-sensitive. "I need to lose 150 pounds" becomes "I am going to lose two pounds or more per month for the next twelve months." This SMART goal may also help you incorporate something else that helps keep people on track: accountability.

For most people, weighing yourself about once a week or so can be a helpful strategy. If there is a week where you "fall off the wagon" and gain a few pounds, then you can simply pick yourself up the following week. Remember: weight loss isn't a sprint; it's a marathon.

Consider a fitness or weight loss goal that you have for yourself. Write it on the lines below. It should be something you can measure. It could be body fat, your weight, or your time running a quarter mile. Also, how long are you going to give yourself to achieve this goal? What you can measure, you can change.

My **SMART goal** is:

_____

_____

_____

3. BE HAPPY

Chapter 5

Think,
Act & Be
Happy

Parent with
Limits & Love

Too Bad You Lost Your Jacket

*"I must do something" always solves more problems
than "Something must be done."*
~Author Unknown

When my children were little we went to Disney World every fall. My friends thought I was crazy, but the kids loved it and I think I enjoyed it even more than they did. Except for one thing. Souvenirs. The kids would drive me nuts asking for souvenirs, to the point that in the stores I would try to block my daughter's view of the stuffed animals and my son's view of the superhero items.

Then I discovered Disney Dollars! The next time we went to Disney World, I gave each child fifty Disney Dollars to spend on souvenirs. They started evaluating every possible purchase as if they worked for Consumer Reports, and we returned home with half their Disney Dollars unspent.

That gave me an idea a few years later when I was at my wit's end over my son's remarkable ability to lose his clothes. Our school had a dress code and it could get expensive. I'll never forget when my twelve-year-old son Mike went off to the first day of school in a brand new navy blue blazer and came home wearing a bedraggled old one that barely fit him. The $100 blazer that I had bought just a little too big for him, so that it would last the entire school year, was gone. He said his friend Gideon needed a larger jacket so they swapped.

That was the last straw in a series of clothing disappearances. I decided it was time to change the dynamic in our household. I sat the kids down and laid out their annual clothing budget. Their father and I would give them half their budget in the fall and half in the spring. My daughter opted for a debit card that I refilled every six months;

my son opted for a savings account.

It was heavenly. I drove them to the stores, we shopped together, and we each paid for our own purchases. If my son lost something, it was not my problem, and he learned a lesson about caring for his possessions. There were no arguments over clothing, no pleading for more, and no frustration on either side. We actually had fun shopping.

The advice columnist Abigail Van Buren summed it up perfectly when she said, "If you want children to keep their feet on the ground, put some responsibility on their shoulders." I gave my children the responsibility for what they wore on their shoulders, literally! My son became much more careful, although he did lose his blazer one more time, the night before an important ninth-grade event. With my new attitude, I just thought it was funny when he had to wear a pastel plaid jacket from the lost and found.

— Amy Newmark —

Mama, Will You Dry My Hair?

It's difficult to decide whether growing pains are
something teenagers have — or are.
~Author Unknown

remember the first time my daughter asked me that question. She was about five and it was obvious she was frustrated. She was fully immersed in her "I can do it myself" stage and had informed me just minutes earlier that she was going to dry her hair all by herself. Until that day, I had automatically pulled out the hair dryer with one hand, comb in the other, and groomed her long brown locks until each shiny strand was dry.

But today would be different. So, after plugging the dryer in the wall and showing her how to turn it on, I passed my five-year-old the dryer with a smile and a cheery "here you go." By the time I reached the bottom of the stairs, I heard her call in frustration, "Mama! Will you dry my hair?" Evidently the dryer was too heavy or maybe she had never noticed how long it actually took to dry her long hair, which hung almost to her waist.

For the next several years, I continued to dry her hair. Then when she was about ten, I decided she could handle the responsibility and she reluctantly took over the task. Being an avid reader, she soon discovered that if she asked me to blow dry her hair, then she could sit on my vanity stool to read one of her many books. So for a while, we took turns drying her hair. Sometimes she would do it, then other times she would appear with a damp towel wrapped around her head and a book in her hand. "Mama, will you dry my hair?" she would say with a smile. "Please?"

Then her teenage years hit, causing our days to be filled with her talking back, me lecturing, her rolling her eyes, me sending her to her room, and so on. On one particular occasion, my daughter approached me at 10:30 on a school night with the infamous question. It was late and I was tired. I had reminded her to take a shower three hours earlier. And on top of that, we had argued earlier that day and I didn't appreciate her rude tone of voice. Who was she to come ask me for a favor after the way she treated me earlier? I disapproved of her disrespectful behavior and I wanted to teach her a lesson.

"No," I simply said. "You'll have to dry your own hair."

Her mouth dropped open. "But..." she paused, "you always dry my hair."

"Not tonight." I stacked the placemats firmly on the counter, trying to look busy.

"But..." she pleaded. "You're not doing anything."

True. Nonetheless, I stood firm.

Over the next few weeks, she didn't ask me to dry her hair. I wondered if she had learned anything. If she now realized that as a family we should be kind and considerate to one another. If she understood the importance of showing respect to her parents. Then one night, she appeared from the bathroom, towel atop her head, and an innocent smile on her face.

"Mama, will you dry my hair?"

I paused for a brief moment. She sensed my hesitation, then offered these simple words.

"One day, I'll be gone and you will turn to Daddy and say, 'I wish she was still here so I could dry her hair.'"

"Ha, ha," I jokingly replied, hoping she didn't notice the truth of her words pierced right through my heart.

Tonight, I'm standing at the kitchen sink scrubbing baked-on lasagna from the dish. Overhead, I hear the drone of a hair dryer coming from my daughter's bathroom. I set the scrubber and dish aside, then quickly dry my hands. As I scurry up the stairs, my husband asks if something is wrong.

"I hope it's not too late," I call as I reach the top step.

After a humble knock on her door, I offer a faint whisper: "Can I dry your hair?"

— Deanna Ingalls —

Dr. Mike...

Amy and Deanna's stories remind me of the story about Goldilocks and the three bears. It's all about finding that sweet spot between "too firm" and "too soft" until you find the spot that's "just right." By doing so, you're training your brain.

Amy started out too soft and was letting her son Mike get away with too much. She needed to get a little more firm to find her "just right" spot.

Deanna started out too firm and realized she needed to get a little more soft. In the end, both of these moms allowed their instincts to teach themselves how to find that "just right" spot.

Maybe you're a Baby Boomer who grew up in a home with tougher consequences than many kids are used to today. If so, did you ever crave more warmth or understanding as a child?

Maybe you're a Millennial. You loved being rewarded and praised for everything, but have you ever suffered when you face the tough realities of the real world?

The truth is that the "just right" spot is the kind of parenting associated with the best outcomes. This is also called an *authoritative* parenting style. It's softer than an *authoritarian* approach but firmer than a *permissive* parenting style.

An *authoritarian* parenting style can create resentment and detachment in children. A *permissive* parenting style creates children who are likely to have poor boundaries and behavioral problems.

The *authoritative* approach allows you to fall somewhere between the "bad cop" and the "good cop." There are still consequences for unacceptable behaviors, but it also tends to create an open line of communication between you and your child.

If you're co-parenting, it's helpful for *both* parents to be *authoritative*... and on the same team. Otherwise, one parent is often forced into the bad cop role *because* another parent has taken the good cop role, which can be the easy way out, because it takes gumption to stick to your guns!

If one parent is a lot softer than the other, it can create resentment *between* parents. It's also not healthy for children, because they quickly learn how to play the parents to get what they want. This prevents children from becoming responsible and accountable human beings.

Amy's story reminds us of a vital truth when it comes to parenting: consequences shape behavior. The only way children experience consequences is if you allow them to suffer a few minor ones. The helicopter parent who swoops in and does everything for his or her children won't allow them the incredible gift of learning from consequences.

Amy taught Mike responsibility by providing him a set number of Disney Dollars to spend on vacation, and later by giving him a twice-a-year clothing budget for his school wardrobe. Imagine how this life lesson came in handy for Mike when it came time to pay a mortgage when he grew up! In fact, he was more likely to get a mortgage in the first place, because Amy's lesson probably helped him become an adult who had a good credit score.

I don't know about you, but I could just see Mike wearing that pastel plaid jacket from the lost and found. What a great visual of the consequence of losing yet *another* $100 jacket!

I wonder what *your* child's proverbial "pastel plaid jacket" will be. It's enough of a consequence to make a kid think twice, but it's not big enough to cause any harm.

And when it came to Deanna's story, I got a little chill up my spine when I read that last line: *Can I dry your hair?*

In that moment, Deanna realized she had been firm for long enough. She had clearly taught her daughter a lesson. There was definitely a consequence for her rude tone and disrespectful behavior, which tend to be the unfortunate side effects of adolescence. She was training her daughter's brain.

But her daughter was right: Deanna would probably miss those precious moments once Deanna was off living a life of her own. I was so glad when Deanna scurried up those stairs.

Now, let's see how we can use *your* brain to find that sweet spot that Amy and Deanna found.

1. Change how you THINK

One pitfall thought pattern that can hold parents back is **paralysis-analysis**. Your brain contemplates all your worries (also known as analysis) about your kids. This leads to anxiety. It also leads to a state of inaction (also known as paralysis) where you fail to find that "sweet spot" action that could have taught your kids limits... with love.

Amy and Deanna could have gone down the endless train of **paralysis-analysis** with their kids.

Amy could have thought: *What if Mike loses every jacket we buy him?! How much money is THAT going to cost? Is he ever going to learn responsibility? This is so terrible. I should be focusing on my work, but I just can't stop thinking about what Mike is doing at school right now. Is he ever going to turn into a responsible young man?*

If Deanna got trapped in this pitfall thought pattern, she would have thought: *Is she ever going to grow out of this? When is this phase going to pass? Maybe it never will. She'll never get a job if she acts like this. Ugh... I just can't stop worrying about her! I should be enjoying my night off, but I'm just so upset.*

Instead, Amy and Deanna took a reasonable action that helped them to find that sweet spot... and teach their kids limits with love.

A lot of parents who are permissive or "too soft" often use **paralysis-analysis** and worry about what would happen if they allowed their child to suffer any type of consequence. They become a helicopter parent. They worry about everything. If Amy had been a helicopter parent, she might have had some thoughts that sounded like: *What would happen if he lost his jacket? I wonder if they even have extra ones. I'm going to wait outside school with an extra one just in case he needs one.*

Some permissive parents actually become afraid of their kids or avoid conflict with them. **Paralysis-analysis** kicks in when they worry about their kids not liking them. *What will he say if I ground him? What if he hates me? What if I totally ruin our relationship... and I end up having a terrible one like the one I had with my dad? I hate it when he's angry at me, so I'm not going to say anything at all.*

On the other side of the spectrum, authoritarian parents use

paralysis-analysis when they worry about their kids becoming unmanageable. *If I'm not strict with my kids, they'll probably fail out of school and become criminals. They need me to be this stern, or they won't learn anything. What I say goes. Because I said so!*

The truth is that there is something valid about both sides of this coin, but remember: discipline is only effective when it's outnumbered by rewards. Kids need to know that limits come from a place of love. Otherwise, they can end up feeling resentment. Or worse: they grow up feeling unloved.

One **paralysis-analysis** worry I've had about my child is:

_____

But my child showed me how capable, worthy, smart, etc. he or she was when this happened:

_____

_____

_____

2. Change how you ACT

Now that you see how the way you *think* affects the way you parent, let's take a look at a **behavioral** strategy that will help.

The first step is identifying where you fall on the spectrum from permissive ("too soft") to authoritarian ("too firm").

Place an X on the line that represents the kind of parent you are:

←---→

Too soft   Too hard

If you co-parent, place an X on this line that represents where you see your co-parent:

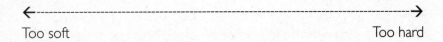

Too soft   Too hard

Now, place an O on the first line where *you* would like to be, and an O on the second line where you would like to see your *co-parent*. (Ideally, both O's will be somewhere close to the middle.)

Let's start creating your desired change in the person you have the most power over — *you*. What's one thing you could *do differently* that would help you to move a little closer to that O?

One thing I could do differently with my child is to:

_____

If you co-parent, there may or may not be some possibility of change. If you have a strained relationship with an ex and share custody, sometimes all you can do is change yourself. And that's okay. Having *one* parent who parents with limits and love is better than *zero*.

If your co-parent is open to change, have a conversation. The best way to have that conversation is talk about what *you* need specifically, what it would *mean* to you, and *why*.

For Amy and Deanna, moving to that sweet spot in the middle helped them parent effectively — with limits and love. I wonder what it will do for you and your family.

3. BE HAPPY

Chapter 6

Think, Act & Be Happy

Thrive with Disabilities

Where There's a Wheel There's a Way

A pessimist sees the difficulty in every opportunity; an optimist sees the opportunity in every difficulty.
~Winston Churchill

Even though I loved a good snowball fight or the stinging frost ricocheting off my cheeks as I picked up speed on the toboggan hill, growing up in a farming community in east central Alberta just made "winter" synonymous with "hockey." The fact that I was a girl and didn't play on an organized team didn't matter. At least twice a week most of the town would gather at the local arena, clamouring for the warm seats under the heaters, to cheer on the hometown team, from the little Mighty Mights to the Old Timers. My brother was a goalie, so through the years I regularly heard the plea, "Take shots on me." Whether it was a makeshift goal on the farm with a tennis ball or playing street hockey in town with a "real" net, I soon became adept at mixing it up between glove hand, stick side and five-hole shots.

Saturday night would find us sitting around our little nineteen-inch TV taking in the latest NHL match-up. Our favourite clash was between our beloved Toronto Maple Leafs and those pesky Montreal Canadiens. From the first note of the Hockey Night in Canada theme song, you could feel the energy level rise in our home. Enthusiastic cheers and homemade replays just added to the excitement. Intermission meant time for a quick round of hand hockey on the living room floor… until Mom told us to "quit before we wrecked something." As the expansion teams began making their way into the league, my loyalties shifted west. Despite several moves throughout western Canada I have remained a die-hard fan of my hometown Edmonton Oilers — in their dynasty years as well as their dismal ones.

Now, years later, my brother coaches his boys' hockey teams and the tradition continues with regular trips to the arena for practices and games. However, as an adult, I had thought that my connection with grassroots hockey was pretty much over. You see, our daughter is an accomplished musician and our son has cerebral palsy. While our son loves hockey and cheers with exuberance, his body does not cooperate with his mind, so his physical limitations made the idea of playing hockey all but impossible... or so I thought.

When he was twelve years old, we were introduced to power wheelchair hockey, and hockey was revived as part of our family's life. For the past few years, every Saturday during hockey season, we join the small army of wheelchair-accessible vans at one of our city's rec centres for the next match-up.

There are four teams in the league, each coached by one of the dads, or someone from the community with passion and heart for both the players and the game. The players' combined fervour and grit are reminiscent of the Original Six. They play on a full size basketball court bordered with custom covered foam "boards" to keep the ball in play. The league is open to both males and females twelve years and older who require a wheelchair, regardless of their diagnosis.

Some players are able to hold their stick in one hand and use their wheelchair controller in the other. Others strategically tape or bolt the stick to the side of their chair. Despite the type or severity of their disability, they arrive ready to play. Some are able to speak clearly, others not. Some are able to use two hands, some can only use one. One player even uses his chin to manoeuvre his chair. For some of them, this is the only sport they can play and they live for Saturdays and "the game."

Now, lest you think this is a nursing home league, do not be fooled. They play with the same rules as able-bodied hockey, with one exception. Cross-checking penalties have been replaced with ramming penalties. In typical hockey a fight often gets fans on the edges of their seats or up on their feet. However, in wheelchair hockey, on the rare occasion when two chairs collide and a chair goes over, both the sidelines and the stands empty as they scramble to set up the chair and make sure the player is unharmed.

Not only were we introduced to power hockey but also to the power of belonging to a community. With approximately thirty-five players in the league, it's a pretty close-knit group. Cheers from the stands often go both ways, acknowledging great plays at either end. Whether it's needing assistance getting their gear on, mounting their stick, or helping players with any number of problems with their wheelchair, capable and compassionate help is readily available regardless of which jersey a player is wearing.

Just like the NHL, the playoffs bring a new round of intensity. The stands are fuller, the stakes are higher and everyone has their "game on." As the intensity increases, so does the commitment to each other and the game. Duct tape solutions and bungee cord quick fixes are freely shared with whoever needs them, as resources are pooled in a collaborative attempt to limp the wheelchairs through the rest of the game until more adequate repairs can be made later.

Perhaps this community is felt the strongest as wheelchairs line the aisles of churches and funeral homes in a statement of solidarity for a lost comrade. As players and those associated with the sport succumb to disease, complications or the simply unexpected, there is an overwhelming sense of community that rises up within the league. At each funeral we've had the sad privilege of attending, I am awed at the number of players and their families that come to show their support.

Indeed, this is a remarkable group of people. Week after week I marvel at the stories behind each of the players and their families — stories of daily struggle and realities that are foreign to many. They are stories that most people would characterize by limitation. Yet, the players and their family's collective tenacity and commitment to the game and to each other demonstrate their ability to live far beyond their limitations. When life would say no, they say a resounding yes. Where there's a wheel, there's a way.

— Cindy Martin —

The Good Fight

You can't go back and make a new start, but you can
start right now and make a brand new ending.
~James R. Sherman

When I was ten years old, I wanted to be a doctor like my dad. I was in the gifted program, played the piano, and loved playing soccer.

My grandparents surprised us with a family vacation to Las Vegas. I was so excited to see the King Tut exhibit, but I never made it.

When we got there, I began to feel sick. My mom thought I had the flu. Then, I started to have severe symptoms. I couldn't talk or move. I was taken in an ambulance from our hotel to the hospital.

Of course, I don't actually remember most of this trip. Why? I had a massive stroke and could no longer talk, read, or write. The entire right side of my body was suddenly paralyzed. I couldn't understand what anyone was saying to me.

I lived in the hospital for three months.

Years later, I learned a few scary things. First, they weren't sure that I was going to make it. They didn't tell me or my brother Mike that at the time.

Second, one doctor told my family that they shouldn't take me home — ever. My stroke was so big and the damage was too bad. His advice was that nothing could be done. No surgeon would operate on a brain this compromised. Physical and speech therapy probably wouldn't work, either. An independent life was out of the question.

Thankfully, my parents didn't believe this pessimistic doctor. Instead, my dad found the *one* neurosurgeon who said he would perform the two brain surgeries I needed. My stroke was the result of a rare brain disease. If I didn't have the surgeries, I would keep having more strokes.

My mom stayed by my side. She slept in a chair every night in my hospital room. Before I was well enough to take an air ambulance to another hospital closer to home, our family's favorite doctor came in.

She usually came to my room carrying my medical charts. This time, she was carrying a small wooden box. She did not use any big words. She did not poke me with any needles.

Her last visit was the most important visit of all. She placed the box in my lap. It was small and had a lid.

She nodded her head and smiled.

"Open it," she said.

Inside, I found a watch with a green band that looked like army camouflage.

On the face of the watch was a soldier. In the box, there was a little toy figure of a soldier. She picked up the soldier.

"This is G.I. Joe," she said.

"He is a fighter. You are a fighter. You must fight to recover, David." She moved her arms like she was fighting, to help me understand.

She said, "Wear this watch. It will remind you to fight and never give up!"

I was only ten years old. I did not understand it at the time. But my fight wasn't over. It was just starting.

The next few years were really hard. I went to tons of speech and physical therapy. I did learn to walk again, but my right arm remained paralyzed.

Slowly, I learned to talk again. I started with one syllable. Then, one word. Then, two words.

For a long time, I was very depressed. Kids at school made fun of me. I became the "kid in the wheelchair who couldn't talk." I went from the gifted program to special education.

People treated me like I was dumb. I couldn't even spell my own name, "D-A-V-I-D." Everything was language and letters. Talking was so hard. So was reading. But inside, I was still very smart.

I had aphasia from my stroke. Aphasia makes language hard, but it doesn't change someone's intelligence. If you went to France and didn't speak French, you'd still be smart. But it might be hard to order dinner.

Eventually, I decided life was going to go on. I decided to live. I co-founded a nonprofit to help other stroke survivors. I started to speak at national conferences and rehab hospitals.

Recently, I was invited to speak at a stroke conference for doctors and tell my story. I won awards for being an advocate for others. *People* magazine did a story on my recovery.

Twenty years later, I've turned this into something that has empowered me and the people I love. My recovery helped to inspire my brother Mike to become a leading brain health expert. We wrote a book on stroke recovery which has become a go-to guide for survivors and family members.

I realize that it was that moment with our favorite doctor that changed everything. While one negative doctor tried to take our hope away, our favorite doctor lifted us up.

Hope was the difference between a nursing home and the independent life I lead today.

Today, I walk, run, and drive. I'm in a relationship. I travel by myself. There are still things that are hard. I still can't use my right arm. But, there are so many things I *can* do.

The fight to recover was hard. Twenty years later, I'm still fighting. And I'll never, ever give up.

— David Dow —

Dr. Mike...

Some people live their whole life with a disability. For example, many of the players on Cindy's son's power wheelchair hockey team were living with cerebral palsy. Perhaps you or someone you love was born hearing impaired. Maybe you're visually challenged.

Many people will unexpectedly become disabled at some point. This was true for my brother David. One day, he was an above-average ten-year-old. The next, half his body was paralyzed and he couldn't spell his own name.

Perhaps you or someone you love has been in a life-altering accident. There may be some things you are unable to do. If you're blind, perhaps becoming a bus driver is out of the question. But there are so many things you *can* do. Sometimes, I wonder if Stevie Wonder's blindness led to the acute sense of hearing that helped him become a world-famous musician.

The focus on what we all *can* do helped Cindy as she watched her son. *His physical limitations made the idea of playing hockey all but impossible... or so I thought.*

If you're living with a disability, could it possibly be that changing your state of mind could improve your life? It's a shift from "I *can't* do this" to: "How *can* I do this in a *different* way?"

I picture Cindy's son on the ice — carrying on the family tradition of being a hockey player. I wonder if he is a Toronto Maple Leafs fan like his mom.

When you're surrounded by other people in your shoes, it can help you feel less alone. This is true for all of us.

I wonder if Cindy's son formed friendships with any of his teammates — who were all living with different types of diseases. They weren't "a bunch of handicapped kids." They were thriving hockey players — who just happened to all be in wheelchairs.

My family also had an eye-opening experience that helped us focus on what David *could* do. When he finally came home from the hospital, we did what most families would do. We tried to help him as much as we could. Although it came out of a place of love, that strategy can sometimes backfire — if you take it too far.

When it comes to stroke, the brain needs to rewire itself. Thus, a survivor needs to finish his sentence. She needs to use the hand that's weak. Otherwise, brain cells won't rewire. Legs won't start working again.

As an adolescent, David was also like any other kid. He wanted to do things on his own.

Our family's efforts to help him may have even held David back sometimes. When taken too far, well-intentioned help can sometimes hurt.

This same phenomenon is true for other disabilities, too. Help your loved ones when they truly need it — without holding them back. Find the sweet spot that lies in between these two extremes. They may end up surprising you. I know my brother shocked us.

Years after David's stroke, he was old enough to be left alone. One afternoon, he was home alone for a few hours. When we returned, all the furniture in his bedroom had been rearranged.

I'll never forget my mom's reaction.

"David, you didn't tell me you were having people over."

My brother's reaction, "I didn't."

My mom: "Well, then who moved all this furniture?"

David: "Me. I moved it, Mom."

We were all absolutely shocked. Our entire family was so busy trying to help him finish his sentences and carry things for him. We didn't realize how many things he was now able to do for himself.

David had *so many* abilities. In our minds, he was "the victim of a massive childhood stroke." In that one moment, he taught us all a valuable lesson. This lesson is a powerful one for anyone with a disability and those who love them.

Train your brain by focusing on what you *can* do — not what you *can't*. It's about being an incredibly *able* you.

1. Change how you THINK

If you are living with a disability, you may struggle with the pitfall thought pattern **pessimism**.

Cindy's son's cerebral palsy may have made him prone to some very serious problems. This could include difficulties with daily needs like feeding and mobility. Perhaps you or your child have trouble with things that other people take for granted.

When this is true, it's easy to spiral into the worst-case, catastrophic outcomes associated with certain diseases. If this **pessimism** is left unchecked, it can even lead to an anxiety disorder.

For my brother David, it seemed like the world was now focused on all the things he *couldn't* do. He *couldn't* use his right hand. He *couldn't* form sentences as effortlessly as he once could.

This **pessimism** can run wild. Like a flame with no oxygen, optimism can flicker. Eventually, the beautiful light of optimism may even go out.

Let's extinguish pessimism — and allow optimism to shine with a simple exercise.

Do you remember that moment when Cindy saw her son on the ice? Or that moment when we discovered my brother David had moved all that furniture by himself?

I want *you* to tap into that type of optimism.

Something that's *right* with me (or my loved one) is:

_____

Something that I (or my loved one) *can* do is:

_____

How does focusing on these things help me to extinguish **pessimism** and let *optimism* shine?

_____

_____

_____

2. Change how you ACT

If you're living with a disability, changing the way you *act* can be a powerful way to train your brain... and your body.

Maybe Cindy's son sat in front of the TV on Saturday nights. As they watched the Toronto Maple Leafs battle those "pesky" Montreal Canadiens, Cindy's son probably enjoyed this family tradition.

However, many people with cerebral palsy (or other disabilities) would have compared themselves to those professional hockey players—and then never played the sport.

I'll never be able to do that. My body is too weak. I guess I'll just always be stuck here... watching from the sidelines.

Not Cindy's son. He didn't just watch from the side of the ice or sitting in front of a TV. He got on it.

By doing so, he met other people. He was exercising his body.

If you're living with a disability, it may take you extra time to do things. It would probably be easier to hide yourself from the world. Perhaps you struggle with self-doubt. But your *experience* of doing something scary or challenging is what trains your brain. Every time you choose this activity, you're teaching yourself an invaluable lesson.

I *can* do so many things.

When David decided to start a nonprofit for other stroke survivors, he was creating a life based on purpose. He fused it with another healing attribute: passion.

You see, my brother's passion is travel. The nonprofit he helped to start has an event he looks forward to every year. It's a cruise for stroke survivors. There is healing, learning, shared experience, and fun... as they sail the open seas.

So if you would like to *thrive* it's time for you to step outside your comfort zone. (If you are the loved one of someone with a disability, go over these questions together.)

What is an *activity* that would help you to *step outside your comfort zone*?

_____

How would this activity bring passion, purpose, or pleasure to *your* life?

_____

What special skill or character trait do you have that makes you unique and capable?

_____

How does this make you more able to do something that brings passion, purpose, or pleasure to your life or to the lives of others?

_____

3. BE HAPPY

Chapter 7

Think, Act & Be Happy

How to Heal from Abuse

My Sobbing, Shaking Strength

Life is very interesting... in the end, some of your greatest pains become your greatest strengths.
~Drew Barrymore

I never thought I would be someone who woke up one day in an abusive relationship. Of course, in reality it didn't happen all of a sudden. My relationship wasn't perfectly healthy and happy one day, and then abusive the next. The changes happened gradually, so gradually I didn't even notice that things were changing between us. Ever so slowly, he became more and more controlling, more and more volatile and unstable.

Yet if you had asked, I would have told you that we were happy. I thought our relationship was beautiful and filled with love. Sure, we fought sometimes, but doesn't every couple? It was true that he was perhaps a little too dependent. He didn't like when I got together with my friends because he missed me too much when we were apart, even for just a few hours. And yes, he made me feel guilty about going home to visit my family during the summer because he couldn't stand to be apart for days, much less weeks.

But these things, I rationalized, were signs that he loved me. If you had told me I was slipping down a rabbit hole of increasing emotional abuse, I would not have believed you. I defined myself as a strong person, and I didn't think that strong people could get tangled up in abusive relationships.

Inner strength has been part of my identity and my own personal narrative since birth. I was born three months prematurely, weighing a terrifying two pounds, six ounces, and I stayed in the hospital for months as I fought to live. I needed a respirator to help me breathe and feeding tubes to help me eat. My feet were pricked countless times for blood samples, and my heart was monitored closely because of a small hole that eventually healed itself. "Your daughter is a fighter," the surgeon told my parents. Against all odds, I battled my way into the world, and throughout my life I have drawn strength from the story of my birth: my experience of survival.

As I grew into a healthy little girl, my underdeveloped lungs grew strong. In middle school and high school I ran cross-country and track, where my teammates voted me "most inspirational" and team captain. I hiked to the summit of Mt. Whitney, the tallest mountain in the contiguous United States. I traveled to England on my own and backpacked through eight countries in Europe. I was the friend others leaned on; I was independent; I was strong. I didn't think of myself as someone who needed help from others.

And then I woke up one morning and found myself in an abusive relationship, engaged to be married to a man who was steadily becoming more and more frightening. Day by day, I could feel myself growing quieter, smaller, lonelier. I was becoming lost. I knew I should reach out to a friend or family member — I had many people in my life who cared for me deeply and who would drop everything to help me, just as I had helped them through various life disasters and problems.

But I felt ashamed. I thought I was strong, but obviously I was wrong about myself — how else could I have fallen so deeply into such a bad situation? And what made things worse and more complicated was the fact that, despite everything, I still loved this man. I was afraid to be on my own without him.

The red flags, however, kept piling up. When we argued, he threw books against the wall in frustration. One night while driving he angrily slammed the steering wheel and the car nearly veered off the road. When I was offered the career opportunity of my dreams, he ordered me to turn it down because it was halfway across the country. He couldn't bear for us to ever be apart and wasn't willing to make any changes in his own life so he could move there with me.

When he coldly shook his head, refusing to even glance at the letter I'd received congratulating me on this opportunity, my heart was ripped wide open. I had reached the breaking point. This was a red flag I couldn't ignore.

That day, the day I finally left, I would have told you that I looked like a weak person. I certainly felt weak. I was a complete mess. My legs shook. I sobbed. I hadn't been able to eat or sleep. It took all the strength I possessed to look into the eyes of this man I still loved and tell him, "I'm sorry, but I can't do this anymore. This isn't a healthy relationship. I can't marry you."

It was the bravest, most difficult thing I have ever done. And I didn't do it alone. My brother hopped on a plane and stayed with me for a week, driving me to work and bringing me dinner, making sure I ate and drank water and slept. My best friend drove six hours to be with me, and for an entire weekend she held my hand and rubbed my back as I cried. I continually received phone calls and e-mails from friends and relatives, checking up on me and asking if I needed anything. Even acquaintances I hadn't known I could count on were there for me, inviting me out for coffee and lunch, making me feel part of the world again. The kindness and love I felt were overwhelming.

Inner strength, I learned, isn't about putting up a façade. Inner strength isn't refusing help from others. Inner strength isn't relying only on yourself. My true inner strength came when I finally reached out to those around me and confessed that I was in a bad situation, and I needed their help to pull myself out. I learned that real inner strength comes from being true to your authentic self, your desires, your needs.

Now, I still draw strength from the story of my birth, from the photo on my desk of my tiny newborn self, hooked up to an array of tubes and monitors in an incubator in the NICU. But I also have a new story to draw strength from. When I was a sobbing, shaking, heart-wrenched-wide-open mess, all I could see at the time was weakness. But now I can see that the opposite is true: I was actually a study in strength. I think of that day — one of the most difficult days of my life — and I am proud of what I went through. I am proud to be me.

— Dallas Woodburn —

Up in Flames

We must embrace pain and burn it
as fuel for our journey.
~Kenji Miyazawa

Five years after my mother's death I realized that I was still hurt and angry. I hadn't dealt with the fact that my parents got separated when I was three years old, I hadn't dealt with the fact that my mother, my brother and I were abused physically and verbally for almost eight years by two of her boyfriends, and most of all, I hadn't dealt with the fact that my mother had died so horribly right in front of my eyes when I was only twelve years old.

"Jenn, write a letter and burn it!" Anne kept telling me over and over again. Anne was one of my mother's childhood friends. She stepped in after my mother's death and has been like a mother to me. She's the one I tell everything to, she's the one I cry with, she's the one I go to for advice, she's the one who knows me best and she's the one always encouraging me and letting me know how proud she is. She told me that burning a letter written to my past would help me get rid of some of my anger, sadness, confusion and stress. At first I really didn't think it would make much of a difference. I felt alone in the world. I was always sick and all I wanted to do was sleep. I was at my lowest point and writing a letter seemed like a waste of time. But, I always listened to Anne, because she always turned out to be right!

I wrote the letter one day after work. "Dear past..." I started. I wrote about my parents' separation and how that led us to having those two abusive boyfriends in our lives. Men who were alcoholics and treated us like dirt, men who I saw kicking, hitting and slapping my mother — men who didn't even deserve to live. And then I continued by writing about my mother's death and how much it hurt me, the fact that I had to see her die and how much I hated the fact that I had to live the rest of my life without a mom. I ended the letter by explaining how unhappy I was. It took all of my energy to write that letter, but four pages later, it was done.

I felt a bit relieved, but it really hadn't made a big difference; I still felt horrible. That's when Anne said: "Come on over and we'll burn the letter." So off to her place I went, crying my eyes out and feeling sick to my stomach. I was greeted with a hug and a chat and then we went outside and lit the letter on fire. As I watched it burn, I thought about all the horrible things I'd seen, heard and felt throughout my childhood. But most of all, I thought about my mother — the mother I lost, the mother I miss, the mother I love and the mother I'll cherish forever. I wanted to get rid of the horrible weight I carried around for all those years, and by burning the letter that's exactly what I was doing!

After the flame died out, I gave Anne the biggest hug ever, told her that I loved her and thanked her for being there. She gave me a box and told me to put a few pieces of the burned letter in it so that I could always look into it and say to myself: "It's over."

I randomly put some of the pieces in the box and when we went inside I discovered that the one word that wasn't burned on the pieces I had chosen was the word "mom." I felt like the happiest person in the world!

"I haven't seen a real smile on your face in such a long time!" said Anne.

This was proof that my mother was still with me and that she was proud of what I had just accomplished. It also reassured me that I can depend on Anne to be my mother now and that she won't ever let me down.

In order for me to be truly happy, I guess all I really needed was to get rid of that negative energy that had followed me around for so many years. And getting a sign from my mother helped me even more! Who knew that burning a letter would be such a life-changing experience? Thanks Mom and Anne, thanks for being a part of my life!

— Jennifer Gauthier —

Dr. Mike...

Abuse — and its aftermath — affect millions of people. If you're one of them, you are not alone.

I'm sure you were touched by Dallas and Jennifer's courage to heal — especially if you are a survivor of abuse.

Abuse can sneak into your life like a fairy tale in reverse. The handsome prince transforms into an angry beast — not the other way around.

That's how it went for Dallas. The signs of abuse can be subtle. Her story is a reminder that you don't have to have a black eye or a broken leg for a relationship to be unhealthy. Would her boyfriend have gone to jail for throwing books against the wall? Probably not.

Even if violent outbursts don't physically threaten you directly, it doesn't mean you should stay in a relationship. I hope her boyfriend worked on his anger management issues in therapy. Perhaps he's in a happy and healthy relationship today.

When people stay in these relationships, the books being thrown at walls *today* have a tendency to be directed at your face *tomorrow*.

Red flags may pop up slowly, so it may take you a while to notice them. Remember Dallas's words: *The changes happened gradually, so gradually I didn't even notice that things were changing between us. Ever so slowly, he became more and more controlling, more and more volatile and unstable.*

Thank goodness Dallas left the relationship when she did. Many don't. Jennifer's story reminds us what can happen when people stay in abusive relationships. Her mother died at the hands of her abuser, and Jennifer had to experience the horrific trauma of watching the nightmare unfold.

Abusers may try to reframe signs of abuse in a positive way. He's controlling, possessive, and jealous because he "loves you so much" — like Dallas's boyfriend not liking it when she saw her friends.

In most abusive relationships, there is a cycle of violence that involves periods of good times between the black eyes and broken plates. You may hear things like *I'll never do it again* and *I'm so sorry.*

You may receive gifts and flowers during these honeymoon periods. These highs are often good — while they last. That's how they get you to stay. And, of course, you *want* to believe the things they say are true… until the nightmare starts over again. Let's train your brain in a way where you now know that this is all *not okay*.

Dallas did something we all need to do in times of need: she leaned on people for help. For her, it was her brother and best friend who helped her when she left this unhealthy relationship.

If you are currently in an abusive relationship and fear for your safety, talk to a licensed mental health professional. Don't know where to find one? Call 2-1-1 from a public phone or go to 211.org from a safe computer like the library (where your abuser can't walk in on you or track your web browser history).

If you're in immediate danger, call 9-1-1 or the National Domestic Violence Hotline at 1-800-799-7223 or the National Sexual Assault Hotline at 1-800-656-4673. Mental health professionals can help you come up with a safety plan for you — and your children if you have them. A safety plan can sometimes be the difference between life and death.

If you are healing from the aftermath of abuse — like Jennifer was, remember that it can be a slow process. If you notice any severe symptoms like distress that interfere with your everyday life, find a mental health professional who specializes in trauma. Post-traumatic stress is a treatable disorder.

There's also a pitfall thought pattern that affects many survivors of abuse: **personalization.** Abusers — or even people who just take advantage of you by treating you like a doormat — will often make you feel that it's something wrong with *you*. Remember: that's the essence of the pitfall thought pattern **personalization**.

When Dallas's boyfriend threw books, slammed the steering wheel, or ordered her to turn down that dream job without talking about it, that pitfall thought pattern **personalization** may have reared its ugly head.

It may sound something like: *You are too loud! Make yourself smaller!* When Jennifer was physically abused by her mother's boyfriend as a little girl, **personalization** might have said: *You are a bad girl! Something is wrong with you!* You need to talk back to this pitfall thought pattern and realize that there isn't anything wrong with *you*. For Jennifer, that meant realizing there was something wrong with *him*!

When people become abusers, it's rooted in insecurity. In fact, many abusers were abused themselves. They feel small and scared. The only way *they* know how to deal with it is to keep *you* small and dependent. Their insecurity and their failure to communicate in healthy ways is what is wrong with *them*—not *you*. Make no mistake: this is no excuse for their behavior.

There are plenty of survivors who would *never* dream of abusing someone else. In fact, many of them become the loudest champions of change. Dallas and Jennifer are in this category.

1. Change how you THINK

When **personalization** rears its ugly head, remember all the ways in which *you are innately good enough*. Remember all the ways in which *your needs make sense*. You don't need to justify basic needs.

I once treated a woman in an abusive relationship who was scared to flush the toilet when she got home. Any noise she made could wake her husband up—and lead to a beating. She is no longer in that marriage… and is free to turn on the television, flush the toilet, and talk on the phone whenever she likes.

There is compromise that needs to occur in any relationship. But if violence, anger, and power is the only way in which the other person makes a point, something is wrong with *him* or *her*—not *you*.

Dallas could have just made herself smaller and smaller. When her boyfriend threw things or slammed the steering wheel, she could have thought *I shouldn't have said that! What's wrong with me?! I'm so selfish.*

She would have learned that she should remain quiet. If she wasn't quiet, anger and violence could have resulted.

I'm sure a similar phenomenon was true for Jennifer. Growing up, I'm guessing there were plenty of times she learned to stay quiet. When you grow up in an abusive household, you learn how to be small and avoid conflict. In other cases, the anxiety of the upcoming abuse is so great that children will do something to just "get it over with." Or, they even sacrifice themselves to protect a sibling from being abused.

In all these cases, your own true needs aren't valued.

Personalization says: *What's wrong with you?* Your abuser says: *How dare you have a dream! How dare you want something for yourself!*

The opposite of this should be your reality: *Your needs, wants, and dreams are valid. They make sense. There's nothing wrong with you.*

Simple desires are often criticized in abusive relationships. Dallas wanted to see her friends. Dallas's boyfriend didn't like that. Many survivors are even degraded for leaving the house. They're falsely accused. *Are you cheating on me?!* They're called degrading names.

The opposite of this is to realize that your needs are valid.

It may sound a little silly at first, but I want you to dig deep and do something people stuck in abusive relationships don't do: consider what you want, and realize that your needs, wants, and dreams are valid.

Write down three needs, wants, and dreams you have for your life. They could be short-term or simple ones like seeing your friends tonight. They can also be long-term ones like realizing your dream of finishing your college degree one day.

Then, consider the "because" of your desires. This is something people in abusive relationships don't do. The "because" of a dream helps people realize that you are allowed to have things for yourself. You could say… *I want to see my friends tonight because I'm an extroverted person. My friends make me happy and make me feel like my voice matters!*

Allow this to set you free from the naysaying voices that told you that spending time with friends made you selfish… or was associated with a false accusation, ugly names, or violence. Realize that you deserve to be happy.

Here are my three needs, wants, and dreams… and my "because."

1. I need to/want to/dream of: _____

_____because:

_____

2. I need to/want to/dream of: _____

_____because:

_____

3. I need to/want to/dream of: _____

_____because:

_____

2. Change how you ACT

Remember when Jennifer healed by writing a letter that said *Dear Past*, and then burned that letter? I want you to do something similar. I want you to consider your past, and then consider what you would *do differently* if you were no longer trapped by it.

Many survivors are afraid to speak up in meetings. Or, they are always putting themselves down or second guessing themselves. They're afraid to make simple decisions for themselves.

Write a quick note.
Dear *Past*, you affect my *Present* in the following ways:

_____

_____

_____

_____

_____

Now, imagine you had a magic wand. What is one thing you could do 10 or 20% differently tomorrow if your past no longer held you back?

_____

_____

_____

When you wake up tomorrow, imagine you have that magic wand. Remember: what you *do* can change the way you *think* and *feel*. This is how you train your brain! So by making this small change, you actually do have a magic wand. And that magic wand is yours to keep each and every day.

3. BE HAPPY

Chapter 8

Think, Act & Be Happy

You Don't Have to Be Perfect

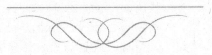

Best Feeding

With what price we pay for the glory of motherhood.
~Isadora Duncan

Most women are walking refrigerators. No, wait, milk comes out warm, so they're more like walking ovens. Or walking stovetops. Whereas men are like table tops, ready to receive the food, women's bodies are fecund like farms, producing life-sustaining milk — nourishment for our children. We are walking, talking food makers.

I am not one of these women.

I used to be one of these women, or at the very least, I assume that I was one of these women before I started down the road of fertility treatments. The mandatory blood work each cycle checked hormone levels. Prolactin, the hormone associated with breast milk, was always in working order.

When we finally became pregnant with our twins, breastfeeding was the way I thought I would take back my body, the way I would learn to love it again after its wonkiness made me rack up enormous fertility-clinic bills. My breasts were going to produce milk for me, and I was going to forgive my body for letting me down in such a big way. The twins and I would be as peaceful as the woman and child on the nursing pillow tag: mother beatifically smiling down at her perfect baby, her modest nightgown hiding the majority of her perfect white breasts, her hair tidily back in a French twist.

The twins arrived and my milk didn't. I hadn't experienced breast changes during pregnancy, but I had been assured that many women don't and this wasn't problematic. The twins were too small and premature to breastfeed, but I hooked myself up to a breast pump eight times a day, dutifully staring at the "breast is best" poster in the pumping lounge of the hospital.

Eight times a day the machine would hum, tugging at my breasts. And eight times a day, I would get only a few drops of liquid that looked suspiciously like boob sweat. After a few weeks, I became certain that if I hooked up the breast pump to my husband's chest, he'd be able to produce the same watery substance. It didn't help that across from the twins' NICU room was a family of triplets whose mother filled the NICU refrigerator with vial after vial of her rich, yellowish breast milk. She would close the refrigerator after putting in her pumping takeaway and inform me that she just didn't know what she'd do with "all that milk."

I did not look like the beatific woman on the nursing pillow label. My hair was not in a neat French twist, my boobs were red and raw from the machine, and the twins certainly weren't calmly suckling. At four weeks post-birth, we were a massive train wreck, both physically and emotionally. I had tried medications and sleeping more and sleeping less and drinking more water and eating more protein. I had been to several breastfeeding specialists, tried holding the twins' sleepy mouths to my breast prior to pumping or sniffing one of their spit-up-soaked burp cloths while on the machine — an idea, I was promised, that would trick my brain into producing milk.

I probably don't need to tell you that it didn't exactly work.

After four weeks, someone had the idea to test my prolactin levels, and lo and behold, the culprit for my lack of milk was found. I wasn't producing prolactin anymore, a possible side effect of the very treatments that brought me my twins. One month of useless pumping finally came to an end, at least physically.

Emotionally, I couldn't move on nor wrap my brain around the idea that once again, my body had failed to do what other women could do easily. It couldn't create a child without help, it couldn't carry said child to term, and now it couldn't even feed a child. This body that I had always loved and treated well certainly wasn't showing me the care I had showed it over the years. And beyond that, I had always been a nurturer, a cook. I was the person who always provided the food, who baked cookies for friends and held dinner parties and had worked her way through an entire cooking school textbook (with the exception of the forcemeats chapter, but I secretly believe that everyone would skip the forcemeats chapter if they could).

I was a woman: food was what we did. Not being able to feed my children in the way that I was led to believe was best from hospital posters and parenting books hit me in the very core of who I was as a person. Was I really the nurturer I saw myself as if I couldn't do this simple task?

One night, in the middle of yet another crying jag over the idea that I had failed so enormously at this whole make-and-keep-a-baby-growing thing, my husband gave me the solution I needed in order to take back that label of nurturer. He asked me to come up with another task equally as difficult as breastfeeding that didn't depend on my body to function in a certain way.

Making my own baby food instantly sprang to mind. Peeling all of those apples and pears, roasting butternut squash and deseeding it, pureeing steamed peach slices: all of these tasks were time-consuming and messy as opposed to simply twisting the top off a baby food jar. So we went to the supermarket and bought fruits and vegetables. We purchased dozens of ice cube trays and Sharpie markers for labeling. We set up marathon baby-food-making sessions after the twins went to bed, turning on some music and creating an assembly line of tasks until the last ice cube tray was in the freezer. And several days later, we did it all over again.

Making baby food for picky twins was a never-ending task. Instead of cracked nipples or mastitis, I had cuts on my fingers from the peelers and knives. Instead of searching for a discreet place to nurse in public, I was constantly seeking microwaves where I could heat-up our frozen baby food cubes when we were on an outing. And instead of feeding being a task solely on my shoulders (or should I say, my boobs), my husband was able to be an equal partner in not only the action of placing the food into the twins' mouths but creating it as well.

Our twins have had exactly one jar of store-bought baby food in their life, but it's not a fact that I hold over the heads of fellow mothers. I have come to realize that everyone has things they do well and things they don't; everyone has special ways they provide that others cannot, either due to time, inclination, finances or ability. There is no single way of feeding that is "best" in the grand sense of the term, but only ways that are best for each individual mother, each individual child.

I never got to be that beatific woman on the nursing pillow label, but like most advertising, I don't think her life was really like that anyway. Instead of a French twist, modest nightgown, and angelic child, I got a messy ponytail, jeans, and the Violent Femmes blasting from the computer while I made baby food, side-by-side with my husband. And that's a memory that is worth more to me than fulfilling someone else's idea of perfect motherhood.

— Melissa Ford —

One Powerful Cookie

*Striving for excellence motivates you; striving
for perfection is demoralizing.*
~Harriet Braiker

"**W**hen are you going to realize you are slowly killing yourself?" My husband sat down on the bed. "Your standards are completely ridiculous, Denise. These gifts don't have to be perfect. The kids don't care."

I ignored him and kept on wrapping. It was true. I suspected I was the only one who had numerous "rules" for wrapping gifts. Each boy needed to have his own paper, and each gift had to be wrapped perfectly.

"Do you want me to wrap the toolboxes?" he persisted.

"Nope." I was in the zone and needed to get this done. There were numerous other holiday tasks that still needed my attention. I did not care how awkward the two giant toolboxes were. I was going to make them look as perfect as the rest of the gifts.

"What else can I do then? You can't do everything yourself. Do you want your blood pressure to keep creeping up because you have to have everything just the way you want it?"

I was exhausted, and fairly certain my blood pressure was, in fact, a little high. I had been feeling awful for months, experiencing anxiety, chest pains, and insomnia. The list went on. But I have three rowdy boys who are all home seven days a week and need tons of attention. I figured that stress went with the territory.

Carefully laying out the paper covered in robots, I placed a heavy toolbox in the middle. The paper ripped as I put it down, and I was forced to lift the unwieldy box off to start over again. Stubborn pride set in. "I don't need any help."

"Fine."

Billy was right. My standards were ridiculous. Everything from how clean I kept our house, to the numerous lists I made each week, to my grocery shopping rules. Our kitchen sink had to be dried out every time I used it, even if I would be turning on the water again in a minute. Every Sunday I made extensive to-do lists for everyone, and heaven forbid if they were not zealously followed. I suspect my entire family lived in fear of my standards.

I told myself I was just taking care of my family, but in reality, I knew my non-stop perfectionism was not doing us any good. My oldest son was clearly used to my ridiculous standards and just did his best to keep the peace by meeting them. My younger two were showing signs that Mom's standards were getting to them too.

"Cooper, make sure you put your books back where you got them," my six-year-old Caleb cautioned his four-year-old brother. "Mom puts the little books there and the construction books over there." He pointed to the different spots on the shelf. "Okay," the younger one agreed, blindly following his brother in adhering to their mom's craziness.

I knew I needed to change.

Two days after Christmas, my husband and I took our two older boys on a trip to Matamoros, Mexico. We were going to participate in an event known as the "Big Feed."

This entire operation could not have been more outside my comfort zone if I tried. I had no control over our schedule. We would be working in a field with strangers. It was dirty, there was no place to wash our hands, and to top it all off, a constant light rain had been falling for days, so we would be out in the mud the whole time.

Upon arriving at the facility, we sat down to orientation and listened to the director, Ben, give his standard speech about serving.

"We are not fair-weather Christians," he boomed in his deep voice, a gentle giant at well over six feet tall. "We won't complain. We won't stay inside because it's raining. And I have something that is going to guarantee all of you stay flexible, something formulated right here in our kitchen."

He passed out a small piece of cookie to each of us. "This is the

Flexi-cookie." He instructed. "You eat this cookie and you are instantly flexible." He sounded so believable.

I listened to him talk about the problems we all have with flexibility. "I think it's a cookie problem," he stated to the room full of families. "When we go into Mexico these next two days, every time you start to complain, or maybe feel a little inflexible, we are going to gently remind you: 'Flexi, Flexi.' And then you are going to remember to be flexible. And if that doesn't work, I am going to keep a few extra cookies in my pocket for emergencies. Now let's eat this cookie together."

It tasted so ordinary, even slightly stale, but it worked in magical ways. I worked alongside my family for two long days in a muddy field. We passed out supplies and cooked for several thousand people, trudging through mud so thick our shoes quickly doubled in weight. I watched my oldest son skin raw chicken for five hours straight, with nowhere to wash his hands, and did not have a second thought as to the cleanliness of the operation. My middle son shared candy and played games with the other children all day in the rain, and I never once cleaned him up.

Late both evenings, I walked with my family across the International Bridge leading back into the United States in the dark; all of our clothes were caked with mud. And I thought about what happened when I made the choice to follow the cookie, when I chose to be flexible. Could I somehow package this Flexi-cookie and take it back home with me? The thought stayed with me on the three hundred-mile drive home.

And each morning since, I have prayed my new mantra during my morning devotions. "Flexi, Flexi." I mutter it throughout the day, reminding myself that I need to be less rigid. I cannot say I have completely conquered my crippling perfectionism, but I have made enough progress that the physical symptoms I was experiencing have diminished significantly.

And once in a while, on a really rough day, I sneak a cookie.

— Denise Valuk —

Dr. Mike...

For Melissa, it was breastfeeding. For Denise, it was the cleanliness and order of her house. Is there something in *your* life that you feel has to be perfect? Have you ever had something in your life where you needed to be a *complete* success… because you would feel like a *complete* failure if you were not?

Perfectionism can sometimes be a piece of life-threatening mental illnesses that may require hospitalization (e.g., anorexia), but it's usually found rearing its ugly head in less extreme forms. Even when it's more of an everyday problem, it can strain relationships or hold you back in your life.

If you don't learn how to train your brain, perfectionism and the anxiety it causes can eventually lead to some very real health problems. Did you know untreated anxiety disorders *do* increase your risk of developing high blood pressure? Denise's husband was worried about hers. Did you also know that panic attacks — often associated with a sense of rigidity and perfectionism — increase a person's risk of a heart attack? So there are actually some really good reasons to find balance.

I recently caught a scene of a show where a woman was served a glass of wine at a dinner party. She had been served her preferred type of wine in the incorrect type of glass, and she told the host that she needed the glass to be changed. This rigidity led to a downward spiral and what appeared to be a very intense fight between two ladies… over stemware.

In my private practice, I've treated many writers and artists. Perfectionism can lead to writer's block. I help my patients to just move forward, and I'll help you do the same. Write. Paint. Create. Whatever it is you like to do: do it. Move forward. You can always go back later and change what you don't like.

If every single sentence or embroidery stitch has to be perfect, it can sometimes become difficult to move forward at all. Perfectionism prevents progress.

Melissa wanted to be a mom and breastfeed her kids so badly. I understand that. It meant something to her. Maybe you have a similar experience, or maybe there's something in your life that means something to you.

And yet, the *meaning* of not being able to breastfeed could have led to Melissa feeling like she was a *complete* failure at being a mom. In reality, nothing could be further from the truth.

Being a true nurturer isn't about the number of ounces of milk you can produce. It's about the amount of love in your heart.

Previously, Melissa attached being a mom to the ability to produce milk. Now, she found something else she can do. Melissa glided through this experience with grace and resilience. Way to bounce back!

The yardstick that Denise used to judge herself was different. Her self-worth was tied to a measure of millimeters of dust present. To Denise, her rigidity in the house was coming from a wonderful place: love. Her extreme cleanliness was how she was trying to show her love to her family. When taken to the nth degree, though, that obsessiveness actually *blocked* love.

I know Denise is a great mom. I hope her family appreciates it when she tidies rooms or makes presents look Martha Stewart photo-worthy. But I'd guess the reason these kids love their mom has very little to do with cleanliness... and more to do with love.

Let's analyze how to address this kind of perfectionism, the kind that gets in the way of happiness.

1. Change how you THINK

One pitfall thought pattern that often holds perfectionistic people back is **polarization**. It's like your brain can only see things through a black or white lens. It's all good or all bad. If it's not picture perfect, it's a total disaster. If it's not spotless, it's a wreck.

Imagine you have a pair of brain-training glasses that you're putting on right now. They suddenly allow you to see things in 1,000 different shades of gray. You're able to see all the possibilities that lie between the pole of "perfect" and the pole marked "failure." Isn't this so freeing?

Melissa put on her magic "shades of gray" glasses and turned off polarized thinking when she said this to herself: *I have come to realize that everyone has things they do well and things they don't; everyone has special ways they provide that others cannot, either due to time, inclination, finances, or ability. There is no single way of feeding that is "best" in the grand sense of the term, but only ways that are best for each individual mother, each individual child.*

For just a moment, consider all the things you do well. And more importantly, give yourself credit for the things you already do fairly well. In the school of life, you don't have to get an A+ in every single area. I don't know anybody who does… at least not in the long run. Being perfect 24/7 just isn't a sustainable life goal.

One area in my life where I tend to be a perfectionist is:

_____

This turns into a pitfall thought that sounds something like…

_____

_____

_____

(e.g., "If I'm not a picture-perfect mom, I feel like a total failure.")

If I could put on a pair of glasses that allowed me to see the "shades of gray" and would magically allow me to see all the things I already do pretty well, I would give myself credit for:

_____

_____

_____

2. Change how you ACT

Remember when Denise had an experience—the magical "Flexi-cookie"—that allowed her to be flexible? That "Flexi-cookie" helped to train her brain. She was able to do things she would have never done before. I imagine that experience changed a deeply held belief she had. Things weren't perfect. And you know what? She was okay.

Consider a patient with obsessive-compulsive disorder who has to wash his hands for an hour. If he doesn't, he fears something bad may happen. But it's changing "the ACT" of *not* washing his hands for an hour… and being okay… that creates change.

If there is some element of perfectionism preventing progress for you, you can change it—right here and right now.

Imagine Denise is sharing a bite of her "Flexi-cookie" with you. You'll notice that this bite allows you to be instantly flexible. Isn't that fascinating?

Now, what do you see yourself doing differently?

See it unfolding in your mind's eye.

Make a written commitment to yourself that you will now actually make this change in your life.

I commit to doing the following a little less "perfectly":

_____

If I did this, I think my life would be a little better because:

_____

_____

_____

3. BE HAPPY

Chapter 9

Find Forgiveness and Liberate Yourself

We Did Our Best

*Forgiveness is beautiful and it feels good when someone
gives that gift to you. But it's one thing for someone you
wronged to forgive you. It was another
to forgive yourself.*
~Kristen Ashley, Fire Inside

The door slammed. I yanked it open and watched my husband of almost thirty years tromping across the front lawn. As he opened his car door, he looked back and saw me silhouetted in the doorway.

"You're wrong, you know," he said so quietly I had to strain to hear him. "There was never anyone else but you. No one. Ever." With those words, he disappeared into his car. Perhaps as emphasis, the car sputtered and shook before the engine turned over and he pulled away.

Tears ran down my cheeks. I became the twenty-year-old who fell in love with a slender young man with curly black hair, soft brown eyes, a tender but tentative smile, who was exactly a year older than me. A birthday wasn't the only thing we shared. We were both hard working, loved our families, espoused similar political beliefs, loved children and knew how to live on a tight budget.

In four years, we had bought our own house, had three of our four children and established a comfortable, if frugal lifestyle. We agreed that I would be a stay-at-home mom and he would be the breadwinner. We made a good team. On our ninth anniversary we conceived our fourth child, who joined our family nine months to the day later. It was also our shared birthday.

My husband gained prestige and acknowledgement at his job while he pursued a college degree. He became the first college graduate in his family. When I expressed pride in his accomplishment, his eyes flattened and darkened with something I couldn't identify. This was the first time I suspected all was not well.

Our children grew and thrived, we became more financially secure, but the seeds planted earlier cast shoots of discontent through our relationship. Our children attended college or secured jobs and I stepped back onto a road I had abandoned when I married and gave up my dream of a college degree. People often refer to stages in failing relationships as pounding nails into a coffin. Although I don't believe it was my intention, that stage of my journey added nails.

Once begun, there seemed to be no turning back. Again, relying on hindsight, I wondered that fateful day in the doorway why we had ever fallen in love and how we had stayed together as long as we had.

When I described our meeting and what we shared in common, I failed to point out where our paths diverged. I was gregarious, outspoken, and loved a good conversation, especially one with a suitable amount of controversy to jack up the interest level. I was quick to say I love you, never able to stay angry, and optimistic to an annoying fault. My husband was my polar opposite — quiet, introverted, someone who refused to discuss religion or politics and was content to sprawl on the couch and watch sports during the few hours he wasn't working, going to school or playing sports. I found it difficult to engage him in a conversation of any length.

John had a guttural laugh that seemed reluctant to emerge. I tried to make him laugh, but he withheld his laughter and I began to wonder what else he was withholding.

We argued about disciplining our children, what they could and couldn't do. And we blamed each other when we didn't approve of their behavior. The tenuous thread that held us together showed serious signs of fray. Angry words replaced words of love.

We made deals to get through activities. My studies intensified as I neared graduation. When I began working, I continued to prepare microwaveable meals, but we ate separately. I began to wonder if he had found someone else.

"Are you having an affair?"

"Yeah. What's for dinner?" he replied, head buried in the refrigerator.

I never knew if it was true, but I realized later he was trying to tell me our relationship was over.

We battled endlessly through the long divorce. Each of us took steps to move on but we never forgave each other. All the paperwork that accumulates in a divorce serves as one big tally sheet of wrongdoing that each partner carries in his or her head, sometimes for years. It makes for a major roadblock in moving on.

I joined a divorce support group. Although the support helped, I felt stuck. One of the speakers hit the nail on the head for me.

"Repeat after me," she began. "In my marriage I did the best I could." I did as requested and heard my words echoed by others in the room.

"Now, say my spouse did the best he or she could." This time there was silence. The heck he did, I thought, and imagined others saying the same.

Because she had oozed compassion and understanding when she began her talk, the occupants of the room stayed in their chairs, albeit in silence. She continued to make the case that, up to that moment, all of us had done the best we could. "After all," she asked, "who would choose to do the worst?"

It took a while before I could embrace that idea and forgive my husband and myself. He wasn't the best husband for me and I wasn't the best wife for him. But I had loved him and had really intended to do my best. And I believed he would say the same.

And my past, sorry as my efforts might have been, was the best I could do at that time. The speaker reminded us not to use the past as an excuse for poor future behavior. Seeing the limitations of my past is a strong motivation to do better in the future. My past is indeed made up of all my best efforts.

— Judythe A. Guarnera —

Road to Forgiveness

*Forgiving is rediscovering the shining path of peace
that at first you thought others took away
when they betrayed you.*
~Dodinsky

As an only child of separating and then divorcing parents, I didn't understand where I fit. I lived in an adult world where dreams were abandoned and futures were uncertain. My parents were suffering, moving, changing jobs, struggling, and healing.

And there I was from age six on, holding their outstretched hands, but only one at a time. For many years I was confused about almost everything: who, what, where, when, why and how. No one offered me any explanation that made sense.

But there was one thing I wasn't confused about: nasty people. And the nastiest of them all was my grandfather. He was cruel to everybody, not just me, and he exploded with rage if I was too loud one day or if I didn't speak up another day. I couldn't win. He told me to sit, stay, and be still, or he ordered me to leave when I wasn't welcome anymore.

One summer evening when I was thirteen we were having a formal "adult" dinner at my grandfather's house. Since I was the only grandchild I was included with my seven aunts and uncles and my grandfather. What this meant was that we all sat at a large round dining room table and listened to my grandfather talk. He wasn't interested in what anyone else had to say, and if anyone else was talking he would interrupt when he had had enough. Even at thirteen I knew that these dinners were dreaded events for everyone.

I was a pudgy young teenager. Food gave me solace when I was feeling sad, and I felt sad a lot. What I didn't realize then was that my grandfather had no respect for overweight women, and I seemed to be heading in that direction. All of the other women around that table were very skinny, so I was the outlier, and thus in danger.

At the end of the meal my aunt brought in a plate of chocolate chip cookies for dessert and put them down in front of me. My grandfather immediately changed the focus of what he was saying: "For God's sake don't put those down in front of her! She'll eat the whole damned plate!"

Everyone turned and looked at me. I was on the verge of crying and quickly asked to be excused — no one could leave the dinner table without permission from my grandfather.

As I scurried away I heard my father try to defend me. "Dad," he said. "She's still growing. It's just baby fat."

For years I held onto the anger I felt toward my grandfather, never missing a chance to say a spiteful word about him when his name came up. Then he died when I was in college, and not long after I was recounting one of the many stories I had heard of his ruthlessness to my father over the phone. After listening to me complain about my grandfather yet again my father said, "Gwen, try to forgive him. Do you realize how much energy you are spending feeling angry? It's just not worth it."

These were shocking words to hear — especially since my dad had suffered far, far worse physical and mental abuse than I had from his father.

It took me five years to put my dad's words into action. To take them in and let them transform me, to really apply them to my emotions. Forgiving my grandfather took practice, took reminding, and took going over my feelings and adjusting them.

Finally, one day it happened. When I thought of my grandfather I felt not even a sliver of anger. For the first time ever, when I thought of him, I felt free… and thankful.

My grandfather was the first person I ever forgave, and like so many things, the first time you do it is the hardest. Since then I have had to forgive many more people, and I am so thankful that I know how to do it.

Today, I like to think that part of my father's family legacy is not the cruelty I remember, but the lesson in how to forgive and feel gratitude.

—Gwen Daye—

Dr. Mike...

Wouldn't it have been nice if Judythe and Gwen had one of those Hollywood movie moments?

Perhaps it would have been like that scene from Nicholas Sparks' *The Notebook*. In the movie, Ryan Gosling and Rachel McAdams play young lovers. During a torrential downpour, they both realize that her mother had been hiding the daily love letters he had been writing for a year. And just like that, the healing they both needed happened in an instant.

For Judythe, the camera would have panned in.

"Are you having an affair?"

The lights dim. Her husband turns. His eyes well up with tears.

"My darling... How could you even think such a thing? You are the love of my life!"

They kiss.

Cut to Gwen's grandfather. He apologizes to his granddaughter for his unkind words. They hug, and he sees the error of his ways.

Of course, that's not how the stories went.

Judythe's husband actually replied with a dry *Yeah. What's for dinner?* Even though he told her later that there really wasn't anyone else.

And, Gwen's grandfather never apologized.

These probably weren't the movie moments you were waiting for.

But in the end, both Judythe and Gwen's stories did have happy endings.

Under the fluorescent-lighting of a divorce support group, Judythe had that "aha moment."

In my marriage I did the best I could.

That caused her epiphany: Her spouse did the best he could, too... because who would choose to do the worst?

At some point, you will probably have someone in your life who presents you an opportunity to mend a relationship and heal. You'll probably also have someone like Gwen's grandfather, a person who is no longer in your life, refuses to talk to you, or has passed.

In these cases, you may end up carrying resentment and hurt around with you. This can negatively affect your current relationships. You have an Achilles' heel that flares up when someone makes an insensitive comment.

Gwen managed to find forgiveness though. There would be no deathbed apology from her grandfather, but she looked for the silver lining and found that in some way, her relationship with her grandfather taught her how to forgive others. And it's something she is now "thankful" she knows how to do. Sometimes, the only thing we can change is ourselves, not the past, and that works, too.

Is your problematic person a "Gwen's grandfather" type — except one who is still in your life? This may be a person who will never change. He or she will continue to say hurtful things. If this is the case, sometimes the healthiest choice is to minimize the time you spend with that person. Or, you may wish to no longer have this person in your life. Fill your life with people who fill you up — not those who cut you down.

Without forgiveness, you are still letting that person affect your life. Forgiveness doesn't mean you are condoning his or her behavior. It simply means you are releasing yourself from the prison of resentment.

And forgiveness is possible whether a person remains your closest friend, an acquaintance, or someone who is no longer healthy for you to have in your life.

The answer in all these cases is forgiveness, because remember Judythe's epiphany — chances are that person was doing the best he could, even if he wasn't doing a very good job.

As Maya Angelou said, forgiveness is one of the greatest gifts you can give yourself. Forgive everybody!

I. Change how you THINK

When it comes to the disagreements that cause hurt or anger in our lives, **psychic** thinking is a pitfall thought pattern that often shows up.

There are two types of **psychic** thinking. The first type is falsely assuming that *you* are the mind reader. You assume you know exactly what others are thinking or feeling — even though they have not verbalized it.

The second type is expecting *others* to be mind readers. You want them to know exactly what you're thinking or feeling — without you verbalizing it. Judythe was in a marriage where it would have been hard *not* to be **psychic**. She describes herself as *gregarious, outspoken, and loved a good conversation, especially one with a suitable amount of controversy to jack up the interest level. I was quick to say I love you.*

Her husband was *quiet, introverted, someone who refused to discuss religion or politics and was content to sprawl on the couch and watch sports during the few hours he wasn't working, going to school or playing sports.*

Judythe even said that it was difficult for her to *engage him in a conversation of any length.*

Eventually, she had to become a **psychic**.

He wasn't *verbalizing* how he felt — so she had to read his mind. This is problematic. When **psychic** thinking isn't remedied, it causes serious rifts in relationships. If those rifts aren't remedied, then divorce is often the end result.

If you're in a relationship where there is a lot of **psychic** thinking going on, stop all that mind reading. If you're the Judythe, communicate in ways that are going to help open the lines of communication. If you're like her husband, say what's on your mind.

And yet, perhaps there is forgiveness in this story when both people realized that they did the best they could. While opposites attract, perhaps Judythe and her ex-husband were just *too* different.

Perhaps Judythe needs someone who is more extroverted and sensitive. Perhaps her ex-husband would be best suited with a fellow introvert.

Psychic thinking tends to affect people who grow up in Gwen's shoes in the opposite way... especially if they haven't yet done some of the healing that Gwen has.

If you grow up hearing that your voice doesn't matter, you are likely to become quiet. Maybe you grew up "a pudgy young teenager" like Gwen. Or, you're black, Jewish, gay, poor, a woman, didn't finish high school, not as successful as your friends... You fill in the blank. Is there a reason that you felt different... or were made to feel that your voice didn't matter? If so, your voice can become stifled.

If so, you may fall prey to **psychic** thinking in its other form. Instead of thinking that *you* are the psychic and know what other people are thinking, you expect *other people* to be psychic and know exactly what *you* are thinking. Instead of other people failing to verbalize their feelings, *you* are the one who's not talking about how you really feel.

This can harm relationships in other ways. Eventually, resentment and negativity build. **Psychic** thinking leads to a kind of energy that can block forgiveness. Open communication and honesty make it more possible.

The opposite of **psychic** thinking is open communication. If there is someone in your life you need to find forgiveness for, let's examine how you can change it.

Here's a meditation that can be an antidote to **psychic** thinking....

- *In your mind's eye, see one person you love easily. This is someone you communicate with openly. You tell them how you feel, and they do the same for you. Feel all the love you have for this person. You may wish to see the love you have for them traveling from your heart to theirs. Silently say: "May you be happy and peaceful."*
- *Now in your mind's eye, see a person with whom you've had a few minor conflicts. Perhaps this person hasn't always communicated what he or she thought or felt, and perhaps you haven't done the same in return. Hear yourself telling this person exactly how you feel with kindness and compassion... explaining exactly how you feel and why.*
- *Hear yourself saying, "I am sorry for any hurt or misunderstanding I have caused you. And in return, I forgive you for any hurt or misunderstanding you caused me." Silently say: "May you be happy and peaceful." Send as much love to this person as you did the first person.*
- *Now in your mind's eye, see that person you still need to forgive most. Hear yourself telling this person exactly how you feel with kindness and compassion... telling him or her exactly how you feel and why.*
- *Hear yourself saying, "I am sorry for any hurt or misunderstanding I have caused you. And in return, I forgive you for any hurt or misunderstanding you have caused me." Silently say: "May you be happy and peaceful." Send as much love to this person as you did the first person.*
- *Now in your mind's eye, see yourself. Perhaps you realize all the ways in*

which you have kept yourself small and silent. Know now that you are just as worthy as any other human being, and the way you feel matters.

- *Perhaps you now realize the ways you have deprived yourself of this gift of forgiveness. As you give yourself the gift of forgiveness and extend it to others in your life, silently say: "May I be happy and peaceful." Send as much love to yourself as you did everyone else.*

How did this meditation change my thoughts?

_____

_____

_____

How did this meditation change the way I feel?

_____

_____

_____

2. Change how you ACT

Changing the ACT is simple. Take the meditation and turn it into action. Extend an olive branch to the person in your life who you need to forgive. It can be in the form of a dinner, a phone call, or a card. If the person has passed away, write that person a letter. Turn right thought into right action.

Identify a person you need to forgive:

_____

How will you extend an olive branch and find forgiveness?

_____

_____

_____

Pick another person you need to forgive:

_____

How will you approach this person and find forgiveness?

_____

_____

_____

Finally, what do you need to forgive within yourself?

_____

Grant yourself forgiveness.

3. BE HAPPY

Chapter 10

Think, Act & Be Happy

Thrive after Cancer

I Don't Want to Die!

There's no disaster that can't become a blessing…
~Richard Bach

"I don't want to die!" was all I could say, all I could think about. Nothing else mattered. No other thoughts intruded. I felt as if I was drowning and my husband was the life preserver I clung to.

"We'll beat this," he assured me, holding me tightly.

I heard the words, but the reality of the moment was just too terrible to accept. I wasn't old. I felt wonderful — except for the insidious cancer that had just been diagnosed. That news hit me like a blow to the heart, to the soul. This wasn't possible. It had to be a mistake.

At that time I was fifty, with my children raised, my husband moving up in his job and our finances finally stable. Life was good. I felt I was in the best physical shape of my life. I felt accomplished in my career. I felt — a lump in my breast.

"It can't be anything bad," I kept assuring myself, even as I kept that first, fateful doctor's appointment. Of course not. Those kinds of things happened to other people, not to me. There was nothing like it in my family history.

"How long has it been since your last mammogram?" the nurse asked as I sat there shivering, more from fear than from the chill in the air of the examination room.

"I don't know. Two years or so, I guess." At that time, the recommended interval between mammograms for women under fifty was every two years. Thankfully, that has now been changed to once a year after the age of forty.

"Well, we'll need to see the old films and I'll schedule you for a new series," the nurse said, so businesslike it seemed hardhearted.

"Since they weren't taken here, you'll have to request them."

"The old X-rays? How do I do that?" My mind whirled and I wondered how I was going to function, let alone handle all the details alone. Why was I there by myself? Because, in my panic, I had decided to shelter my husband from the trauma until I was certain I was all right. I had not told him what was going on or what I feared. After all, I was still assuring myself that this threat was nothing but a figment of my overactive imagination.

The doctor entered the exam room. He glowered at me. "Why are you here?"

"I found a lump."

He checked the nurse's notes. "I see that. But why come to me? Why not see your regular doctor?" Still, he scowled as if I were annoying him.

There was something in his tone and in my own mental anguish that pushed me over the edge. He was young, yes, but that was no excuse for his attitude.

I blinked back tears and spoke my mind, raising my voice. "Do you know how hard it was to come here at all? Do you? My regular doctor wasn't in today and I said I needed to be seen urgently so they sent me to you. Do you want me to leave?" By this time I was weeping openly. I slid off the table while clutching the paper gown to my body. "I can go. I will go."

He seemed to come to his senses and looked truly surprised. He also apologized, more than once, and I got my cursory exam before leaving for the mammogram. When I did hear from my regular physician the following day, he also expressed empathy and explained that my mini-tirade had actually helped open his colleague's eyes.

That event, as unwelcome as it was, also taught me to stand up for myself. To ask for whatever I needed and to demand that my concerns be addressed. It was a new role for me, but it has become part of the advice I now pass on to other cancer patients. "This is your life. Your body," I say. "Take responsibility for your care."

Which brings me to the evening my husband brought me the bad news. I was away from home, attending a conference, and my husband, who was now aware of the tests that had been done, was to join me for the weekend.

I greeted him with a grin, then saw his expression. My jaw dropped. He reached for me. I think I may have said, "No," or maybe merely thought it.

"The doctor called," he said. "He gave me his home number so you can talk directly to him instead of having to wait till Monday morning."

Nothing else was said. I fell into my husband's arms, sobbing, "I don't want to die."

I don't really know how long we stood there together. Perhaps it wasn't long, but in my memory the scene stretches eternally because so much of what happened next is just a blur. I telephoned my regular physician and he explained what to expect next. He was patient with my confusion and I thanked him for giving me his home number, an act of unusual kindness that I remember to this day.

As I hung up, my husband asked, "What do you want to do now?"

The answer was easy. "All I want to do is go home."

No banquets, no speeches, or party atmosphere appealed to me as it had just a few minutes before. I wanted peace. Quiet. Home. And now, as I relive that day, I sit in the special place that was the ultimate result of my illness. You see, we both got a wake-up call that day. Jobs were no longer as important. Money and career advancement took a back seat to survival.

I had surgery, then chemotherapy, and seventeen years later I am cancer-free. I still get nervous from time to time, sure, but I have learned to live with that lingering uneasiness about my health and it has kept me aware of the narrow escape I had. That's not a bad thing, especially since I have been given many chances to reach out to others who are battling the same disease.

Through it all, I came to understand more about what really matters than I had in my whole adult life up to that point. Friends matter more. Family is paramount. Expressing my love and affection for everyone takes precedence over the many mundane tasks that had monopolized my previous hours on earth.

I still feel enormously blessed to have accidentally discovered that lump and to have survived to talk about it. Each day, each breath, each opportunity is an unimaginable gift.

Always remember that others have walked the same path that you are on, whether it was through illness or financial trials or other disastrous calamities.

You are not alone. Reach out. We're here to take your hand.

— Valerie Whisenand —

The Ten Best Things

The best things in life aren't things.
~Art Buchwald

"Y̶ou know what I really can't stand?" Wendy asks rhetorically. "It's when people say cancer is a gift. I mean is that really something you'd like to receive? Would a friend give a friend cancer?"

"Yeah," chimes in Alice. "Some gift. Can I give it back? Say I don't want it? Maybe exchange it for something different?"

We are all getting in the spirit of it now. "Can we rewrap it and give it to someone else?"

"Or donate it to a white elephant sale?"

"Say politely, thanks but no thanks?"

As we all erupt into laughter, I sneak a glance around the room at the eight or so women assembled in a loose circle. The only prerequisite to joining this writing group was having received a cancer diagnosis at some previous point in our lives. A positive (in the clinical sense, that is) pathology report was our ticket for admission. A perk of getting cancer, if you will.

It's kind of funny to group cancer and the idea of perks in the same thought, but for all that we are chortling about it, there has been a silver lining to being diagnosed with cancer, even if it wasn't immediately apparent. *Pollyanna* wasn't one of my favorite childhood books for nothing, and almost as soon as the initial shock of my diagnosis began to subside, I tried playing the "glad game," like Pollyanna.

In the first place, I had to be grateful for all the technology and the vigilance of my doctor that enabled my cancer to be caught early, when it was, as they tell me, the most treatable. I held this thought close as I endured the treatment, reminding myself continually to focus on the future, and that this was merely the means to an end.

Time passed, and as my family and friends pulled around me, I slowly, almost imperceptibly at first, began to heal. The physical recovery, surprisingly enough, proceeded more rapidly than the emotional recovery. It took much longer to accustom myself to the uncertainty of life post-cancer. I was to discover that cancer challenges all of your basic assumptions and beliefs and causes you to reassess your priorities. Given that the average life expectancy for women in this country is somewhere around eighty years of age, I'd always figured I had plenty of time before I had to give serious thought to my own mortality. Cancer changed all that.

The voice of Sharon, our group facilitator, cuts through our laughter. "Let's get started now," she says. "While we're all thinking about cancer, I want you to write about something that is different about your life as a result of being diagnosed with cancer. Take about fifteen minutes."

Heads bend to the page, and pens move as everyone else begins writing. I alone stare vacantly out the picture window, tapping my pen, and thinking. What should I write about? How I stopped stressing so much about every little thing because suddenly everyday petty concerns didn't seem as important? About all the compassionate people I met along the way as I embarked on my cancer journey? About how I became more open to taking risks, like walking into this writing group with absolutely no writing experience whatsoever, because after cancer nothing else looks really scary?

Slowly, I begin to write "The Ten Best Things about Cancer." I stop and underline it several times before I continue.

There has to be a bright side. Every cloud has a silver lining after all.

Ten: I can never repeat the shock of the initial diagnosis.
Now that's something. Isn't that a bit like lightning never strikes twice? (Although sometimes it does.)

Nine: I appreciate each and every day now.
Even more than I did before.

Eight: I have something to talk about with people, if conversation ever lags.

Seven: I can almost guarantee that anyone I talk to has a cancer story of their own — themselves or a family member or a friend of a friend.

Six: I belong to an exclusive club of fighters and survivors.

Five: People tend to cut you some slack when they find out you've had cancer.

Four: I've met some truly amazing and inspiring people that I cannot conceive of having become acquainted with under any other circumstances, and for this, I'm truly grateful.

Three: I've learned that looking out for myself is not a luxury anymore, but a necessity.

Two: I've learned to stop and smell the proverbial roses (and tulips and crocuses and daffodils).

Finally, One: I am a survivor, as my pink shirt at next year's Race for the Cure will surely attest to. I have battled my arch-nemesis, Cancer, and for now, I have prevailed.

The gong gently calls us to attention. "Come to a stopping place," Sharon tells us, and there is a sudden furious scribbling of pens as everyone scrambles to wrap up their piece. As we go around the room sharing our writings, I am struck once again by the determination, courage and cautious optimism shown in the face of adversity by all the women in this room.

Over and over, I hear common themes echoed in the writings.

"I've learned not to take anything for granted," Amy reads.

"I stopped putting things off for the future. Besides attending this writing group, I've signed up for a watercolor class, something I always wanted to do." This is from Kristy.

And Donna: "I take the time now to explore life's highways and byways, and enjoy the ride."

And it gets me to thinking. Knowing what we know now, would any of us actually have chosen to have been diagnosed with cancer? The answer has to be emphatically no. I'm sure that I am speaking for all of us when I say we would have been glad to avoid the nerve-wracking wait for pathology results, the life-altering shock of diagnosis, being poked and prodded endlessly with needles, the surgeries, chemo and radiation treatments that tried the very limits of our endurance, and the relentless scans and blood tests to ensure that we remain, for the moment, cancer-free.

Yet for all that, one thing becomes patently clear to me. I doubt very much that any of us would give back what we have learned along the cancer journey: to be kinder, more compassionate, more life-affirming people and never to forget how much we still have to be grateful for. Cancer may not have been a gift, but it was certainly a wake-up call.

— Cara Holman —

Dr. Mike...

If you have a family history of a disease or have just found a lump in your breast like Valerie did, mammograms or other types of tests or exams can be downright terrifying.

Here's where our brain can start to play some real tricks on us. This can be a scary time for many people. Health anxiety can lead to avoidance. When it comes to our health, avoidance can lead to serious consequences.

Remember how Valerie started her story? *I don't want to die.* But that was just a *thought.* Fearful thoughts want to take *us* by the hand. They grab us and say, "Let me lead the way. Come over here. Bury yourself down here with me. Put your head in the sand, and don't come up!"

Instead, do what Valerie did. Take *fear* by the hand. *You* lead the way. Show fear who's in control. Every time a doctor, nurse, or friend supports you along this journey, that fear will shrink 1%. Taking action is fear's kryptonite.

Valerie's story also reminds us that our journey may not always be perfect. People may not always say the right thing. Some people get really uncomfortable around illness.

Remember when that specialist's tone of voice made her cry when he said: *But why come to me? Why not see your regular doctor?*

I can't imagine how hard it must have been for Valerie as she wept openly, clutching her paper gown as she said, *I can go. I will go.*

Thank goodness she didn't.

Remember: doctors are people, too. Maybe he had seen one too many patients that day and was tired, or maybe he was just one of those people who doesn't make great first impressions.

Regardless, this specialist cared and apologized repeatedly. Thankfully, Valerie was brave enough to stay.

One of my favorite parts of Valerie's story was the advice she passes on to other cancer warriors: *This is your life. Your body. Take responsibility for your care.*

Once upon a time, we thought medicine would be the cure-all

for everything. Now, we realize that the best health outcomes are the result of patients who empower themselves.

Yes, doctors can be brilliant. I hope we continue to come up with advancements and treatments that save lives. Yes, we will cure cancer one day. In the meantime, we need to empower ourselves. Smoking cigarettes, drinking soda, and eating French fries today and expecting doctors to fix you tomorrow isn't the answer. As they say, an ounce of prevention is worth a pound of cure.

There are so many things we can control in this world... and so many things we can't. In fact, I'm often reminded of the Serenity Prayer when it comes to our health. Accept the things you can't change (e.g., your family history, your age). Change the things you can (e.g., your diet, how often you get a mammogram). And have the wisdom to know the difference!

Valerie can't change her age or family history. But she did follow the recommended screening interval for a woman her age. That was something she *could* control.

Is there something in your life you *can* change or control?

Can you cut down on foods you know aren't good for you? Eat more veggies? Exercise more? Have you done a self-screening? Have you been to your doctor lately?

Maybe you can even do something deep and meaningful in your life. Did you know that your emotional life also falls under the "change the things you can" column of the Serenity Prayer?

Cara was forced to have some emotional "aha" moments when her group facilitator made her write "The Ten Best Things about Cancer." For Cara, cancer forced her to appreciate every day more than ever. She learned the importance of self-care... something so many of us neglect. What "aha" moment would you like to have right now?

Maybe you're sitting in a chair right now, and you're nauseous from your latest round of chemotherapy. Maybe you've been cancer-free for ten years. Maybe you've never been diagnosed with cancer. In any case, we all have a lot to learn from cancer survivors.

One researcher looked at people with some of the most remark-able cases of cancer remission. She found these survivors had a few things in common. They all took control of their health, changed their diet, embraced social support, deepened their spiritual connection, and had a strong reason for living.

There are so many things we can't change in this world, but yes, there are also so many things we can….

1. Change how you THINK

One pitfall thought pattern that cancer survivors or people who worry about chronic illness fall prey to is **pessimism**. It tends to be a specific type of **pessimism** — one that considers the doom-and-gloom, worst-case-scenario, and catastrophic outcome.

And when it comes to cancer, that type of **pessimism** can even be the most catastrophic outcome: death. That was Valerie's overwhelming fear.

This kind of pitfall thought pattern isn't just anxiety provoking. In fact, stress may actually play a role in spreading cancerous cells more quickly throughout the body — *six times* faster in a recent animal study that made headlines around the world.

Stress — the kind that pessimistic, catastrophic thinking can cause — acts like a fertilizer and allows a cancerous cell in one part of the body to travel to other parts of the body. But guess what? The cognitive behavioral tools you're learning in this book can help you to feel less stressed! And more optimistic…

Here's a meditation that is a great antidote to this type of thinking. Pessimistic, worst-case scenario, catastrophic thinking is obviously a negative way to think. It's also a future-oriented type of thinking. So instead of focusing on what's going to happen tomorrow or at your follow-up appointment, let's just focus on what's happening *right now*.

Take the next few minutes to do the guided practice. After you memorize it, you can do this meditation with your eyes closed.

• *Imagine you're sitting in front of a stream, and that stream represents your thoughts and feelings. You can see all your pessimistic, worst-case-scenario thoughts. But look upstream! See that silly thought floating toward you?*

Now look upstream again! See that other thought about that errand you forgot to do today?

- Just let all these thoughts float… whether they're positive, negative, or neutral… as if you were watching a stream. The thoughts and feelings just gently float… just like water flowing in a stream. Do this for a few moments… or a few minutes if you'd like.
- You may notice something else that's interesting here that happens for most people. At some point, you may notice a care-free ease around these thoughts. When that happens right now or in a few moments, you'll become a bit more relaxed than you were before.
- Now, can you notice the difference between you and your thoughts? You're so much more than just your thoughts, aren't you?
- Knowing that you're more than just your thoughts can help you to feel so easy, comfortable, and calm. You're a spiritual being. Know that. Feel that.
- Now, just reflect on something else… as you sit here watching this beautiful stream: If your stream is flowing, it means that you're alive.
- Do you know how many miracles it takes for you to be alive? Even Albert Einstein said there are two ways to live: as though nothing is a miracle… or as though everything is a miracle. Choose the latter, and know that to be breathing, to be thinking, to be feeling… is a miracle in and of itself. Yes. You are already a miracle. I wonder what incredible things you'll do with this precious gift.
- The fact that you are sensing these thoughts and feelings in your river means that there's so much more right with you than wrong with you. In fact, it means that you are alive! And the more you know that— and feel that— in the moment, the more you're giving your precious body the ability to heal… as you harness the power of your own mind.

The pitfall thought pattern of **pessimism** comes in many different forms. Catastrophic, doom-and-gloom, worst-case-scenario thoughts are some examples of **pessimism**, and they're quite common if you've been diagnosed with a disease like cancer.

Pessimism spirals out of control when you stew in these negative thoughts. It's like you're jumping into a river. You get swept away.

That's why this meditation is such a fantastic antidote for **pessimism**.

It helps you to stay grounded in the here-and-now. It's a mindful approach to train your brain — and even boost your immune system.

If you used this thought stream meditation regularly, how would it prevent you from spiraling out of control with pessimistic thoughts?

_____

_____

_____

At the end of this meditation, you reflected on "what's right" with you. Perhaps you had a mini "aha" moment. Remember what Einstein said. *There are two ways to live: as though nothing is a miracle... or as though everything is a miracle.* Yes. The fact that you are breathing, seeing, hearing, and reading this sentence right now *is* a miracle.

How does the focus on "what's right" with me and a "miracle mindset" help me banish **pessimism**? How do I turn living, seeing, hearing, and breathing into a miracle — right here and right now?

_____

_____

_____

2. Change how you ACT

Remember when Valerie took control of her life? She took the advice she now gives other survivors: *This is your life. Your body. Take responsibility for your care.*

Cara took control, too. When she walked into that group with no writing experience, she was taking a risk. When she didn't storm out of the room after being given the assignment "The Ten Best Things about Cancer," she was taking control over something in her life.

What are *you* in control of? The Serenity Prayer is a fantastic way to create **action**.

Grant me the serenity to **accept** these five things in my life:

1. _____

2. _____

3. _____

4. _____

5. _____

Give me the courage to **change** these five things in my life:

1. _____

2. _____

3. _____

4. _____

5. _____

Circle which one of these tasks you will do first (today or as soon as you're well enough to be able to do so). And how will you specifically go about making this change?

_____

_____

_____

…and grant me the wisdom to know the difference.

3. BE HAPPY

Chapter 11

Think, Act & Be Happy

Move On and Reclaim Your Life

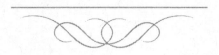

Singing in the Rain

I don't sing because I'm happy;
I'm happy because I sing.
~Author Unknown

It had been months since my dad went to work one night and never came home, but we were nowhere near over the divorce. My siblings didn't talk about it. Kelly went out a lot and my brothers, John and Matthew, just sort of wandered around doing what they always did, but in a kind of fog.

My mother cried night after night. Of course it would affect her differently. She had not had a clue Daddy was leaving. The shock of it alone made her cry. She screamed a lot, too, misdirecting her anger at my dad towards us, mostly me. It was one of the hazards of being the oldest child.

Then our house burned down. Neighbors actually stood outside in the street and chatted and laughed as our house burned one January morning. I stood there, shoeless, watching my mother weep and all I could think was, "We are broken."

We moved into the Ramada Inn, where my mother worked, five of us crammed into one tiny room. In no time, we were on each others' nerves. After four months of not having any of our own air to breathe, we were on the verge of just giving up. We were never going to have a home again. Putting one foot in front of the next felt impossible.

One day Mother stood up, looking frenzied. "Let's go for a ride."

Kelly, John, Matt and I looked at one another warily, not sure we had heard right. There were two issues. One, Mother had just been learning to drive out of necessity since Daddy left. Two, she was very bad at it.

"Come on," she urged. "It'll be fun."

This confused us further. We didn't have fun in our family. We fought and cried. Our mother's anger at our father's abandonment had seeped slowly and surely into each of our lives. Fun was something we might have known about once, but which seemed foreign to us now.

Still, we minded our mother and piled into our 1972 blue Ford Torino, a blue so faded as to appear almost white. As the oldest, I sat in the front seat with our mother, while Kelly, John and Matt sat in the back. Mother started the car and backed out of the parking lot. "I thought we'd go look at all the houses we've lived in."

We had lived in quite a few places. Mother drove us by the house where we'd lived when I was just a kindergartener and then down the road a few houses to where we'd lived when I was in first grade. We even hazarded the main drag to see where my parents had lived when I was born, a tiny one-room apartment over a pharmacy that looked about the size of the motel room we inhabited now.

We talked about everything you could imagine — all the things we had to avoid talking about in that motel room. When there were lulls in the talk, we sang. We had always been a singing family, growing up with two parents who loved music. We started by singing "On Top of Old Smokey" the right way and then we sang every strange variation we could think of. We laughed a lot.

After this first foray, going for a ride in my mother's car became a regular thing. Every night we piled into the car and the world changed. We told jokes and sang and looked at houses we wished we had the money to live in.

I loved riding in the car. As spring turned to summer, the breezes blew through the car and cooled us even on the hottest of nights and we were spared the sticky, humid nights of anger in the motel. The singing allowed us to vent emotions we couldn't face back in that cramped space. It was during one of those nightly car rides that my mother taught me how to harmonize.

We sang "You Are My Sunshine" and "K-k-k Katie" and a million other songs. The hope we seemed to have lost in the rest of our life was real again in the car as we sang.

So was laughter. We sang a Lynyrd Skynyrd song, "What's your name, little girl? What's your name?" at the top of our lungs to a tiny girl in another car at a stoplight and fell into hysterics when the occupants of the other cars pointed and laughed at us.

The hymns were my favorite. Mother didn't go to church. God had become a taboo topic since our dad had left. The hymns we sang—"Amazing Grace" and "How Great Thou Art" and "Shall We Gather at the River"—let us connect on a different level than we'd ever been able to in the past and calmed us down at evening's end for the return to the motel. More often than not, Mother and I ended these nights by carrying our sleeping boys, her sons and my brothers, in to bed, exhausted but happy.

One night as we were singing loudly, "In the pines, in the pines, where the sun never shines and you shiver when the cold wind blows..." Mother suddenly slammed on the brakes. "This is it!" she cried.

"This" was a house, and a for-rent sign in the front yard brought me more joy than I could believe.

"Really?" I asked.

My mother jumped out, excited, and ran to peer in the windows of the house. My siblings soon followed, and when I realized we might really have a house again, I got out, too. "This bedroom is mine!"

I realized that night that my mother was just a person, just like the rest of us. She was no better and no worse and she had been through a lot. And her driving had improved dramatically!

We moved into our new house the following weekend. We were very busy and the nights in the car became a thing of the past. The following summer we tried again with the car, but the times had changed and the car was never the same kind of haven for us again. Better off, we had moved on. New jobs and activities of every kind used up our time now. But we knew that one summer in the blue Torino had saved a vital part of us all. My dad had left, it was true, and we had lost our home, but my mother, whether by accident or design, had found a way to bring us together and keep us that way.

—Marla H. Thurman—

Breaking the Cycle

Could we change our attitude, we should not only see
life differently, but life itself would come to be different.
~Katherine Mansfield

Dropping out of high school and becoming a single mom by the time I was eighteen years old was certainly not the dream I had for myself as a little girl, but that was the hand that I was dealt. I don't think I ever realized what a difficult journey it would be trying to become a successful adult while also raising a child.

As a young girl, I experienced sexual abuse as well as parents who battled an addiction to drugs and alcohol. Once I reached my teenage years, I found myself alone and becoming my own parent. By the time I had my son in 1989, I was depressed, 110 pounds overweight, and a high school dropout with no self-esteem. I could not even hold a job. By the time I was twenty-one, I had my second child, a daughter, but still struggled with obesity, depression and a poor work ethic. I knew I wanted a better life for my kids and for myself but I just could not find the motivation within myself to get us there. By the time I was twenty-six, I got a job at a hotel and had finally found a place that gave me the opportunity to grow and learn and start to feel like I was worth something. I was there for six years and had been promoted four times to be second in charge.

Today I am the General Manager of a fifteen-million-dollar company, have been named one of the Best 50 Women in Business in Pennsylvania, a top forty business professional under the age of forty, and have lost 140 pounds. My proudest moment was in May of 2007 when I officially graduated from high school at the age of thirty-seven.

How has all this affected my life as a woman and a mother? I have broken the cycle! My kids have watched me work very hard to grow as a person, a wife and a mother. They have seen firsthand what hard work, passion and dedication can bring into your life. My son is now twenty and has completed his first two years of college. I am so proud of where he is in his life. He is a hard-working, bright, funny, well-rounded young man and watching him grow, learn and become his own individual has been scary, wonderful and exciting all at the same time. My daughter is sixteen and is strong-willed and outspoken just like I am. I hope that I have taught her how to love herself more than anyone else will and to never settle for anything less than what will make her very happy.

My kids have been the motivators in my life. I worked so hard because I wanted them to have a role model that they could look up to. But I also wanted to show them that the blessings in your life are something you need to give back to others and that people are not defined by the mistakes they have made but by the content of their character. Being a mom is more than just feeding, clothing and providing a roof over your children's heads. They are empty books that we fill throughout their lives and you can never erase the pages.

I felt the need to show my kids the importance of giving back to others who are not as fortunate as we are. I started mentoring other kids, young people who lost their way and were dropping out of school, and young girls who have had babies in their teenage years and just need an understanding ear. I am also a mentor to women living in homeless shelters and transitional housing, teaching them life skills as well as work ethic and job interviewing techniques. In addition to all of this, I sit on three corporate boards and countless other commit-tees. Somehow, in my crazy life, I still find the time to go home every evening, make dinner for my family and spend time with my kids.

When you have a love and a passion for your life and your children, you find the time to do it all. No complaining, no feeling sorry for yourself. I am now blessed not only with my two amazing children, but also with a loving marriage to their father, and a network of people who can say that I have touched their lives in some way.

—Aimée Urban—

Dr. Mike...

Some children are dealt lucky hands in this world. They have great, loving parents. They are given every advantage. They go to the best schools. If this were poker, some kids are dealt a royal flush. Flip the cards over, and you see an ace, a king, a queen, a jack, and a 10.

Other kids are dealt different hands. Marla lived in a Ramada Inn hotel room with four other family members — after her dad left and her house burned down. Aimée was a teen mom and high school dropout — who was also the daughter of addicts and the survivor of sexual abuse.

Marla and Aimée had the equivalent of five numbered cards. No pairs. Different suits. The highest card: a 6.

It would have been easy to say, "I'm so unlucky! This isn't fair!" It would have been easy to give up, become hopeless, and throw in the towel.

Marla shouldn't have laughed in that 1972 blue Ford Torino. How could she be singing "You Are My Sunshine" at a time like that?! Stay angry! Did she see the unfair hand she was dealt? But she and her family did laugh, and they powered through their dire situation, all of them learning a lesson on perspective that surely enabled them to handle many negative situations in their future lives.

It would have been easy for Aimée to repeat the cycle. Looking at her hand, she shouldn't have become the General Manager of a fifteen-million-dollar company, been named one of the Best 50 Women in Business in Pennsylvania, a top forty business professional under the age of forty, or lost 140 pounds.

Aimée should have been one of those "statistics" — an addict, a physically abusive mother repeating the cycle of abuse, or spending her life scraping by on government assistance. Nope. Not Aimée. She took the hand she was dealt and won the poker tournament... all on what they call a "nothing hand."

How did she do that? I guess in many ways, both of these ladies acted like they were the casino — not a gambler.

You know what they say in Vegas: the house always wins. How does it manage to do that? It just stays the course. The house takes emotion out of it. The house advantage is simply that mathematical edge the casino has in every game you may play — from slots to blackjack to poker.

While an irrational, reactive gambler is busy feeling sorry for himself… and then gambling his rent money to try to make up for the money he just lost… and then losing that… the house is steady.

One gambler may have just won a $10,000 jackpot, but 100 other gamblers have just gambled away $20,000. Every time you win a small jackpot, your brain releases a small hit of dopamine. That feel-good chemical keeps you coming back for more.

Marla's mom and Aimée remind me of the tortoises in the Aesop's fable *The Tortoise and the Hare*. And you know what they say about that tortoise: slow and steady wins the race. Vegas casinos are like the tortoise, too. Over time, hard work, diligence, and rationality wins. A healthy dose of hope comes in handy, too.

Every dollar that Marla's mom made at that Ramada Inn slowly helped her to move her family into that house. And every shift Aimée worked at that hotel for six years helped her. Her hard work helped her to be promoted four times!

Compulsive gamblers aren't tortoises. They're the hares. They think they can outsmart the house. They go all in all at once with their rent money. They put all their money on red. They lose their shirt. They get frustrated with their luck. Their emotions are all over the place. That gets them in trouble.

If there is something in your life that's hard right now, become a tortoise just like Marla, Marla's mom, and Aimée. Maybe you've been dealt a bad hand. Pick yourself up… one day at a time. Set goals, and stay the course. The largest building starts with a single brick.

When you do so, you may even find yourself singing "You Are My Sunshine" in your car one day.

1. Change how you THINK

Permanence is a pitfall thought pattern. You need to change that thought if you want to move on from something in your life, because that way of thinking makes you believe that the way you feel *now* is the way you will *always* feel. It falsely tells you things will never change.

Remember when Aimée was 110 pounds overweight, a high school dropout, and a new teen mom? If she had let this **permanence** weave its nasty spell in her brain, it would have told her, "You'll always be this depressed and won't amount to anything. You'll always be this overweight, too. And by the way, you'll probably always be stuck in this situation."

Imagine Aimée is with you right now, and she's telling you, "I've been there. If I can do it, so can you! Don't believe that nasty thought!"

Yes, she lost 140 pounds. Yes, this high school dropout was named one of the Best 50 Women in Business in Pennsylvania. Imagine what *you* are capable of. Whatever it is you're going through or whatever it is you need to overcome, the tools you need are right here within you.

Memories in the brain are mood-congruent. That means when you're sad about something, all the sad memories light up. It *feels* like your life is filled only with sad memories, and this creates the false illusion that your life is always going to be sad. Don't believe it.

Train your brain right now. Rewind the tape of your life.

What are the three accomplishments that you are the most proud of?

1. _____

2. _____

3. _____

How does focusing on these wins help you to train your **permanence** away?

_____

_____

_____

2. Change how you ACT

Aimée's story began when she was just a young girl. Now, she has broken the cycle as a wife and mother. When Aimée wrote this story, her son was twenty and was two years into college. Her daughter was sixteen, strong-willed, and outspoken.

While you may have read Aimée's incredible journey in a few minutes, her journey from high school dropout to successful businesswoman or from abused teen to awesome mom took decades to unfold.

There will be mundane days. You'll wake up. You'll go to work—just like Aimée did at her first job. You'll pick yourself up. This will allow you the time to heal. Slowly but surely.

And so, it's time to see your future. Do you see that sun peeking out from the clouds? There! In the distance!

Become that tortoise. See your recovery unfold. Take it day by day. And see how that, day by day, can turn into healing, progress, and change over the years… just like Aimée's did.

A goal I have for myself today is to:

_____

This will help me to reach this goal next week:

_____

This will help me to reach this goal next month:

_____

This will help me to reach this goal next year:

_____

This will help me to reach this goal in the next five years:

_____

How will my story end? I will:

_____

3. BE HAPPY

Chapter 12

Tips that Work to Overcome Insomnia

Insomnia

Don't fight with the pillow, but lay down your head
And kick every worriment out of the bed.
~Edmund Vance Cooke

Most people look forward to hitting the sack, but I dreaded going to bed — I associated it with thrashing around until the sheets were bunched up and wrinkled, and watching the minutes turn over on my nightstand clock. I flipped my pillow so often there was no longer a cool side.

"I'm so tired!" I would moan in the morning when the alarm went off.

My husband would snort. "It might help if you went to bed at a decent hour."

"But if I go to bed before I'm sleepy, all I do is toss."

Sometimes I stayed up till 2 or 3 a.m., but still couldn't count on falling asleep when I finally turned in. Every cell in my body screamed with exhaustion, but I couldn't lie still. I was so hot. Off flew the covers. Pretty soon, I was cold — time to bundle myself back up.

When it became unbearable, I would stumble downstairs for a cup of tea, a snack, or a book. After a bleary hour or so, I'd head back upstairs to try again.

I avoided caffeine in the afternoon. I prayed. I took hot showers. I actually tried establishing a "decent" bedtime. I drank soothing chamomile tea right before my decent bedtime — and then I had to get up to go to the bathroom a couple of hours later.

The worst were the nights when the worries surfaced — everything I'd managed to push aside by keeping busy during the day. My life looked bleaker, scarier, more hopeless at night.

"I have the worst insomnia," I would tell my friends. "I never get a good night's sleep. When I was a little girl, I never wanted to sleep. One night, my mom decided to call my bluff and told me just to stay up if I wanted to, because she was going to bed. So she turned off the lights and pretended to go to bed, but all I did was keep playing with my toys in the dark!"

When I was in elementary school, I went through a sleepless period that went on for months. I was obsessed with worries and fears, and the only way I knew to keep them at bay was to stay up and read or play with the lights on, until exhaustion overtook my feverish brain. My mother was so concerned, she took me to the doctor, who gave me "nerve medicine," which I now suspect was sugar pills. They helped a little, but she only gave them to me when absolutely nothing else seemed to work.

"I hate bed," I said now — the same way I did when I was seven or eight. "I just can't sleep."

One day, I ran across an article with "sleep remedies." I never passed up articles on insomnia, even though I already knew all the tips before I read the first word.

"Okay, let's see what this one says…. Good sleep hygiene, limit caffeine, blah, blah, blah…" Then, incredibly, I saw something new — positive self-talk.

Most insomniacs, I read, tend to tell themselves and others they "just can't sleep." Over and over, day after day, they go to bed saying, "I know I won't sleep." Even people who otherwise appreciate the power of positive thinking in their daily lives fail to apply it to their sleep habits. The author of the article had interviewed sleep experts, and several had seen significant improvement in patients who had decided to change their inner self-talk.

I was dubious… but desperate. I couldn't believe that just telling myself I could sleep would produce any dramatic results, as several of the article subjects claimed. After all, like Patsy Cline, I'd been "walkin' after midnight" for many, many years. But I had to admit, it certainly couldn't be helping me when I told myself over and over that I was a hopeless case. And, like several of the subjects interviewed for the article, I had already seen the power of positive thinking in other areas.

Tips that Work to Overcome Insomnia | 137

Could I change my thought patterns? All I could do was try.

When I went to bed that night, I smiled as I smoothed out the pillowcase and laid down my head. "I'm going right to sleep," I told myself with a confidence I was far from feeling. "I feel so relaxed. I'm so tired."

A worry tried to assert itself, but I just pushed it down and told myself, "I don't have a care in the world."

Miraculously, that very first night, I fell right to sleep! When I woke up the next morning, I felt a new sense of power—I could actually control this thing.

The next night, I repeated my new bedtime routine, despite a little lingering doubt. Maybe it had just been a coincidence. But once again, I fell right to sleep.

By now, I was beginning to believe what I had been telling myself. The following night, I repeated my routine with more confidence—and the same result.

After a while, I no longer even had to talk myself into sleeping. Of course, as time went by, I still had the occasional restless night. But they became the exception, and were no longer a way of life.

I'd never really realized the enormous power of our thoughts, even in controlling what seemed to be physical circumstances. I was sixty years old, and had struggled for so long—yet the answer to my years of misery lay right inside my own head.

—Susan Kimmel Wright—

Secret Soup

Love is the poetry of the senses.
~Honoré de Balzac

My husband Matt and I have a secret nighttime ritual. It's one that even our closest friends and relatives don't know about. To the rest of the world we probably seem just like any other average middle-class, mid-life couple. Our philosophy is that whatever happens between two consenting adults is okay, as long as no one is harmed. We have decided to come out from behind closed doors and share this glimpse into our private life. Our secret… Matt reads stories to me from the *Chicken Soup for the Soul* series.

To me, the most beautiful sound in the world is Matt's voice. It has a rich masculine resonant quality. Whenever he sings in church, his powerful baritone voice can be distinctly heard above the rest of the congregation. After the service is over, the ladies in our church often compliment him on his singing. I believe it is the combination of his robust voice and boyish enthusiasm that captures their attention.

While we were dating, Matt and I would meet each other for coffee after I finished work at the hospital. We sat for hours in our favorite booth holding hands, sharing our dreams, and planning our future. Afterwards, he waited patiently for my call to let him know that I had arrived home safely. We then spent several more hours talking on the telephone. Matt's voice was the last sound that I heard before drifting off to sleep. It is amazing how little rest you need when you are falling in love. He still teases me, "I married you so that I could get some sleep at night."

Matt learned the art of reading aloud from his mother, as she read to each of her nine children. He continued the tradition with our own children. Danielle and Michael always enjoyed it when he read stories to them. His characters leapt off the page, as he brought them to life by varying the pitch and tempo of his voice. I loved listening as he read, treasuring this time together as a family. Gradually, as the nest emptied… I began to miss hearing Matt's stories.

Over the years Matt and I have shared the joys and challenges of life together. One of our most devastating setbacks was immediately following my back injury. A back injury is disastrous to the career of a bedside nurse. Along with severe pain, emotional and economic loss, there has been an extensive rehabilitation period with many relapses. Matt has been loving, supportive, and patient throughout my recovery.

One of the most troubling symptoms that I experienced during this stressful time was insomnia. I tried every known remedy including: establishing a regular bedtime, eliminating caffeine, drinking warm milk with nutmeg, lavender aromatherapy, and relaxing music. For a brief period, I resorted to taking sleeping pills. I hated the drowsy feeling the next morning and feared becoming dependent on them.

One particularly difficult night Matt suggested that I try reading a book. I was too tired to read and too restless to sleep. He offered to read to me. A natural choice seemed to be *Chicken Soup for the Nurse's Soul*. The book is a collection of encouraging uplifting stories about how nurses make a difference in the lives of their patients. This simple gesture combined the happy memories of hearing his voice over the telephone and listening to him read stories to our children. As he read, I began to feel more relaxed and after a few stories I was able to drift peacefully off to sleep. Thus began our nightly ritual of Matt reading stories to me from the *Chicken Soup for the Soul* series.

An added benefit has been the inspiration that we have both received from the stories themselves. As soon as we finish one book, we start another. Many of the volumes have been re-read several times. Others have been passed on to friends or family members. We select titles related to whatever is going on in our life. From time to time, the power of a story will cause Matt's voice to crack with emotion or a tear to roll down his cheek.

"That was a good one."

"You know… one of these days, one of my stories will be in *Chicken Soup for the Soul*."

"Yes, Laura, it will and I will read it to you."

— Laura Wisniewski —

Dr. Mike...

Sleep is a funny thing. It reminds me a lot of surfing. If you've ever taken a surfing lesson, there are lots of things you need to do.

Pick the right size surfboard for your body. Position your feet correctly on the board. Learn timing. If you stand up too soon, the wave knocks you down. If you stand up too late, the wave leaves you behind.

And even when you've done everything right, sometimes you still have to wait a long time for the next good wave to come in.

Sleep is that wave. Sometimes, it's right there. Tonight, you may be that lucky surfer who catches a perfect wave moments after paddling out. Tomorrow night, you may have to wait twenty or thirty minutes for the perfect wave to come to you. Despite being a good surfer, there's nothing you can do but be patient.

Like a surfer fine-tuning his or her technique, there are a few tips that are likely to help. There's actually quite a bit of skill involved when it comes to healthy sleep. That's where cognitive behavioral therapy for insomnia — or CBT-I — comes in.

A lot of the common sense strategies Susan and Laura instinctually used are part of the CBT-I program.

It's also a natural program that helps you use the power of your own brain to restore natural sleep-wake rhythms. Remember when Laura said she briefly "resorted" to taking sleeping pills and "feared becoming dependent on them." She's not alone.

In fact, the American College of Physicians now recommends CBT-I as the primary treatment for insomnia — not medication. There are many reasons for this.

Recent research has shown some women's bodies don't process sleeping pills very effectively. This means some of the medication could still be in your system eight hours after you take it. Obviously, this could be a problem for a mom who drives her child to school in the morning. For the elderly, sleeping pills have been associated with falls.

CBT-I is a natural, drug-free program. Whether you have trouble falling or staying asleep, CBT-I can help you. You can train your brain to restore your natural sleep-wake cycle.

Let's look at some of the CBT-I principles that Susan and Laura were using… whether they knew it or not.

Susan's husband's snorts: *It might help if you went to bed at a decent hour.*

Susan replies: *But if I go to bed before I'm sleepy, all I do is toss.* Who's right here?

Trick question. They're both right!

Going to bed at a decent hour is one of the most effective strategies when it comes to overcoming insomnia. Many of us have what researchers call "social jet lag" as so many of us stay up until the wee hours on the weekends and go to sleep early on weekdays. This wreaks havoc on our sleep-wake cycles. In our brains, it's like taking a plane from Los Angeles to New York and back every week.

The solution: pick a bedtime — and wake up time — and stick to it seven days a week.

This may mean you have to make some adjustments to your schedule. Look at your life and your commitments. Look at your family's commitments.

If you wake up at 5 a.m. to go to the gym before work but then stay up late to see friends, it's time to change one or the other. Move the workout to your lunch hour so you can sleep in later on weekdays. Or, you could choose to see your friends for Sunday brunches instead of late Saturday dinners. That way, you could get to bed earlier.

But what do you do if you toss and turn like Susan does?

Susan was right. You *don't* want your brain to associate your tossing and turning with your bed.

If you toss and turn for a long time, get up and do light activity. Don't turn on bright lights. Don't watch TV or play with your phone. That's training your brain in the wrong direction — to stay awake. The type of light that electronics emit shuts off melatonin production in your brain, and you want lots of melatonin at night.

Under dim lighting, read a book (like this one!), knit, or do a crossword puzzle until you're sleepy. Even the type of light bulb matters. Try a good, old-fashioned incandescent bulb on a dimmer or get a dimmable LED bulb that filters out the blue light. They're marketed as "night" or "good night" bulbs. Compact fluorescent bulbs have too much light that turns off melatonin in the brain — just like TVs and phones.

If you haven't slept a full eight hours and have reached your wake-up time, get out of bed anyway.

But wait! I thought eight hours of sleep was crucial for my brain!

It is! That's why you're getting out of bed. Natural rhythms of sleep that include eight hours are vital for brain health. It's *so* important that we'll sacrifice *one* day of you being tired... so that you can fall asleep naturally and easily the following night. This will keep you on your natural sleep-wake cycle for the long-term... and give you many eight-hour nights.

And what about temperature?

Susan's body temperature was all over the place... *I was so hot. Off flew the covers. Pretty soon, I was cold — time to bundle myself back up.*

We often think of a healthy body temperature as a nice even 98.6 degrees. Actually, your body temperature should go up and down slightly every day. It can be as much as a degree or two cooler at night than it is during the daytime.

Guess what? You can trick your body into thinking it's tired. Here's how: If you have a programmable thermostat, change the temperature to go down by a few degrees an hour before your scheduled bedtime. Or, change it by hand.

While you're at it, shut down all your electronics. Put your phone in airplane mode, and turn the wifi off. It prevents the temptation to look at your phone. Looking at your phone makes melatonin levels go down (the light) and stress hormone levels go up (the e-mail from work). No wonder you can't sleep! Get yourself ready for the day ahead of you... in a calm and comfortable way.

Another great way to cool your body temperature is to take a warm bath or shower. That will relax your muscles. When you get out, your body temperature dips. This will tell your body it's time for sleep.

This may be part of your wind-down ritual. For Laura, her ritual was Matt reading her a *Chicken Soup for the Soul* book. For you, it could be a bath and setting out your kids' clothes for tomorrow's school day. This trains your mind and body for restful sleep.

1. Change how you **THINK**

People with insomnia often struggle with the pitfall thought pattern **pessimism**. Did you hear how profoundly Susan's pessimistic thoughts were preventing sleep?

Let's take another look at Susan's self-talk at the beginning of her story:

I hate bed.
I have the worst insomnia.
I just can't sleep.

For Susan, insomnia's magic bullet was training her brain by changing her thoughts. She was skeptical, but as she said: *All I could do was try.*

What's *your* pessimistic sleep worry? And how much do you believe this thought? For example, do you talk to yourself in a negative way — like Susan did?

I have the worst insomnia.

Also: how much do you *believe* this worrisome thought?

Perhaps after reading Susan's hopeful story, you're now thinking to yourself… Hmmm… I guess my insomnia is about as bad as hers… and hers got better… maybe mine will, too… maybe this isn't a life sentence if hers wasn't. I'm starting to believe this is something I can change!

Perhaps you'd write a 65% next to your pessimistic sleep worry. That means that 65% of you believes this worrisome thought. But 35% of you is hopeful that something you're going to do could change this. You could be free of this worry soon. See, you're already admitting to *yourself* that your worry may be overblown! By doing so, you're *already* starting to train your brain.

My pessimistic sleep worry is _____

_____

and only _____ % of me believes it.

2. Change how you ACT

Now, let's change some of your *behavior* around sleep. Then we'll circle back to that worrisome *thought* in a few days or weeks. That's why cognitive behavioral therapy is so great. The ways you think, act and feel all affect each other. This brain training is like a domino effect that's never-ending.

First, set a bedtime and wake-up time. This is a time that you can stick to seven days a week.

My bedtime is _____ p.m.

My wake-up time is _____ a.m.

Note: these times should be roughly eight and a half hours apart.

Second, set a wind-down time that's sixty minutes before your bedtime. You can set a timer in your phone if that's helpful. When this timer goes off, do a few things: Dim all the lights. Turn off your ringer. Better yet — turn your phone off completely. Turn off all electronics. Make any last minute preparations for tomorrow. Turn down the thermostat or take a warm bath or shower. Get ready for bed. Make this wind-down time a ritual. Rituals are fantastic. Maybe you could even do what Matt did for Laura — make reading this or another *Chicken Soup for the Soul* book before bed — a ritual.

When it's time to actually go to bed, be *realistic*— not *perfectionistic*. Did you see how I set the times eight and a half hours apart? That's because it often takes people thirty minutes to fall asleep. Falling asleep in five minutes every night is *perfectionistic*. Allowing twenty or thirty minutes is *realistic*.

If you fall asleep right away, great! If you notice yourself lying there awake for a very long period of time like an hour or more, get out of bed and do some light activity until you feel sleepy again. If there's one day where you wake up really early and can't fall back asleep, know that you'll probably sleep really well the next night. Just avoid driving or operating machinery that day, since your reaction time will be affected.

One more thing: banish clock watching! Alarm clocks are meant to be heard — not seen. Turn your clock around if you're tempted to look at it during the night. Looking at the time during the night makes insomnia worse. If you're one of those people who gets nervous about missing your alarm and that 8 a.m. meeting, you could even set two alarms if that helps to avoid anxiety about oversleeping — get two clocks or set an extra alarm on your phone, the phone that's in the next room by the way (not by your bed).

Don't take naps unless you need them. If you do need a nap, make it a short one during the day — only twenty to thirty minutes. If you're still feeling exhausted despite sleeping eight hours, talk to your doctor. Long naps can disrupt the natural sleep-wake rhythms that CBT-I helps to establish.

CBT-I is a very effective treatment for insomnia, but it's important to note that it doesn't work to treat the potentially dangerous but treatable sleep-related condition sleep apnea. If you wake up gasping for air, are tired all the time despite sleeping eight hours, or snore loudly, talk to your doctor. There are now in-home sleep studies available to diagnose sleep apnea and they're covered by most insurance.

Keep using all these behavioral strategies for as long as you need them. Some people will notice improvements in just a day or two. For others, with more significant problems, more time will be needed.

From time to time, revisit that pessimistic sleep worry. Day by day, have you started to believe it a little less as your sleep improves? I wonder when you'll notice that your *actions* banish that worrisome thought completely.

If you're anything like so many of the patients I have treated, your actions will leave you with positive thoughts that may sound a lot like Susan's:

I feel so relaxed.
I'm so tired.
I don't have a care in the world.

Which optimistic, relaxing thought is the one that lulls you right to sleep?

_____

_____

_____

Once you've used all these behavioral strategies to improve your sleep, come back to the sleep worry you wrote down in the last section. Remember how you identified your sleep worry — and identified how much of you believed it to be true?

Let's take another look at your sleep worry — to see how you may have shifted it. Many people will notice that they believe these pessimistic thoughts less… thanks to all the strategies you have put into place.

My old pessimistic sleep worry was _____

_____

and now only _____ % of me believes it.

3. BE HAPPY

Chapter 13

Think,
Act & Be
Happy

Stepfamily Strategies
that Work

Worth the Wait

*When you look at your life, the greatest happinesses
are family happinesses.*
~Dr. Joyce Brothers

I accepted Bruce's invitation to dinner at his house with a tiny bit of discomfort. This time, his children were going to be there, too. I'd met Megan, Brent and Kevin once before at a picnic. But my sister and her family were also there so I wasn't alone with them. This time it would be obvious Bruce and I were a couple. I was uncertain how the children might react to that idea.

The weather was unusually hot, even for July. Bruce wanted to keep it casual but thought we needed something to do so we wouldn't be sitting around staring at one another. He decided we could wash our cars. Playfully spraying one another with the hose kept us all cool and provided the diversion we needed. Everything seemed to be running smoothly and I was beginning to relax.

Bruce had planned bacon, lettuce and tomato sandwiches for dinner and Megan insisted on cooking the bacon. I was a little skeptical about letting a nine-year-old work with hot bacon grease, but Bruce said she'd be fine. Even so, I went inside to supervise.

The aroma of maple bacon already filled the room. Seizing the opportunity to avoid her father's censorship, Megan wasted no time commencing her own agenda. The questions came quickly. Did I have a husband? Kids? What kind of jobs had I had? Which one did I like best? Why? Where did I live? Did I like dogs? Had I ever owned any? I'd been in job interviews that were less comprehensive. I was amused and suggested I'd set the table while I answered her questions. Forgetting the kids had no idea I was familiar with the kitchen, I automatically went to the cabinet containing the plates. Four-year-old Kevin eyed me with suspicion.

"You don't have to steal those," he said.

Megan didn't notice my faux pas and began yelling at him for being rude. I was about to ask him for some clarification when she let out a yowl. Distracted by her annoyance with her brother she'd brushed the hot tongs against the bare skin of her thigh.

By the time Bruce and Brent came inside, I was finishing up the bacon and Megan was perched on a stool on the other side of the room cooling her burned leg.

"Nice job, Megan," cracked seven-year-old Brent, surveying the damage and shaking his head.

She'd barely paused my interview, so I knew the damage wasn't bad. Bruce took a cursory look and pronounced it "no big deal." Still, I wished it hadn't happened.

After dinner, the kids begged Bruce to pull out the projector so they could show me photos of "when they were little." I was curious, so I went along with the idea — until I understood which pictures they wanted me to see. They were combing through slide carousels in search of the photos that showed each of them being born! I had some friends who'd taken some pretty graphic photographs of their kids entering this world. I was definitely not prepared for that much information and began to squirm. Bruce and I exchanged stressed looks as he tried unsuccessfully to dissuade them. But they were so excited for me to see these particular photographs that I couldn't say no. I searched out a good spot to focus my eyes so I could look away without being obvious, but I didn't need to. Bruce quickly pulled most of the shots that included his ex-wife so he could focus on the individual photos of each child swaddled in pink or blue blankets. All three were convinced I'd taken in every detail and they were thrilled.

By the time we were married I had read every book our library had on stepfamilies. Most were about stepparents with full custody. Our situation was much different. Bruce's ex and her husband lived nearby so the kids popped in and out unpredictably. One moment we were newlyweds and the next we were a family of five. By our first anniversary I was struggling. I'd had no problem moving to the house

Bruce had shared with his first wife. In fact, I rather liked the cozy little Dutch Colonial. And it was the best possible situation for the kids as they still had loads of friends in the neighborhood. What I wasn't prepared for was the growing feeling that I didn't belong.

Bruce put everything he had into helping me feel comfortable. He let me redecorate the kitchen with beautiful hickory cabinets and new counter tops. He even gutted and tiled the upstairs bathroom for me, installing a wonderful jetted tub. He never questioned my ability to handle the kids. In fact, he had more faith in me than I did. Still, I couldn't shake off the feeling of not being part of the family. Every time they visited, the kids brought their memories of family life the way it used to be. I began to feel like I was the stand-in for the real mother as I listened to a running dialog of "remember when" stories. Initially, I'd found them interesting, encouraging their talk. But eventually, I felt myself closing down as soon as they started. I tried to control my increasing sadness and jealousy. I didn't want to be that person and I felt angry with myself for letting it get to me, for being so immature. I knew they had a life before I arrived. The fact that they wanted to talk about it shouldn't have been any surprise.

I wondered whether this feeling was normal, whether it would go away. I knew of no one else with this kind of experience. So I kept searching for answers in books. I don't remember where I read it, but I finally found the one line that hit home: "You need time to develop your own history."

I can't say that everything was immediately fine. I'm not especially patient so I still went into a funk for a while when the kids had one of their "remember when" visits. But instead of giving in to my feelings, I began planning things for us to do together. We started traditions like make-your-own pizza nights and New Year's Eve hors d'oeuvres parties. We had winter floor picnics — roasting hot dogs in the fireplace and gorging on deviled eggs and potato salad as we lounged on my old quilt spread on the living room floor. I searched out tree farms with horse drawn wagons where we could cut our Christmas trees. And I initiated story times, reading aloud to the kids, often as we snuggled together during raging thunderstorms.

All of a sudden, I began to hear stories about the time we went to the apple orchard where we'd seen beautiful dappled gray ponies pulling a wooden cart or the exciting day we got to meet my sister's new parrot, and I realized it had happened. We finally had our own history. It took time and patience. I don't remember exactly when it began. But I can tell you it was worth the wait.

— Barbara Ann Burris —

The House That Ernie Built

Where we love is home, home that our feet may leave,
but not our hearts.
~Oliver Wendell Holmes

My husband Fred's grandchildren squealed with delight as they leaped from the dock into the cool lake. The cousins laughed and teased each other, just as my cousins and I did when we were young. The sky was blue, the sun was hot, and the breeze was gentle. We were enjoying a family picnic with Fred's sons and their families at Fred's former home. This was a special day in an atmosphere I loved. I knew I should be happy, but I wasn't. Instead, I was numb — lost somewhere inside my memories.

Fred and I were a widower and a widow who were lucky enough to find each other after losing our spouses to cancer. When we married three years earlier, Fred sold this beautiful lake home to his son and joined me in my country house. Now, we were taking the next step. We decided that it was time to sell my house and the forty acres it sat on, and buy a smaller house in town. We wanted a place closer to medical facilities, shopping, friends, families, and church. Yet, it still needed to have big garages like the country house. Fred rebuilds antique motorcycles and has at least forty of them. He needed room for his stuff!

With those requirements, house hunting was a challenge. The real estate market was booming, and it proved almost impossible to find what we wanted. Day after day we studied the computer, but when we found one that looked interesting, it sold before our agent could show it to us. This went on for months. Finally, we gave up.

Then, Fred went online to look for motorcycle parts. Instead, he found a house that was for sale by its owner. It sounded perfect. It was meticulously built, had everything we wanted, and was even my favorite color — yellow. Plus, it had something we hadn't even dreamed of finding. Its huge windows overlooked Lake Superior, and a short walk across the scenic highway would bring us to the lake's rocky shore.

Earlier that morning, Fred and I went to look at it, fell in love, and signed the papers to buy it. We knew it was a place our friends and families would enjoy visiting. This would be *our* house. Now we wouldn't be living in houses we'd shared with our previous spouses. Fred admitted that he'd never been comfortable living in Ernie's house, and I understood. I wouldn't have been comfortable living in the home his wife Suzy designed and loved.

However, instead of being excited about our great find, I now found myself strangely preoccupied. I adored the sweet little house that Fred and I had just agreed to buy. But, I was surprised by feelings of guilt. Now I would have to sell the house Ernie worked so hard to create.

Usually a social person, I was unhappy sitting by the lake and went for a long walk. I was crazy about Fred and loved the new life we had together. It was important to me that we live in a house that made him happy. What was wrong with me? My stomach churned with unexpected second thoughts. Ernie designed the house, then he built it all by himself. Usually, he was at work all day, then worked on the house until late at night.

There were so many memories there: the sunrises over the little lake, the magnificent rock garden he created for my birthday, and the antique pump he bought from an old farmer, painted bright red, and attached to our deck to surprise me on Mother's Day. Some of his ashes were scattered by his deer stands in the woods. What would he think of me selling his creation?

Was I being disloyal to Ernie? Fred managed to keep his house in the family. I'd be selling Ernie's house to a stranger. Yet, Fred and I prayed over and over about this decision. Why was I having doubts now? I walked back to Fred's old house and joined his family for dinner.

I was quiet on the long drive home and prayed silently. I'd been praying to God about this for months, but I was still confused. I felt silly about it but I asked God for a sign.

And that's when we drove up to our mailbox and pulled out the day's mail. There was a large manila envelope that was addressed to me, had no return address, and had something heavy in one corner.

Opening the envelope, I didn't find a letter or an explanation. It simply contained a pile of 35mm pictures. They were pictures of Lake Superior and most of them had Ernie in them — sitting by the lake, walking by the lake, or simply smiling at the camera with the lake in the background. Ernie and I had gone to the big lake whenever we could. I was puzzled. Where had the pictures come from? Fred and I sat in silence, gazing at the stack of pictures.

Pictures of Ernie by Lake Superior on the very day that we bought a house on the lake. How could this be?

Then, I remembered. About fifteen years before, I sold a story, along with these photos, to a travel magazine. The story was about travel along Lake Superior's north shore, but it was never published because the magazine went out of business. These were the pictures I took for that article.

How was it possible they arrived the day we bought the Lake Superior house?

Fred looked at the pictures, then spoke gently. "What's Ernie telling you?"

When I grasped the meaning of Fred's words, I began to sob. My dear Fred held me close as I struggled to put this miracle into words.

"Ernie's telling me it's time to move on. I think he's glad I'll be living by our precious lake."

Somehow my beloved Ernie found a way to reach down from heaven. He gave me the help I needed to move on with my life.

— Lou Zywicki Prudhomme —

Dr. Mike...

Whether you're struggling to become a new stepmom like Barbara or a healing heart searching for an answer like Lou, there is one thing for certain: you do it one moment, one day, one deviled egg, and one walk around the lake at a time. Creating family traditions and moving on aren't things that happen overnight.

For Barbara, one of the most anxiety-provoking experiences was that first night at Bruce's house with his kids. Remember what four-year-old Kevin said to her when she reached into the cabinet for extra plates?

You don't have to steal those.

Of course, young Megan was quick to come to her defense moments later. You have to admit, it was a *little* cute when an accusation of "plate theft" comes out of the mouth of a four-year-old.

But imagine you had a *sixteen-year-old* accusing you of theft. And imagine you were now *living* at that house. This story wouldn't be as cute, would it?

Whatever your circumstances may be, remember those words of advice that hit home for Barbara: *You need time to develop your own history.*

For Barbara, another tough time was that "remember when" game the kids played. Don't take it personally. It's fantastic for kids to love their parents.

Let's reframe the way someone like Barbara could look at this: What sensitive and sentimental kids these are! How nice. If they're softies with Mom, then they'll probably be softies with me one day. The more they have learned to love their mom, the more they'll know how to love and be loved.

Love isn't like apple pie. If their mom gets a bigger piece of pie, it doesn't mean they're going to run out of dessert for you. You can still get a piece one day, too.

Love is like outer space. Every day, it seems like scientists are discovering yet another planet or solar system, and the universe keeps expanding. Love is infinite. There is plenty for everyone to have a piece. The more you give it away and wish that others have it, the more you will have for yourself. Haven't you found that to be the case?

The role of a stepparent can be tough. If you fear being seen as Cinderella's wicked stepmother, you may be tempted to overcompensate. You become more best friend than stepparent. Family rules and boundaries get broken.

Or, perhaps you swing in the opposite direction. Unlike Barbara, who liked her new "cozy little Dutch Colonial," perhaps you feel completely uncomfortable in your new surroundings. You feel like a total outsider living in someone else's home. Someone else's kitchen. Another family's traditions. Rules you don't agree with.

So, you decide that *something* of yours is going to be injected into this family… and it's all going to happen right now! You end up being too stern… and letting them know who's boss. Perhaps you decide to redo the entire house the day you move in.

Your feelings are valid. This transition is tough for everyone. The truth is: many things of yours *should* become part of this family and this home. It's important for you to find ways to feel at home and at ease immediately. It's also important to allow things to unfold at their own, natural pace.

Plant a seed today. Add water and sun. Then wait. You'll see the first signs of life in a few months. Then, a bloom. One day: a fully-formed tree.

There are stages that a blended family goes through. These stages don't last days or weeks. They last years. It's completely normal to feel like an outsider in a band of insiders at first. But, that will slowly change. Be patient.

Of course, easier said than done… right? Barbara said it was hard for her to be patient. Even with a welcoming stepfamily like hers, she said that "remember when" game could send her into a "funk." You're not alone when you feel that way.

Eventually, Barbara and Bruce put in those hickory cabinets and new countertops. But, Barbara also didn't bring her measuring tape to redo that kitchen at that first dinner with the kids. She was patient.

The best role you can play to would-be-stepkids is a supportive role. Be the co-pilot, assisting your significant other as he or she is piloting these kids to their final destination: that place where responsible, confident, and kind adults live.

By playing the supportive role, you can hopefully bypass some of the dreaded: "You're not my real mom/dad!"

If you happen to hear that phrase at some point in the stepparent journey, it's fairly normal. This will be especially true in the teenage years.

As far as relationships with exes goes, Barbara and Bruce were lucky. It sounds like Bruce had a good relationship with his ex-wife with no horrific custody battles.

If you're not so lucky, try and live by the mantra *If you can't say anything nice, don't say anything at all*, at least when the kids are present. If you need to "let it all out," then do it with each other or your friends during "adults only" time.

If there are real concerns for children's safety and wellbeing, voice them directly from parent to parent whenever possible — and only if it make things better. If the relationship is strained or if there are real concerns for a child's health or wellbeing, it may sometimes be necessary to let courts, custody agreements, or your attorneys figure things out.

In general, try and take the high road. Try and steer clear of the conversations about "your deadbeat dad" or "your mom… who, if I'm being really honest, is probably going to be single for the rest of her life." By doing so, you can let your kids be kids. They can focus on being four and six and ten. They don't have to choose sides.

Kids can love their mom, their dad, their stepmom, and their stepdad. If this family were a pie, then kids would get to have seconds… and thirds… and fourths!

I. Change how you THINK

If you're anything like Barbara or Lou, that pesky pitfall thought pattern **permanence** can prevent you from seeing how things will get better.

Permanence would have prevented the Barbara, who showed up at that dinner the first night and was accused of stealing plates, from knowing that this new blended family would create its own traditions one day. Remember how they ended up having make-your-own pizza nights, winter floor picnics, and thunderstorm story times? That less-than-ideal first night was not *permanent*. It got better.

Permanence would have told Lou, "You won't be able to love again. This dark cloud is here to stay. You won't be able to find love after Ernie." It probably would have robbed her of the energy that she needed to even meet Fred.

It also would have kept Lou clinging to her old house filled with so many memories…. She wouldn't have been able to buy that dream home with Fred.

Luckily, those pictures that arrived that day were the message from Ernie she needed. As Lou said, *Ernie's telling me it's time to move on.*

If their love was true, then Ernie wouldn't have wanted **permanence** to keep Lou trapped. Loving someone means wanting the best for them. Grieving is normal, and it's a process. There may always be some sadness. But if you really love someone, you also want that person to eventually move on to a full life again.

Here's a brain-training exercise that will help you free yourself of **permanence** right now. All you have to do is to imagine you have a miraculous device that allows you to travel through time — like Michael J. Fox in the movie *Back to the Future*. Only, you don't need a fancy car to make this piece of science fiction a reality.

The power of this miraculous time travel machine is already available to you right now — in your own mind. After all, doesn't your mind have the power to revisit the past in great detail? And, it can consider endless possibilities about your future, can't it?

This mental time travel device allows you to see your life in a whole new way with clarity and positivity. This miraculous device is going to help set you free of the **permanence** that is holding you back from seeing the positive possibility in a new type of family or relationship.

If you are struggling today, I wonder how this mental time travel machine may help set you free. Let's figure this out right now.

Something I am struggling with today is:

_____

Now, use this "mental time travel machine" to go back to a time in your life. See something you didn't think was going to change… but did. Do you see how it all got better? See it all so clearly — step by step. Do you see that? Isn't that amazing?

What did that "mental time travel machine" help you remember about the way gray clouds cleared for you in the past?

_____

_____

_____

Now, come back to the problem you were dealing with in your present. Then, use your "mental time travel machine" to go into the future. See it all unfolding in the best possible way over the course of days, weeks, months, and years. And, see your part in what you need to do. Perhaps you need a little more patience? Or do you need to take an action? Or employ some optimism? Or have some faith?

What did you see?

_____

_____

_____

How did seeing this unfold help you to get rid of the illusion of **permanence** in your present life?

_____

2. Change how you ACT

Now, connect the thoughts you saw in your "time machine" and connect them to positive action. Many people will notice that once they have seen the outcome unfold in their mind's eye, they are able to glide through dinners, conversations, and anything reminiscent of Barbara's "remember when" game with calm and confident ease.

In many ways, this is one of the brain-training tricks of cognitive behavioral therapy. You can act "as if" you know things are going to get better.

Barbara would have known that, one day, the winter floor picnics would come.

Lou would have known that although her home with Ernie would always hold a place in her heart, the house with windows overlooking Lake Superior will be filled with memories… and feel like a home one day, too.

By knowing that your tomorrow will get better, your today is filled with hope. Thus, you choose *actions* based in faith — not fear.

For Barbara, that choice was to smile and listen with love and interest when her stepchildren-to-be talked about their mother and played the "remember when" game.

And even if you do sometimes go into a "funk" for a moment, just go back into that time machine… and remind yourself how many memories of your own you all will have ten years from now. It may prevent you from storming out of the room or reacting in anger.

For Lou, the next step she needed to take in her life was helped along by a little nudge from Ernie. Remember when she got that miraculous stack of photos of Lake Superior in her mailbox, right when she had been wishing for a sign? The message? This future, that house, this man — this is your next chapter.

But what if you don't get some miraculous, clear-cut message like Lou did?

Well, then realize your life is already filled with miracles. As the late, great Dr. Wayne Dyer said, "Miracles come in moments. Be ready and willing."

I remember a miracle that happened to me just a few years ago. I had always admired Wayne, but I'd never heard him in person. Then, we were both invited to speak at the same conference (a miracle "moment").

Luckily, our talks were at different times (another miracle "moment"). I snuck in and sat in the back of the auditorium after my talk and book signing was over. I finally got to hear this great man and author in person! That was one of the last times Wayne spoke in public before he passed away. Yes, miracles do happen in moments. They happen to all of us. All the time.

Let this new day, a second chance at life in any form, and an opportunity to love and be loved today be the miracle. Create another miracle by choosing an action today that's based on faith and hope for a better *tomorrow*.

What does that *action* look like for you?

_____

How will I live my life: as though nothing is a miracle, or as though everything is a miracle? Why?

_____

_____

_____

3. BE HAPPY

Chapter 14

Think, Act & Be Happy

Caring for Elderly Parents While Caring for Yourself

Trading Places

We can only be said to be alive in those moments when
our hearts are conscious of our treasures.
~Thornton Wilder

My mother was one of the strongest, most independent women I've ever known. Her mother died the day after her birth, and she survived a horrendous childhood, filled with two or three stepmothers and an abusive father.

Like so many in her generation, she became the single mother of two small children when my dad was drafted into the army during WWII. Only months before he left, they lost their third baby to whooping cough three weeks after his birth.

My mother struggled through the illness and death of my father when they were both only 41. I was married and had a baby girl at the time, so I did not witness firsthand how strong she really was, but I heard about it.

So it was with dismay and sadness that my two siblings and I received the news that, at the age of 88, our indomitable mother was diagnosed with stage III lymphoma. We had recently faced the fact that dementia was progressing quickly, and that the woman we knew and loved was disappearing before our eyes. With the lymphoma, her prognosis was six months to one year.

Since my mother lived in the same town in Southern California as my sister, Mom's care fell to her youngest child. My brother and I both live in Illinois. Our sister kept us informed of Mom's condition, and my brother and I both flew to California to be with her that last spring. When Mom's doctor told us that our mother could fly to Illinois for one last visit, our reaction was combined joy and sadness.

The three weeks my mother spent with my husband and me in

our home is a time I will always treasure. There were moments when she called me "Sweetie," and I knew that she did not remember my name, perhaps did not know who I was. Only weeks before that, she had introduced me as her niece, even once asking my sister who I was. That was tough.

Often, as she napped in the rocker, I sat and watched her with tears in my eyes, knowing that it would be the last time she would be in my home. I cooked the foods she liked, ate with her, sat with her, and tucked her into bed every night. She had never liked showers, but one day I asked if she would let me help her bathe.

She thought about it for a moment. "That would be nice," she said. "I've been afraid that I would fall, so it's been a long time since I took a shower."

I don't know how to adequately describe my emotions as I helped my mother undress and get into the large, walk-in shower in our master bathroom. I eased her into a secure shower chair, padded with a thick towel for her comfort. I soaped and washed her back, and she said, "Oh, honey, that feels so good!" I swallowed tears as I gently washed her pale skin, taking the same care I would have for a small child.

During those three weeks, I did everything I knew to keep her comfortable. I reassured her when she could not find her way out of a room, calling "Barbara?" as she had done when I was a child and she could not find me. Her confusion progressed quickly during that fleeting time, and her short-term memory became nearly nonexistent.

I accompanied her back to California, reassuring her every few seconds that our plane tickets were safe. I left her in my sister's capable, loving hands and flew home, knowing that I would not see my mom alive again. Only 12 short weeks later, she passed away.

Three years later, following a hip replacement, I found myself in need of care. Luckily, I had close friends and family members nearby to provide the assistance I needed. My son loves me, but he was not one to provide hands-on care. My daughter, older granddaughter and my grandson's wife did the hard stuff!

But it wasn't until the day that my daughter told me she would help me shower that I realized I had, so to speak, become my mother.

I took a deep breath, knowing that the moment could be traumatic for both my daughter and me, before I shed my robe and put myself in my daughter's hands. She had never seen me nude. Gently, she soaped and washed my back, and I closed my eyes, so very grateful for her compassion and willingness to help me.

"Oh, honey, that feels so good!" The words popped out of my mouth without a thought, and I was instantly transported three years back in time. For a moment, it was almost confusing, for I had suddenly become the older woman, dependent upon care from a loving daughter. I didn't let her see the tears that spilled down my face, but I could have blamed them on the shower.

There is no other vulnerability quite like sitting naked, and helpless, while someone else washes the body we have always cared for. Gratitude, however, far outweighed any shame or embarrassment I might have felt. I am still a distance from being the age my mother was when she died, but I'm aware, up close and personal now, how fragile we are, how quickly we can lose our proud independence, how possible it is that we can become like a helpless child again.

What makes it bearable is knowing, hoping, that there will be someone to love us, to care tenderly for us when we can no longer do it ourselves. I'm grateful for my "trading places" moment, for I now know how my mother felt when, for a short time, I was privileged to be her caregiver. I treasure that moment, holding it close to my heart, remembering.

— Barbara Elliott Carpenter —

How I Learned to Lie

*A little inaccuracy sometimes
saves tons of explanation.*
~Saki

And in the beginning, there I was… a fairly nice person with an excellent sense of ethics; kind to others, both human and four-legged; brought up properly; good manners; church-going; good values; helpful; polite; and always, always honest.

Then I learned to lie — and it felt good!

My mother's journey through her dementia altered my preconceived, well-established viewpoints on many things. As her dementia progressed, she began to travel first class down the road marked "Delusions," with dynamic side trips to the land of "Obstinate Refusal."

How was I to know in advance what this was going to mean to my belief system? Flying by the seat of my pants was my new mode of travel; there were many stopovers and the tickets were nonrefundable.

Delusions are rigid false beliefs and Mom had them in glorious abundance — this was her reality. She was amazingly good at embroidering around the edges of the imaginary fabric she wove and I had to enter her world, as she certainly was not able to function in mine.

She became delusion driven, filled with turmoil in her false beliefs. I stole all of her money. I was hiding the mail. I hid or stole her stamps. All I bought was rotten food. I hid her favorite bedspread. I used her money to fly to Europe and buy jewels. I threw away her favorite clothes and purposely bought only the worst toilet paper. And, she did not wet the incontinence undergarments, somebody poured water on them. Yes, indeed.

I tried to explain, to accommodate, mollify, plead, and grovel. I was especially good at groveling.

One exhausting day, my wits had completely left me and Mom once again railed at me about my taking her good toilet paper and substituting "the cheap junk." Instead of explaining, pointing out, trying to educate or argue, I wistfully said in a weak voice, "I'll do better next time and buy the good stuff."

Expecting a thermonuclear explosion, I girded myself for the blast and fallout. But something strange happened. She stopped ranting, became calm and moved on. Huh? What?

Okay — let's try that again. A few days later, there was another delusional accusation fueled with agitation, "Gosh Mom, it must feel terrible when that happens, I will watch out for that." And again, there it was, the same outcome with return to calmness. I was on to something!

This is when my lying began in earnest and it was awesome in its rewards. The fixation on rotten food was from time to time a hugely difficult problem because then Mom would not eat. But by now, I was such a good liar, there ought to have been a medal.

"Let me get rid of that and go to the grocery store and get some fresh food." So, there I stood, putting various items from the refrigerator into plastic grocery bags and pretending I was taking them out to the garbage. I waited outside for ten minutes or so and re-entered the house with the same bags and same items, happily declaring, "Hi Mom, I got some really wonderful stuff at the market; so fresh and on sale, too!" I proceeded to put the same items back into the refrigerator and she was happy.

Initially, it was difficult for me to lie; I felt as though the earth might open up and swallow me for some of my whoppers. But as I developed insight, I came to understand that these fibs were a great kindness and not a moral lapse.

Later I learned this intervention is called "therapeutic fibbing." It was one of the best tools in my caregiving toolbox. These fiblets kept Mom from becoming agitated or having unnecessary meltdowns, which made her life so much better.

When Mom demanded we go somewhere, but there was no time, or it was stormy, or the middle of the night, I would say the car battery was dead and I had to wait until tomorrow for the garage man to come.

She insisted on controlling the remote control for her heating system and would crank it up to stifling. There was a spare controller so I took that one for myself and took the batteries out of hers. I told her that she was "now in charge of the heating system." She loved clicking that darned thing and it gave her great satisfaction. There was so much out of her control in her compromised life that this small bit of ersatz control was a delight for her.

If she refused a doctor's appointment, I would pretend it was for me and she just came along, or that the doctor could not refill her treasured blood pressure pills until he saw her and, by the way, we would stop for ice cream on the way home.

Was this always perfect? No, not always, but it was for the vast majority of the time. It kept my mother from having to suffer the irritability, agitation, and upset from the false beliefs her compromised brain was inducing. It was so, so much better.

As I grew in knowledge, I learned that my lies were actually "validating her feelings," and not her words. That made sense, as she was driven by her feelings. I also learned that when I validated what she was feeling it brought her comfort because she was being heard. And when I swiftly changed the subject after validating her feelings, that was called "re-focusing," and permitted me to move her from the delusion onto something more pleasant and comforting.

Therapeutic fibbing worked so well through our journey that I now recommend it to friends who have a loved one with dementia. Who knew lying could be ethical? One more lesson in life that not all things are written in stone. It was worth all of the prevarication to see Mom calm and even smiling. It all goes into the basket called quality of life.

— Johanna Richardson —

Dr. Mike...

Life's ultimate switch. The parent becomes the child, and the child becomes the parent.

Although it sounds like the family version of the reality show *Wife Swap*, it's actually the real-life story of Barbara and Johanna. It's also one that most human beings will experience at some point in their lives.

For Barbara, there was both joy and sadness as she flew to Illinois. She would get to see her mom. But, this would be the last time.

Barbara also felt the pain of her mother not knowing her name. If you have had this experience, perhaps you told yourself: *It's just the disease talking.* But you're also only human. When it happens, it still hurts.

Do you remember when Barbara bathed her mother? She swallowed her tears as she washed her mother's pale skin. *Oh, honey, that feels so good!* said her mother.

Most of us will easily and instinctually give tender loving care to babies.

I'd guess Barbara did this effortlessly and with great joy when her son and daughter were adorable infants. Now it was time to turn to her motherly instincts and shine the love in her heart onto her own mother.

Barbara also did something so simple that many people fail to do: ask directly and specifically if someone needs help.

The conversation may sound something like this:

"Mom, do you need help bathing? I'd be happy to help you."

Perhaps you'd get the same response that Barbara got from her mom:

That would be nice. I've been afraid that I would fall, so it's been a long time since I took a shower.

Now, there's no denying that some people struggle with pride or embarrassment when it comes time to allow others to take care of us.

Barbara would be forced to face those feelings just three years later. Now, Barbara was the one who needed help being bathed. Was there shame and embarrassment there? Perhaps a little. But for Barbara, she said those feelings were outweighed by a stronger emotion: gratitude.

I wonder what positive feelings you might experience if you allowed yourself to be taken care of.

Perhaps we should all take a moment to do a quick reframe. Instead of dreading the day that someone needs to take care of us, perhaps we should focus on how lucky we are to have people who love us enough to care for us. If you find yourself in a long-term caretaking role like Johanna did, perhaps you can focus on being given the opportunity to give.

After all: "it's in *giving* that we *receive.*"

1. Change how you THINK

Caregivers can sometimes struggle with the pitfall thought pattern **polarization**. When you think in these terms, there are only black-or-white, yes-or-no answers. It's like we're thinking in the binary code of computers when we're actually spiritual human beings.

For Johanna, who was raised with good values and was taught to always be honest, this created problems.

If you see something in absolute terms, then something must be an absolute truth or an absolute lie.

There's nothing in between. The circumstances don't matter. The backstory doesn't matter. You've become that cold attorney grilling a defendant, "Yes or no, Mr. Smith? Is this your signature on this document?... No further questions!"

When it comes to human beings, intent matters. The outcome matters. The emotion *behind* the words matters.

If polarized thinking had its way, Johanna couldn't let her mother get away with lying — ever. Despite the dementia, a lie is a lie is a lie.

But Johanna learned a technique that can be helpful when a loved one has dementia: therapeutic lying, or what she called "fibbing" or "fiblets." Her mom insisted on controlling the remote control for the heating system and crank it up to stifling, and they could have fought.

Instead, Johanna told her mother she was now in charge of the heating system. And... it worked. Her mother loved clicking that remote — the one with no batteries in it.

How does one make sense of this? Here's a quick brain-training trick. Shift from left-brain, analytical *thinking* to right-brain, emotional *understanding.* Try to understand what's *behind* the words. You'll often find a human need that's relatable.

When it came to that heating remote, Johanna's mother needed a sense of control. She was living in a world — and with a disease — where so much was out of her control. Doesn't that make sense? If you were in her mother's shoes, wouldn't you need to feel in control of something?

If your father thinks he's going off to work on Wall Street today when he's in a memory care assisted living facility in Wisconsin, he has a human need to be valuable. Doesn't that make sense? Don't we all want to be valuable… and be valued?

If your mother asks where your father is every thirty minutes, a polarized way to deal with this would be to say, "Dad died seven years ago, Mom!" Then, you could watch her feel pain every thirty minutes. Talk about gut wrenching.

But consider her need, and you could understand that she is yearning for connection and love.

So how could *you* respond to, "Where's your father?"

One helpful way to respond to this that actually doesn't actually involve lying. You could try and refocus her attention.

"Mom, remember that one Thanksgiving where you and Dad forget to defrost the turkey and we all ate macaroni and cheese?!"

If that doesn't work, sometimes a "therapeutic lie" can be the most compassionate way to deal with this question.

"He went to the store, Mom."

Of course, this is a strategy that's specific to people with Alzheimer's disease and other forms of dementia.

However, understanding the need behind a person's words is an incredible strategy for so many of life's dilemmas.

How can you maintain your compassion for people who can sometimes be hard to love? The person who bullied you as a child probably had someone who was unkind to him or her. Some of the people who are the hardest to love are the people who have had the toughest lives.

Whether we are teaching our children how to relate to others or we are becoming a caretaker to our parents, perhaps letting go of **polarization** can make room for a bit more compassion and understanding in this circle of life.

Think back to a time when **polarization** had you thinking of something difficult in your life in absolute black-or-white or right-or-wrong terms. For a moment, imagine you are turning off the left side of your brain. The logical, analytical, and rational side of you is temporarily offline. This side of your brain thinks in binary code: 0 or 1. The most complex programs are simply a long string of 0's and 1's. This side of your brain can't even consider anything between a 0 and a 1. A 0.25 or a 0.75 don't exist!

For a moment, imagine that only the emotional, relational, and understanding right side of your brain is online. For a moment, you can only consider this situation through the lens of emotion. There is no "right or wrong" when this side of your brain is online. You can only consider what makes sense emotionally — to you or others. This side of your brain only sees shades of gray. In fact, there are no absolute 0's and 1's. All you can see are 0.33, 0.5, and 0.7341, because every situation has so many different sides you need to consider.

What's different when you look at this situation with the emotional side of your brain?

_____

_____

_____

How does this help you to turn off **polarization**?

_____

_____

_____

2. Change how you ACT

It's vitally important that caretakers create balance and self-care in their lives. This is especially important if you are a long-term caregiver like Johanna. You can't take care of others if you don't take care of yourself.

There are **two** specific steps in creating balance and self-care.

Step 1. Ask for the help you need in specific language.

Most people who are caretakers don't ask for enough help. They also don't know how to ask for it.

Here's a quick brain-training hack for that: Use positive, specific, and time-based language to ask for help.

If you have a brother or a few best friends who help you from time to time, you may have been saying something like: *I'm so exhausted!*

But that doesn't provide people the instructions for how to help you, or the permission to do so. Sometimes, people want to help but they don't know what you *need*, and they're not even sure that you want their help.

Try this instead: *John, can you take mom to her doctor's appointment Thursday at 12, please?*

Or try this: *Can I give you a grocery list tomorrow morning of twenty or so things I need? It would be a great help if you could pick those things up for me.*

Or this: *My mom loves to watch* Jeopardy *and* Wheel of Fortune *but can't be alone. Can you come to my house and sit with her for an hour or so while I get my hair cut?*

Step 2: In that time, do something for you.

You should do something that fills you with one of the following: **pleasure**, **passion**, **peace** or **productivity**. There are self-care activities that, at the very least, are **productive** — like getting a haircut. Even better, do something you're **passionate** about like going to your daughter's recital. Or, do something that gives you a sense of **peace**. Perhaps you like to meditate or go for walks. Sometimes, the simplest activities give us **pleasure**, so you can try one of those during your time off. Get your nails done. Buy yourself a nice shirt. Do something for *you*.

Step 1:
What's a positive, specific, and time-based request I can make to someone I trust?

_____

Step 2:
What's something I can do at that time that fills me with **pleasure, passion, peace** or **productivity?**

_____

3. BE HAPPY

Chapter 15

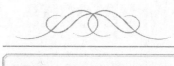

Think, Act & Be Happy

Ten Baby Steps to Conquering Your Fears

Kryptonite

Fear is only as deep as the mind allows.
~Japanese Proverb

Tucked in between farmland and rivers in upstate New York is a small "ranch" consisting of one shack-like building, a lot of grass, three airplanes and dozens of insane people who jump out of planes every day for a living. On a busy Saturday, up to twenty flights carrying eager twenty-somethings and bored fifty-somethings fly 13,500 feet above the ground, only to promptly throw said customers out of the plane while attached to an instructor.

"You are a student," one of the instructors informs us. "Your job is to listen to your instructor, follow his directions, and have fun."

I'm standing in line with five of my co-workers as this cigarette-smoking skydiving expert tightens my harness, makes a joke about the placement of my genitals, and explains how to stand at the edge of the plane once the door is open right before we jump. He tells me to keep my feet together and my head back, putting emphasis on looking up when I jump. A friend of mine told me this was to protect us from snapping our head back, knocking out our instructor and having to land with our parachute by ourselves.

It was about the scariest thing I'd ever heard.

I'm a fairly confident guy in most situations, but put me a few hundred feet above the ground, and my equilibrium gets thrown off. Heights are my kryptonite. My knees feel weak, I get clammy hands, and my heart races. I can't focus on anything except how high up I am.

Yet, somehow, my co-worker Rafa convinced me to drive two hours north of New York City, pay $200, and spend a day living out my worst nightmare.

A few weeks before, Rafa—who happens to be a Stanford graduate, engineer and pilot from Mexico — took me on a flight in a four-seater Cessna airplane as a little warm-up for skydiving.

We did a "skyline tour" of New York, where we flew south down the Hudson River, did a U-turn, passed the World Trade Center within a few hundred feet on our right, avoided helicopters flying at 1,500 feet, and got one of the coolest views of New York City I'd ever seen. But throughout the whole flight, my legs numbed with anxiety at every bump or turn.

I never really imagined I'd go through with skydiving.

And then, there I was, shaking hands with a guy named Danish to whom I was entrusting my life.

"Once we're in the sky, the order of priorities goes: 1) my comfort 2) your safety," he says with a Hungarian accent, smirking. I laugh, knowing this big-brother, trash-talking instructor is exactly who I need.

As a group, we board the plane, which is about four times the size of the Cessna I rode in weeks before but still much smaller than a commercial airliner. Inside are two long benches that we straddle, with our instructors behind us and the jumpers who would go alone sitting on the floor near the door.

"What are you scared of?" Danish asks seriously.

"I don't know," I say, pausing for thought. "Dying? Being scared of heights?"

"It's not about a fear of heights," he says curtly. "It's only about the altitude."

With that, Danish straps his harness to mine as the plane takes off and climbs toward the clouds.

"I know, I know... I should have bought you dinner first," he quips as he hooks himself to my harness inside the plane. "This is part of my job, alright?"

"I think I'm going to puke," I tell him honestly.

"If you puke on me, I'll pee on you," he says, and I don't get the sense he is joking this time.

On this trip, we'll be climbing 13,500 feet into the air, where the temperature is about 40 degrees Fahrenheit, a nice relief on a hot 93-degree summer day. As the plane continues to rise, Danish checks in by showing me his altitude watch. 3,000 feet… 5,000 feet…. 8,000 feet…

"We'll be at altitude in about five minutes," Danish tells me.

This is about the point where my phobia starts to kick in. I feel my eyes widen and my chest tighten. My knees get weak.

"No matter how scared you are," another instructor had told me, "one thing is for certain: Your body loves adrenaline and dopamine. And when you jump out of that plane, you're going to get a shot of both of them."

At 13,500 feet, a light goes on in the plane. One of the skydivers yells something, and seemingly everyone else in the plane chants something back. I didn't get the memo. Instead, I am burying my head into the back of the instructor in front of me, begging every god I know to help me get out of this plane and make it to the ground in one piece.

"DOOR!" someone shouts.

And just like that, a five-foot-tall side door on the plane swings open, and I am staring down at the clouds, at New York, and at my imminent death.

"You ready, *mijo*?!" Rafa shouts to me.

"F---, yeah!" I scream back, pretending to be ready.

The scariest part of skydiving is seeing the person in front of you jump out of the plane. Imagine driving on the highway, rolling down the window, and then reaching out and letting a piece of balled-up paper go flying down the road. It's just like that, except the piece of paper was my boss. One second, he's there giving me a thumbs-up, and the next second he's a speck in the clouds, flying away at what looks like light-speed. Suddenly, I realize I am in a plane going hundreds of miles per hour with the door open and, oh my god, he's pushing me out!

Before I know it, I'm belly down trying to scream, but I can't really scream because the wind is so strong it fills up my mouth and lungs. For a brief moment, all I feel is the distinct sensation I'm probably not going to survive, but then I acclimate. I find the horizon, see the trees, and remember that a dude who does this for a living is attached to me. And then he taps my shoulders, the sign to put out my arms. I think for a second and then remember where I am, willing myself to take my hands off my harness.

And in that moment, I feel it. I'm freefalling from a plane, I'm safe, I can breathe, and it is one of the most gorgeous things I've ever seen. There is no stomach-dropping, roller-coaster feeling in my stomach, just the sensation of flying, of control. The clouds pass by quickly, and now I have a clear, 360-degree view of everything around me. Freefall speed is about 55 meters per second, so in ten seconds I've covered 1,800 feet, five hundred feet more than the Empire State Building. By the time I'm oriented, I'm about 12,000 feet off the ground. Flying.

The instructor reaches around and gives me a thumbs-up.

I give him the thumbs-up back and nod furiously with joy.

Danish shows me his watch, which says we are at about 11,000 feet and gives me another thumbs-up. I give it back, remembering what my friend Casey — a frequent skydiver — said before I jumped. "Don't just look down. Make sure you look up and down and all around." I do. I look at the horizon and up to the clouds, which seem only feet away, closer than I've ever seen them without a thick airplane window between us. It is a beautiful, sunny, blue-and-green day, and I look to my left and see the massive Wallkill River. I can see the first of the parachutes below me and know that Rafa's freefall is up; he was about twenty-five seconds before me.

Before I know it, Danish is guiding my hand to the golf-ball-sized attachment that he told me I could pull to release the chute. I rip it, and suddenly there is the loud thunder of nylon catching air, harnesses doing their jobs, and the force of the parachute slowing us down in what is now the scariest part of skydiving.

And then there is quiet.

"Holy crap!" I scream, elated at the incredible rush that is the last fifty seconds.

"Welcome to my office," Danish says with a laugh behind me.

And what an office it is. Lush green trees and farmland are all around. Cities are on the horizon, and I see small-town suburbia built along the rivers. Danish pulls at the steering controls, or brakes, and starts to rotate us in a circle as we descend, giving me a view of everything around us.

I am out of breath now and quiet, but the beauty of everything around is stunning. It is so much better than flying over a city in an airplane. I can see both sides, and down and up and straight out in front of me.

As we work our way closer to the ground, I am already feeling the urge to go again. The fear, the rush, the panic, the camaraderie — it all feels so addictive. In that moment, I realize: *I want to go back up in that plane and jump out… again!*

I can't believe that in a matter of minutes what was once my biggest fear became something I would do over and over again if it weren't such an expensive hobby.

As we get closer to the ground, Danish reminds me to lift my feet up in the air as we come in so we can land on our butts.

One by one, my co-workers and I slide into the grass field, safely and smoothly on our behinds, ending five of the most exhilarating minutes of my life.

The jump reminded me that our fears are usually built around what we don't know, as opposed to what is actually dangerous or worrisome. In the span of a few hours, I went from being someone who couldn't look over a balcony without feeling queasy to thinking about how I could save money to jump from a plane for a second time.

But more than anything else, conquering my fear didn't just feel good because skydiving is fun; it felt good because I had overcome my kryptonite. In the legend of Superman, kryptonite is his weakness but gives regular humans super powers. That day, flying like Superman 13,000 feet above ground, I realized that my kryptonite had indeed turned into a power source for me, one that encourages me to face my fears to this day.

— Isaac Saul —

I Can and I Am

If you want to test your memory, try to recall what you
were worrying about one year ago today.
~E. Joseph Cossman

My early twenties were rough. And I don't mean that in a
"Woe is me, I was struggling to find direction" sort of way.
I mean that I was housebound with a severe panic disorder
that left me unable even to check the mailbox many days.
Sounds were amplified, everything seemed too big, and my world
closed in on me.

It all happened out of the blue right around the time of my college
graduation. Before then, I was very social and adventurous. People
were my thing. I always had friends around and I was a stage actress
and singer — briefly professionally. My plan was to move with a friend
of mine to Los Angeles and try for our big shot… and then the panic
disorder derailed me.

I had to find a way to make a living without leaving my house
because I could no longer perform. There had been too many close
calls when I had panic attacks on the way to the theater. Professors had
encouraged me to be a writer, so I figured I would give that my best
shot. First screenplays and magazine articles, and eventually books.
It took some time to earn a decent income, but I managed to build
my credits quickly because I literally had nothing else in my life — I
never went out, and at its worst, the panic disorder even robbed me
of the ability to have friends come visit. They tried, but I wound up
locked in the bathroom, shaking from head to toe.

Hope was in short supply. I didn't think I would ever get better,
and I was running out of reasons to get out of bed. I sat at the computer
nearly nonstop from the moment I got up until I went to bed. Often I

didn't change out of pajamas (what was the point?) and I ate at my desk.

But after four years, something amazing happened: I got better. It was a gradual process that involved a patient boyfriend, a hearty dose of antidepressants, and small steps to get me back into the world again. There were little triumphs: sitting in a restaurant for the first time in years, getting my hair cut, bringing my cat to the vet. Then there was a monumental turning point for me: I went to a Counting Crows concert and had a great conversation with the young woman standing next to me. She was the first stranger I'd spoken to in years, and she saw me as a normal, healthy woman. She didn't see me as broken.

Getting better was so exciting and unexpected to me — I had figured that I would never leave the house again, let alone live a regular life. Within about a year, I was able to do most things again. I still had some panic attacks and there were some things that were still too scary for me, but overall, I was living again.

Through the worst of my agoraphobia, I had craved success stories… I wanted to hear from other people who'd been as low as I had and recovered, because I didn't really think it was possible. Now that I was recovering, I wanted to be that light for others, so I started writing about it.

One of the people who read my story was Jamie Blyth, who was then on the first season of *The Bachelorette* with Trista Rehn. He had gone on the show in part to challenge himself: He had social anxiety disorder and panic disorder, and he was trying to push his boundaries to get past it. After the show, he wrote to me to ask if I'd help him write a book about his experiences.

"Well, I've never written a book with anyone before, but if you're willing to take a chance on me, I'll take a chance on you," I said — and it worked. We sold his book to McGraw-Hill and I began the process of understanding Jamie's life story. It was pretty amazing. He had methodically put himself in situations that were more and more challenging to get past the anxiety. Among other things, he became a door-to-door salesman just to force himself to talk to people every day, and he flew to Sweden to join a basketball team without knowing a soul there. How brave!

Getting engrossed in his story and success was inspiring to me and made me dissect my own life. Here I was feeling pretty good and comfy about how far I'd come, but I'd hit a plateau. There were still things I was avoiding, and I had been okay with that. But Jamie lit the fire under me: "If he can go to Sweden by himself, I can fly to Florida with my family."

Truth was, I was terrified; it had been eight years since I'd been on an airplane. There was no escape if I did have a panic attack. No way to make them stop and put me safely on the ground again and let me go outside to breathe. But I used the power of positive thinking to get myself ready.

First, I had to combat my worries: What if I pass out? What if I have a heart attack? What if…?

I had to talk to myself: "You have never passed out from a panic attack before, and heart racing doesn't lead to heart attacks. You will be fine. You will feel so good when you arrive in Florida."

But what if I panic the whole flight?

"Then you will listen to music and talk to your sister and focus on your breathing, and it will be over before you know it. It will be worth it, and soon you'll be relaxing on a beautiful sandy beach."

But what if…?

And then I told myself, "I can and I am."

Those five words would become my mantra. No matter what fears cropped up in my mind, I would answer them with that: my shorthand version of "I can do it, and I am doing it." Over and over, drowning out any nervous chatter.

I'd like to tell you that I had a perfect flight, but that wouldn't be honest. I did have a panic attack part of the time and it was hard, but I kept thinking positive: "The hard part will be over soon, and I am so proud of myself for taking this risk."

I was right: the hard part ended as soon as we touched down, and I had a terrific vacation. Taking that trip opened the door for what was to come next: I got a call inviting me to write a book with Céline Dion, and that meant I had to fly to Las Vegas several times to meet with her. I'm not sure I would have done it without having that "practice trip" under my belt, but I said yes even though I was still terrified. When the day came, I spent the whole morning bolstering myself with positive thoughts about how ready I was for this, how much Céline was going to like me, how wonderful this was for my career — and it became one of the best experiences of my life. She *did* like me, too!

Those flights — all of them — were perfect. It marked the final end of my panic disorder.

I don't have to think about panic attacks anymore. It's been seven years since I had even a minor one, and it's no longer part of my head-space. I'm a homeowner and a PTA mom; I've taught writing courses and made television appearances. Nobody who meets me now would ever know that I was once afraid to leave my front door. But what I've taken from that difficult time is my power to reclaim my thoughts from the grips of fear. Whenever I face a challenge now, I remember the power of those five words and how far I've come: I can and I am.

— Jenna Glatzer —

Dr. Mike...

What's your kryptonite? Heights? Snakes? Speaking in public? Driving on the freeway?

Did your kryptonite surface "out of the blue" like Jenna's did? Or, can you pinpoint when your phobia started—that Tuesday afternoon when you got stuck on an elevator? Or, perhaps you're someone who has always had a fear of heights. If so, you can probably relate to Isaac's story of jumping out of a plane.

Fear is a funny thing. Where does fear come from?

Some people learn to be scared of something. If you got stuck on an elevator, your brain has paired elevators with panic. Scary "uppers" like adrenaline surge, and this makes your heart race and your palms sweaty.

Others are hard-wired for fear and anxiety. If your panic attacks popped up "out of the blue" like Jenna's did, it's likely you have a genetic tendency for anxiety disorders. Anxiety can manifest itself as phobias, panic disorder, agoraphobia, OCD, or generalized anxiety disorder.

Speaking of how we're wired, did you know that people with certain personality traits are more likely to experience anxiety? We all process the "upper" called dopamine differently in the brain. Sensation seekers love the way it feels. They become rock stars and travel the world. To sensation seekers, dopamine makes them feel great.

Sensation avoiders don't like too much dopamine. They don't want to play the guitar in front a stadium of people. They're more likely to become librarians and accountants. They'd prefer a boost of other feel-good hormones that aren't as activating.

Both sets of traits come with a unique set of upsides and downsides, so neither one is inherently "good" or "bad." Sensation seekers (e.g., the rock star) are *more* likely to be diagnosed with addiction since they love the way dopamine-releasing alcohol and cocaine feels. However, they're *less* likely to be diagnosed with anxiety.

The opposite is true for sensation avoiders (e.g., the librarian or accountant). He or she is *less* likely to be diagnosed with addiction but *more* likely to be diagnosed with anxiety. Too much dopamine floods these people's brains, and they get jittery, nervous, and feel out-of-control.

But guess what? There's good news for sensation seekers, sensation avoiders, and people in between. No matter how your brain processes dopamine, you have the power to train your brain — just like Isaac and Jenna did.

What's so cool about Isaac and Jenna's stories is that they both used graded exposure therapy — a type of cognitive behavioral therapy used to treat phobias — to conquer their fears. These are just fancy ways of saying using "baby steps" to teach your brain how to turn off fear.

Isaac had his friend Rafa take him up on that four-seater Cessna as "a little warm-up for skydiving."

Jenna also got a "practice trip" under her belt. That practice trip wasn't easy. In fact, Jenna *did* have a panic attack on that practice trip and had to tell herself: *The hard part will be over soon, and I am so proud of myself for taking this risk.*

True progress isn't about having *no* anxiety. In fact, small amounts of anxiety help human beings perform at their best. It's about moving through life *despite* anxiety... even if we have to take anxiety *with* us — just like Jenna did.

Was it worth it? Did it lead to something incredible in her life? You bet! Jenna soon got that call to write a book with Céline Dion! That job required several flights to meet with her... and became "one of the best experiences" of Jenna's life.

Panic attacks, agoraphobia, and phobias can be difficult to overcome. The first time people have a panic attack, they often think they're dying of a heart attack. If you haven't seen your primary care physican or cardiologist in years, then get testing to rule out heart problems. In most cases, I've found they they'll help you confirm what most people instinctually know: the shortness of breath is probably an indication you need to do a better job training your brain — not your heart.

Phobias hold people back in all sorts of ways. You may not think that a fear of cats may affect your quality of life that much, but I've treated many people who won't get out of their car for hours if they've seen a cat cross the street. If you had a job interview but saw a cat on your drive on the way there, now a phobia has interfered with your life in a major way.

Agoraphobia can lead to catastrophic consequences — a life completely unlived. You miss your daughter's wedding because you're afraid to leave the house.

The only way to truly overcome these fears: Go through them — not around them. The brain will try to seduce you. It may try and tell you to take the easy route: choose short-term comfort and avoid what makes you uncomfortable. But that prevents you from choosing the experience that will extinguish the fear once and for all.

As you already know, cognitive behavioral therapy is all about the three-way relationship between thoughts, feelings, and actions. It empowers you to train your brain.

When it comes to conquering fears, lead with action... And let your thoughts and feelings change as a result of those actions. Even if you have to take fear and anxiety *with* you through this process, this will allow you to conquer your fear.

Teach yourself just how brave you are.

Turn kryptonite into a source of power like Isaac did.

Imagine what it will feel like to be able to say what Jenna now says: *I can and I am.*

One baby step, one plane ride, or one meow at a time.

1. First, change how you ACT

This is the only chapter in the book where you'll start by changing how you *act* instead of changing how you *think*. You'll circle back around to the pitfall thought pattern after you act. And this time you'll see how actions can change the way you think. Why is that?

When it comes to anxiety, people often get bogged down by their thoughts. They become paralyzed with anxiety, dread, and worry. They overestimate situations. A bump on the plane means *we're all going down!* Nope, that was just a cloud.... It happens all the time....

The anxious mind *prevents* action from taking place. *I can't do it. Everyone will laugh at me if I get on stage.*

If you are so afraid of the world that you can't even leave the house like Jenna, then it's essential the baby steps start here and now. Why? Your life is waiting.

Jenna pushed herself to take chances and write. We know how that turned out: from a woman afraid to leave her house, to someone flying to write a book with Céline Dion!

Jenna's journey also involved her crossing paths with someone else who conquered fear by choosing to change everyday behaviors. Remember when she wrote a book with Jamie, who was on the first season of *The Bachelorette*?

Jamie's story is another incredible beacon of hope when it comes to conquering fears. As someone with both panic disorder and social anxiety, he *methodically put himself in situations that were more and more challenging to get past the anxiety. Among other things, he became a door-to-door salesman just to force himself to talk to people every day, and he flew to Sweden to join a basketball team without knowing a soul there.*

And then, Jamie went on *The Bachelorette* in part "to challenge himself." If you experience panic attacks and social anxiety, I can't think of anything more anxiety provoking than playing the stressful "game of love" *and* being filmed on national television while doing so.

In many ways, the only way to truly change your brain is to face your fears and stop using avoidance. Action also helps people avoid the other major coping strategy: self-medication. If you are anxious, you may be tempted to self-medicate with food, alcohol, or drugs to cope.

You have the power to change your brain and your life… today. It's time for *you* to conquer your fears.

What is your fear? The kryptonite holding me back is:

_____

Now, let's break this down into baby steps. If your fear is cats and you've never been able to be in the same room as one, perhaps the ultimate goal would be for you to hold your sister's cat. But, we can break this down into manageable baby steps that can slowly teach you to tolerate this fear. This is the ultimate way to train your brain.

Perhaps the first step would be to watch one minute of cat videos on YouTube — something you avoid. Then, maybe the next step would be to watch them for three minutes. Then, you may be able to see some real cats from your car. Then, you'd go to the Humane Society and look at cats from a safe distance. Eventually, you'd be working your way to having your sister's cat in your lap.

In this example, the one minute of watching cat videos would be a "1" and holding your sister's cat in your lap would be a "10."

It's important that these baby steps are personalized to you. The "1" is the least anxiety-provoking. "10" is the most. This helps your brain to rewire itself.

There's no set timeline in terms of how quickly you progress through these goals, as each person is different. What's important is that you challenge yourself.

Remember: the goal is not getting to the point where this was a completely comfortable, enjoyable, or fun situation. It's okay to still be nervous at every step of the way. The goal is to teach yourself that you can do it, and then challenge yourself to move on to the next baby step. Gradually, your fear and anxiety will decrease as you teach yourself *I can do this!*

List the ten baby steps you will take to help you overcome your fear:

1. _____

2. _____

3. _____

4. _____

5. _____

6. _____

7. _____

8. _____

9. _____

10. _____

2. Then, see how that changes the way you THINK

Every time you complete one of your baby steps, look at how this changes the pitfall thought pattern **paralysis-analysis**.

Anxious people tend to get stuck in patterns of worry like a needle on a broken record. That's why I had you start with changing the way you act and then circle back to how you *think*. **Paralysis-analysis** is all about the lack of action.

As you train your brain by moving from 1-10 in the baby steps above, you'll notice that your anxiety or panic will likely decrease overall. You may never be the world's most relaxed flier. You may never be a go-with-the-flow, laid-back person. That's okay.

The point is to let your behavior lead the way... and let your thoughts and feelings change every step of the way.

Go back to the ten baby steps you assigned yourself above. Now write below each one how that step helped you to break the cycle of **paralysis-analysis** in your life... and choose action instead. Look at how you chose to face your fears — even if you had to "take fear with you" along for the ride.

Your *action* cured you from the ***paralysis-analysis*** that the mind traps us in.

3. BE HAPPY

Chapter 16

Make Healthy Choices Because You Want To

My Daughter's Gift

Action is the antidote to despair.
~Joan Baez

was 5'2" and I weighed over 200 pounds. I never felt motivated to change my eating habits despite how uncomfortable simple activities like showering, dressing, walking, and even sitting eight hours a day at my job as a programmer had become.

I was in the doctor's office with my daughter, Amanda, when she was diagnosed with end-stage renal disease. The diagnosis presented a challenge I knew I would not turn away from. I was prepared to give her a kidney.

"Amanda, I can give you a kidney," I assured her confidently.

The nephrologist spoke slowly, not quite looking me in the eye. "Toni, you won't be considered a viable donor because of your weight."

Embarrassed, I glanced at my daughter.

"It's too dangerous anyway," she smiled, as she reached over and took my hand. "I don't want you to do it."

But her sweet acceptance of the situation made me even more determined. That day I made up my mind to lose the weight I had carried for more than twenty years.

"At work, there have been quite a few people who've lost weight going the low-carb route," I explained to Amanda as we discussed diet options. "Charles had success on Weight Watchers. Gail and her husband are on Nutrisystem. And there have been lots of positive results with Jenny Craig, Atkins, and the South Beach diet."

"You know," she cautioned, "you don't really do well when things are strictly regimented."

"Then I'll come up with my own version of a low-carb diet."

My diet consisted of the foods I liked the most and wouldn't tire of eating on a daily basis. Dinnertime staples consisted mainly of lean, braised steak or oven-baked shrimp and fish, with steamed vegetables completing the meal.

I eliminated all fast food, fried food and snack food. Bread, buns, rolls, donuts, muffins and potato chips were exorcised from the house, eliminating temptation. But by far the most difficult challenge was giving up Coca Cola. I never drank coffee, tea, water or milk. For years, the only beverage that passed through my lips was Coca Cola. Some days I'd down as many as four to six twenty-ounce bottles.

Eventually I made new friends: Crystal Light, Nutri-Grain cereal bars, Healthy Choice and Lean Cuisine.

The pain of caffeine withdrawal overshadowed the hunger pains from my decreasing calorie intake. I counted calories religiously and as my daily calories declined my energy level increased. I remembered hearing somewhere that unless you feel hungry, you're not losing weight. As hungry as I constantly felt, I was sure I must be losing weight.

Keeping the big picture in mind, I weighed in only once a week and wasn't preoccupied with minor fluctuations. I didn't have a target weight or an end goal in mind when I began dieting. After all, I wasn't sure I'd even be able to maintain any sort of diet plan, but watching my daughter grow weaker every day gave me all the incentive I needed to stick with it.

It wasn't until I had lost forty pounds that my co-workers, friends, and neighbors even noticed.

"Toni, did you get a new hairstyle?" my boss asked me one day. "It makes you look thinner."

That's one terrific hairstylist, I thought. *Give her a big tip.*

"How much weight did you lose?" asked my neighbor. "I told my wife it's got to be from walking the dog. I always see you out here."

That's a lot of shoe leather.

So I wasn't surprised when five new dogs became members of the neighborhood in the following months.

My slow walks around the block soon evolved into regular jogs throughout the subdivision, a pleasant surprise for our miniature Greyhound.

"Are you sure you're not sick?" questioned my friends periodically. *No,* I thought sadly, *that's my daughter.*

Months flew by and the diet became a way of life. Many of my cravings disappeared. Our days were filled with doctor appointments and medical testing to qualify my daughter for placement on the National Transplant wait list. No longer weighing in every week, I didn't even notice how much weight I had lost.

"I didn't even recognize you," gushed the nephrologist at one of our appointments. "I never thought you'd do it. How much have you lost?"

Hopping onto the scale in the corner of the exam room, I found I had lost seventy pounds.

I placed my arm around Amanda's shoulders, pulling her close. "I think I'm ready to give my daughter a kidney now," I proudly informed the doctor.

"Finish her tests and once she's on the list you can begin your testing," instructed the doctor.

Finally the day arrived when my daughter took her place on the National Transplant wait list. And I was ready. I rushed to the LifeLink office on my lunch hour to fill out a mound of paperwork and begin the battery of tests required to become a living donor. First up, a simple blood test.

"We'll call you this afternoon with the results," said the donor coordinator as she walked me to the elevator.

Four hours later my phone rang. "What test is next on the list?" I practically yelled into the receiver. I was excited to get through all the red tape and get my daughter back on the road to health.

"Toni, I have some bad news." The coordinator hesitated a moment too long. "Your blood type is not a match."

My disappointment was nearly insurmountable. Instead of giving my daughter a kidney, she gave me the gift of a healthier life.

It's a gift I do not take lightly and will value forever, so I continue to count calories and count my blessings.

— Toni L. Martin —

| Make Healthy Choices Because You Want To

Taking Taekwondo

Find something that you love and go for it!
~Author Unknown

When I was twenty-six years old, my left lung collapsed. The surgeon who repaired the damage told me bluntly that I needed to quit smoking — I was at three packs a day — or I would die. I had been told this before, but the facts had never been this convincing. So I quit smoking — and grew heavier and grumpier by the day. I was terrified that I would eventually give in and start smoking again. But I knew that, once and for all, I had to take control of my health by getting in shape and eating right.

In the beginning it wasn't easy. I went for walks, but soon lost interest. I counted calories, but couldn't stop eating. I considered joining an aerobics class, but couldn't imagine myself prancing around with a bunch of strangers.

Then one day I walked by a building: New Horizons Black Belt Academy of Taekwondo. I didn't even pause. I walked right in and took my first lesson. I was too dizzy and out of breath to make it through the first class. But I knew I'd be back the next day, and the next, and the next — I'd fallen in love.

Immediately, I learned my body could do things I never thought possible. I practiced a Taekwondo "form," which is a pattern of movements almost like a dance. As I caught sight of myself in the mirror, I was struck by how beautiful the form was — and how beautiful I was. I had never thought of my body that way before.

Every Monday night, the instructor demonstrated self-defense techniques. One evening, she asked me to show the other white belts, my fellow beginners, how to do a technique. It was intoxicating. I'd been practicing for only a few weeks and I had already mastered something. I had achieved something physical—me—the playground klutz, the sideline spectator.

A few weeks later, I earned my yellow belt and began "sparring," a form of mock combat that involves kicking and punching other people, and getting kicked and punched back. At first, I couldn't hit anyone. Jeanne, a tall black belt, patiently coached me. She simply stood there, hands lowered, saying, "Okay, go ahead and hit me." I did so, timidly at first, then with mounting confidence, until one day I hit her hard enough to matter and she hugged me.

It wasn't the sort of thing that would make my mother proud, but it made me proud. It made Jeanne proud, too. I realized that I was worth defending.

Getting hit also frightened me. A punch or a kick didn't even have to touch me for me to flinch. But after enough practice I learned not to be afraid. I grew bolder, I hit harder, people hit me back just as hard, and I discovered a profound and electrifying truth: You could get hit, you could get hit hard, and it didn't have to demoralize you. You didn't have to fall down and cry, or wait for a man to come along and rescue you. You could take it, smile, and defend yourself.

Years later, after I earned my black belt, I visited a new physician for my annual exam, and he said, "I see you've had rheumatoid arthritis for more than ten years, but you seem to be getting around okay."

I grinned. Oh, boy. "I can do a jump spinning-wheel kick to your head," I wanted to say, but did not. "Yeah," I said, instead. "I do all right."

—Jennifer Lawler—

Dr. Mike...

Toni and Jennifer both learned some very important lessons in their journey towards health. I think these lessons are pretty universal and ones that we all need to be reminded of every day.

Lesson #1: Health is the ultimate wealth.

Lesson #2: The person who has the most power over your everyday health isn't a doctor. It's you.

Lesson #3: The seemingly insignificant actions you take today can change the entire course of your life.

For Toni, there was something supremely valuable at stake: her daughter's life. It helped to motivate her to put down those sodas. Fast food, fried food, and those blood-sugar-spiking snacks also became instant no-nos.

But when you stop to think about it, don't we *all* have something supremely valuable at stake? *Your* health is incredibly valuable, isn't it? If you don't have your health, then you can't enjoy time with your family, friends, or enjoy that boat ride on the lake.

Even the most successful people in the world need to be reminded of this. Ariana Huffington was working eighteen-hour days building the *Huffington Post* until she collapsed from exhaustion. Waking up in a pool of blood was her wake-up call.

Do you have high blood pressure? Are you prediabetic? Are you overweight? Achy? If you are experiencing symptoms, that's your body trying to tell you that *something* needs to change.

For Toni, that wake-up call was her *daughter's* life. Once that was at stake, Toni was willing to do whatever it took to prevent her daughter from suffering. Sadly, she couldn't give her kidney to her daughter. But, she ended up changing her *own* life.

Here's something to think about right here and now: Do you think *your* loved ones would suffer if something happened to you? While some diseases are inevitable no matter what, most modern diseases are affected by what we choose to do today.

The healthy choices you make today will make you healthy tomorrow. They also will make those around you happier and healthier, too.

Did you know people who live with people who are healthy are more likely to be healthy, too? Become that pebble dropped in a lake… with ripples of "health wealth" extending out to all your loved ones.

Of course, the opposite is also true. If you smoke, don't move, or eat fried foods, the people around you are likely to do the same.

If you're a mom who would do anything for your kids (like Toni), picture them every time you choose fresh foods over French fries. Food is the single most important decision that affects our long-term health. We all make that decision multiple times every day.

Every day, set an intention. Before you decide *what* you will eat or do, remember your *why*.

Why are you eating this food? *Why* are you going for that jog — even when it's hard to get started?

Is it to live a long and healthy life — and see your grandchildren graduate? Is it to feel your best — so you can serve the world with your unique set of gifts? When you connect with your *why*, the *what* you eat or how much you move becomes easier.

But wait, you say. I have a family history of disease, so I'm doomed!

So do I. My grandmother was in a wheelchair from debilitating arthritis by the time she was in her thirties. My father had three heart attacks. The last one took his life. My little brother and grandfather are both stroke survivors.

My family history is why I follow what I call a "Kediterranean Diet." It's a term I coined that emphasizes brain-healthy Mediterranean foods like fish, olive oil, veggies, and whole fruits — combined with some ketogenic (lower-carb) practices. Vegans or vegetarians can use it as a modified "Kegan" diet — plant-based but lower carb.

This is the diet that works for me personally. As a researcher, I also know it's a program that has science to support it. For me, it's one easy-to-follow way to eat. And, it's compatible with other programs. For example, you can follow my "Kediterranean Diet" while following Weight Watchers. I also exercise just about every day and regularly practice relaxation techniques.

There are two ways I could have looked at this. I could have looked at my genes as a death sentence. Instead, I chose a different way *because* of my family history.

In fact, people who *do* have a family history need to make healthy living a priority far more than those who *don't* have a family history of disease. Don't get mad at your history. Just get moving!

When it comes to that question of nature versus nurture (e.g., is illness determined more by your genes *or* is it the everyday choices you make), recent science has given us the answer: it's your choices.

Genes load the gun, but those everyday choices you make determine if that trigger gets pulled. Every decision is a game of Russian roulette. Fruit or fries? Tennis or TV? Spin class or smoking a cigarette?

Every person has different genes and therefore a different tipping point for when that gun's "bullet" gets fired—in the form of obesity, diabetes, cancer, heart disease, or other major illnesses.

That's why one person can eat fries and stay thin, but most people can't. Do you want to take that risk? Which French fry will be the one that puts you into prediabetic territory? Which cigarette is the one that pulls that trigger—allowing a malignant cell to form and then spread?

But wait, you say… *I can't do it. I have*_____.
(Fill in the blank with the condition you've been diagnosed with. You're not alone. Chronic conditions are now the norm; not the exception.)

Or, I'm just too _____.
(Fill in the blank with one of the following words: out of shape, old, sick.)

Remember when Jennifer took her first Taekwondo class? She couldn't even finish it: *I was too dizzy and out of breath…*

Perhaps she should have just given up. After all, her left lung had collapsed at one point after years of smoking. I guess she could have just thrown in the towel. She could have just watched more TV from her bed. But what did she do? She went back the very next day… and the next… and the next.

Immediately, I learned my body could do things I never thought possible.

Make Healthy Choices Because You Want To |

I wonder what *you* will learn about yourself, your body, and your mind. You'll learn your everyday choices have the power to change your history.

If you have been diagnosed with an illness, talk to your doctor before starting a new routine. Once you get the "all clear," then it's you, your sneakers, and the open road.

Your doctor can't lace them up for you. Those everyday decisions are up to you. Go out and create a brilliant, healthy future. And watch it influence your family and friends!

Every seemingly insignificant decision you make today will end up creating a "health wealthy" tomorrow. Go get filthy rich in health.

1. Change how you THINK

If you aren't as rich in health as you'd like to be, you may be struggling with the pitfall thought pattern **polarization**.

When polarized thinking is applied to your health, you consider your life through a black-or-white, all-or-nothing, yes-or-no lens.

For Toni, polarized thinking may have sounded something like:

I'm doomed with genes that make it hard for me to lose weight. There are people who can eat anything they want, and there are the people who can't. I'm in the latter category. Guess I might as well eat those chips.

Do you see how there are only two categories here?

For Jennifer, polarized thinking may have sounded something like: *There are smokers and non-smokers.*

When she was becoming smoke-free, there may have been a really bad day. Perhaps she couldn't resist, and she thought to herself:

Well, there goes my entire plan to quit. I'm not a non-smoker... and I never will be! I guess I might as well finish this pack.

Do you see how polarized thinking also spirals into negative patterns of behavior?

The opposite of polarized thinking is gray-area thinking. So perhaps she *did* slip up. A gray-area thought would sound something like:

I wish I hadn't just smoked that cigarette, but you know what? I went two weeks without one. That's the longest I've ever gone. So, some of the changes I've been making must be working. But I also need to possibly look at what wasn't. Hmmm. It was the stress that led to that last cigarette. I think perhaps I need to add twelve minutes of meditation to my daily routine. I'll try that this afternoon.

Do you see how gray-area thinking can help people become more successful in their health goals?

Speaking of cancer, recent advances in science have made it possible for us to test for genes. A few that most people have heard of are BRCA's link to breast cancer and APOE's link to Alzheimer's disease.

If you test positive for one or more of these genes, a polarized way to look at this would be:

There are people who have the genes for this disease and people who don't. I'm doomed… I guess I'll just eat whatever I want. After all, I'll probably die from that disease no matter what I do.

Now, polarized thinking has also given way to pessimism — another pitfall thought pattern — and it's negatively affecting your health outcomes.

Now that you understand how genes work (genes load the gun, but your everyday choices pull the trigger), you'll be able to take a more balanced, gray-area stance on health.

Your thinking now sounds something like:

I have this gene which makes me more likely to develop this disease. This means that my choices like diet, exercise, and sleep are more important to me than someone else. I guess I better get moving!

You shift from *powerless* to *powerful*, and this helps you to make healthier choices every day.

Identify a health goal where you have used **polarized** thinking. What did you tell yourself?

_____

_____

_____

Now, train your brain away from all-or-nothing and towards gray area thinking — which tends to help people feel more empowered. My new thought process sounds like this:

_____

_____

_____

2. Change how you ACT

Now, let's look at **behavior**. Before we look at *what* you are going to do, let's look at *why* you will do it. For Toni, it was her daughter's life. For Jennifer, it was the moment she wanted to take control — after her lung had collapsed and she knew the time had come for her to live a smoke-free, healthy, and vibrant life.

You can train your brain to make these choices for your health and happiness. First, let's identify your own personal *why*.

* *Just take a quiet moment here for yourself, and consider all of the incredible gifts you already have in your life*
* *Family, friends, children, grandchildren…*
* *Blessings in the form of a career that feels like a calling, animals that bring you joy, and all the other things that bring a smile to your face and love to your heart*

* *And don't just think of others, think of your own health, your own body…*
* *Remember a time in your life when you felt pain-free and empowered*
* *And now, connect to your own personal WHY*

* *See that image of you smoke-free or enjoying that sensational strawberry*
* *Feel what it's like to move, to run, to be in nature, to break free of pain*

Doesn't that feel so good?

- *And now, you're probably beginning to remember your WHY: all the people you love*
- *And the love you have for yourself*

My WHY is:

_____

_____

_____

And something I will DO a little differently from now on is:

_____

_____

_____

3. BE HAPPY

Chapter 17

Think, Act & Be Happy

Enjoy that Empty Nest

All Things New

They must often change, who would be constant
in happiness or wisdom.
~Confucius

"Mom, you don't need to call all the time to check on me," our twenty-year-old son, Joe, said. "I've got to go. And Mom, you need to get a life."

Before I could say goodbye, he hung up. His words echoed in my head. "Get a life." I felt like I'd arrived to work at the best job in the world and been handed a pink slip. Being a mom meant everything to me.

It seemed one day our house bustled with activity, and then the next day it was quiet. There were no teenagers bursting through the front door asking, "What's for dinner?" There were no more late-night chats about school, crushes, or jobs.

In an effort to lift our spirits, one weekend my husband Loren said, "Let's go for a drive." We caught the ferry and drove up Whidbey Island. Standing on the bluff at Fort Casey, Loren and I watched tugboats drag barges through the Straits of Juan de Fuca. We'd visited the favorite Washington state park dozens of times with our kids.

Tears dripped down my cheeks as a chilly March wind whipped off the water. "It feels strange to be here without them. I can hear their laughter in the air and see Ben chasing Joe down the beach, whacking him with kelp."

"I know." Loren pulled me close under his arm while we strolled to our car. "I wonder what they're doing today."

Scenes from their childhood played in our minds as we drove from the park. The emptiness we felt with half our family missing ruined our outing. A few miles from the ferry I interrupted the silence. "Well, we can't just mope around the rest of our lives. I think we need to go to new places, places we never took the kids, places not already filled with memories. We need to build new memories of our own."

"Hmm… " Loren nodded. "You might be right."

While my idea simmered, Loren and I talked of dreams long left dormant. We considered changes we needed to make to move forward. Plans took shape as we envisioned our future together.

In May we traded our family car for a sporty SUV. In June Loren took a two-week vacation. We packed our clothes, loaded an ice chest filled with fruit and sandwiches into our new car, and hit the road. Instead of heading north or east like we'd always done as a family, we drove south.

Traveling down Highway 101, we explored the Oregon and Northern California coastlines. Whenever we needed a rest, we pulled off the highway at the nearest beach. Seated on the tailgate of our vehicle, we ate meals from the ice chest. We held hands, strode miles of oceanfront beaches, and sat on driftwood logs to watch the sunset.

We booked a room at a B&B, something we'd never done. The innkeeper operated a side business making fused glass and offered classes to guests. We marveled over glass vases and platters, swirled with color, displayed in the dining room. "Do you want to sign up for a class?" I said to Loren.

He gave me a skeptical grin. "I don't know. We've never done anything like that before."

Smiling, I shrugged my shoulders. "That's the point. Come on, it'll be fun."

We paid our forty dollars and signed up for an afternoon class. Huddled over a workbench in the innkeeper's studio, we spent several hours learning the process of fused glass. I watched Loren select colored glass chips from numerous supply bins and arrange them in unique patterns. We each made two coasters, had hours of fun, shared a new experience, and learned a new craft.

We had so much fun on our trip we started a list of other places we wanted to visit.

However, when we returned home once again, we faced a quiet

empty house. After twenty-two years of raising kids, we felt lost until we realized we finally had time to focus on our own interests. We cleared out the kids' bedrooms and turned one into a study. Loren registered for college and earned a degree. We repainted our daughter's old room and transformed it into an art studio. Loren built me a painting table and I signed up for watercolor classes with a local artist.

We skated along fine until that first holiday season approached. Without the flurry and excitement of our kids it was miserable. Alone, we slogged through the field of the Christmas tree farm our family visited each year. From a dark corner of our closet Loren retrieved cardboard boxes labeled "Christmas." I loved the sights, sounds, and smells of the season, but when we unwrapped the first decorations, I held up a calico cat fashioned from wallpaper with buttons sewn on to attach the legs. "Bethany made this," I sniffed. "And here's the rabbit Joe made, but he's not here to hang it on the tree."

Loren wrapped his arms around me and pulled me onto the couch. "Hey, I've got an idea. Why don't we buy new ornaments?"

His suggestion seemed a wild extravagance. I gazed into the box of homemade decorations. Each one came with years of memories. "Okay." I jumped up from the couch. We rewrapped the ornaments in tissue. Loren carried the boxes back to the closet.

On Saturday we went to the store. "I feel like newlyweds on our first Christmas together," I said.

Loren laughed. "We're a long way from those days." Eyes wide with delight we strolled each aisle. A string of twinkly lights for the tree and several packages of shiny ornaments lifted our spirits and helped us glide through the season.

One evening early in the new year Loren said, "Hey, let's catch a movie."

"What, right now?" I glanced at my watch. "It's nine o'clock."

After a moment's thought I raced to grab my coat. "You're on."

Near midnight, stars twinkled in the sky as we strolled from the theater. "I don't remember the last time we went to the late show."

Loren gave my hand a gentle squeeze. "Not since we were dating."

When we arrived home we spotted the answering machine blinking.

Loren pressed the button and we heard Joe's voice, "Hello... Hello... Pick up the phone... Hey, it's ten o'clock. Where are you guys?"

I laughed as Loren and I snuggled into bed. "He told me to get a life."

— Kathleen Kohler —

A Different Life

Fun fact: There are more than forty varieties of Tabbies, making them the most common breed of cat.

After thirty-six years of marriage, I was alone, living in a nice rental townhouse near my work. My three wonderful kids, now grown, had families of their own. Thankfully, I had a job that took up my days, but the nights were long and lonely. My life fell into a dreary routine: wake, work, home, eat, sleep, repeat.

A few months after my move, a co-worker found a stray cat living under her porch. She could not take him in because she already had three cats. I was reluctant, even though I was allowed to have a cat in my unit. I had always been one to nurture and care for helpless critters. I had even raised two orphaned robins to adulthood. But right then, to agree to adopt a homeless cat, sight unseen, seemed a little crazy. But perhaps I was feeling a little crazy that day because I suddenly blurted out, "Okay! I'll take him!"

At first, he huddled in a tight ball inside the carrier and refused to come out. I could see that he was a tan-and-black Tabby, fairly nondescript. Well, that was exactly how I felt. I went about some quiet chores, and eventually he ventured out to hide under a chair and watch me suspiciously with his big yellow eyes as I moved about. I spoke to him in a soft, soothing voice, and slowly he loosened up. Crouching low to the floor, he began to work his way around the perimeter of the first floor, slowly investigating every corner and piece of furniture. At any little noise or unexpected movement, he would jump and tense, then continue on his timorous exploration.

As I watched him, I could see that he had an impression in the fur around his neck where a collar had been. I looked at my hand where there was still an indentation left by my absent wedding rings.

We had similar losses. Neither of us belonged to anyone.

The Tabby looked directly at me now. I looked back, with my eyes half-closed so as not to seem threatening, and wondered: What happened to you? What have you gone through out on your own? I thought it must have been very frightening for him, suddenly out fending for himself, because that's how I felt. The world was so big, and I felt so small. He was pretty thin, too, so he obviously had not been doing very well. I could also relate to that. I had lost twenty pounds.

Watching him creep along the baseboards, the boundaries of his new world, I saw exactly how I had been living for months, creeping around the boundaries of my own newly single life, peeking around corners, afraid to venture too far out into the open, keeping to the routine. I no longer knew where or how I fit into the world, just like that poor, homeless cat.

Later on, I lay stiffly in my bed, straining to hear any sound from my feline guest. Where was he? What was he doing? Did he use the litter box? I did not even know if he had come upstairs yet. Cats are so quiet! Time dragged on. I got up once and looked for him to no avail, so I went back to bed, straining to hear any sound. At some point, though, tense as I was, I must have dozed off because I was suddenly wakened by a solid thump at my feet. I lifted my head ever so slightly and peered toward the foot of the bed. The cat stood facing me, statue still. Neither of us even twitched. My sleepy brain wondered: Was he going to attack me? Had he ever been vaccinated? I dared not move. The small nightlight in the room gave off a soft glow that reflected eerily from his big, round eyes. Was he glaring, staring, or just look-ing? My imagination had to choose which before I could decide what to do next, like defensively burying myself under the covers. I chose "looking," and slowly put my head back on the pillow, took a deep breath and resolved to be calm.

Then an extraordinary thing happened! The cat uttered an audible sigh, sucking in a deep breath that I could hear as he expelled it in a soft *whoosh*. I felt movement, then warm pressure on my feet as he curled up against me with his head resting on my ankle. Relaxed. Another sigh, and he closed his eyes. He had made the choice to trust me and began to purr, that gentle, contented rumbling that seems to say "all is well." My heart melted. We chose each other that night and spent the next day bonding before I had to go back to work on Monday. I named him Bailey. I no longer had to come home to an empty house because he was there, always sitting on the back of the chair by the window, looking for me or curled up beside me on the sofa, warm and comforting.

My three-year-old granddaughter was sleeping over one night and asked me to tell her the story of how Bailey came to live with me. I told her a brief version, and since I was scrapbooking at the time, I thought it would be fun to gather pictures of him and create a storybook for her. I bought a spiral notebook to begin writing what I imagined his life had been like while he was lost. I took the notebook to work every day and wrote longhand on my lunch breaks and more during the evenings. The words and situations poured out from my heart onto the pages, and I realized that I wasn't just writing a fiction story of a lost cat; I was writing my own story. It became a way to release my feelings in a safe way through creative writing. My anger and anxiety flowed onto the pages as I eagerly wrote, to see what would happen to my reluctant hero. I had to purchase a laptop in order to write more and faster!

I told my friends about my new "hobby," and they urged me to self-publish. The result was an actual book I could hold in my hands, with a cover and 247 pages filled with my words! Those who read it loved it, but I wondered how that could be. Me? An author? I couldn't write a book! I had not set out to write a book, after all. But I've always believed that God works in mysterious ways, opens windows when doors seem closed, and works all things for good. In my case, God opened a window and let in a cat I named Bailey... and a new and different life began.

— Beth DiCola —

Dr. Mike...

Perhaps you and your partner find yourself empty nesters together like Kathleen and Loren did. Or, perhaps your nest is empty after moving on from a marriage with adult kids like Beth did. No matter the circumstances, this transition is a tough one for any loving parent.

Kathleen, Loren, and Beth were all at a crossroads. A certain amount of loneliness is normal in those circumstances.

I always say: thoughts and feelings are *information*. What is this information that you are receiving right now telling you about you? Pretend it's like one of those personality tests you might find in a magazine.

Is this sadness telling you that you're an inherent caretaker? If so, perhaps you can eventually channel that strength of yours in a different way like Beth did. Just because you are no longer the mother of twelve-year-old boys doesn't mean you should extinguish your loving, motherly heart. Beth became a momma all over again... to a cat named Bailey.

Is the loneliness an indication that you're an extrovert... and that you get your energy from being around other people? If your kids are all at college, surround yourself with friends — old ones or new ones.

When it came to their daily lives, Kathleen, Loren, and Beth did so much *right*. They filled their lives with novel activities. Did you know that they you can actually help you grow new brain cells?

Eventually, Kathleen and Loren changed their brains. They did all sorts of things they had never done with their kids. But, it wasn't easy at first.

Remember when Kathleen and Loren caught the ferry and took that drive together? She said to him: *It feels strange to be here without them.*

Tears dripped down her cheeks. This mom's transition was not easy. Perhaps you've had that same feeling... those same tears...

After that initial hump, they took risks. Kathleen and Loren tried new things.

Remember when they drove south on the 101 Freeway on a road trip to Oregon and Northern California instead of their usual northbound route? And that other first: a room at a B&B.

I loved Loren's response when Kathleen asked if he wanted to take a glass-vase-making class: *I don't know. We've never done anything like that before.*

Great! That's exactly the point!

Beth tried new things, too. She was not a middle-aged woman twiddling her thumbs all day long. Beth is a busy woman. Her life was filled with joy knowing she had rescued a cat. She was working a job during the day and found time to write a 247-page book… which also helped her to manage her anxiety about her transition.

Did you know that reading and writing are both incredible activities for aging brains? When you're done reading this book (and writing in it), maybe you could pick up another *Chicken Soup for the Soul* book… or submit a story for a future edition of the series!

Maybe you're still working forty-hour weeks. Maybe you still have other responsibilities at home. Right about now, retiring in Mexico and doing nothing for the rest of your life but sipping daiquiris and napping in hammocks sounds like a dream.

I'm sure that would feel nice for a week or two. After that, napping all day on the beach is more apt to feel like an empty existence. Where's the purpose? Where's the challenge? And doing nothing all day is terrible for your mental *and* physical health. When it comes to training the brain, it's "use it or lose it."

If you're ninety-five and can still make it out to see your friends and family for lunch, walks, and to play Bingo… great! If you're seventy and can go on road trips like Kathleen and Loren, fantastic! If you're still working a 9 to 5 job like Beth, wonderful!

By challenging your brain, your daily life will be full of activities. May they bring purpose, passion, and peace to your life. Allow your brain to help heal your heart.

1. Change how you THINK

If you're going through a transition like empty nest syndrome, beware of **pervasiveness**. If you let it, this pitfall thought pattern will seduce you into allowing it to affect every single area of your life.

Remember when Kathleen had tears streaming down her cheeks?

When **pervasiveness** wins, it tells you: You feel sad about something specific (e.g., your kids leaving), but you interpret this as your *whole life* being sad.

If **pervasiveness** would have held Beth back, she might have called in sick to work. She would have allowed her sadness about her kids to keep her from her normal activities and her normal interactions with other people. If that had happened, maybe she wouldn't have had that conversation with a co-worker about the cat she found under her porch. And that Tabby wouldn't have ended up being Beth's sweet Bailey. She might not have her new passion for writing, either.

Do you see how **pervasiveness** can seduce us? It's like when one area of our life isn't going well… now *other* areas of our life aren't going well, too.

When **pervasiveness** is telling you to sacrifice other areas of your life because you're struggling in one particular area, make sure you talk back to it. Don't allow **pervasiveness** to seduce you.

Let's do a positive reframe. Do what Beth and Kathleen did. They didn't allow **pervasiveness** to drag down their lives.

If you looked at your longing as information, what is it saying about you? What does it tell you about what you need in your life now? Do you need to add some caretaking like Beth did when she adopted Bailey? Or perhaps some novelty and adventure like Kathleen? Or perhaps all you need is some time and a few kind friends around you for a few months.

Just take a moment to breathe in any and all feelings related to this transition, and honestly evaluate how you're handling it.

When I take a look at them in a non-judgmental way, my thoughts and feelings sound something like:

_____

_____

_____

If I look at these thoughts and feelings as *information* about what I *need*, what are these feelings telling me I should add into my life?

_____

_____

_____

How does this reframe help me to avoid **pervasiveness** — so that I won't allow this one area of difficulty to affect all areas of my life?

_____

_____

_____

2. Change how you ACT

Another way to help you avoid **pervasiveness** is to change the way you act. Become unsinkable. Imagine you are a ship with nine watertight compartments. Each compartment represents an area of your life: family, hobbies, health, and so on. If you spring a leak in one or two areas, seal them off.

Pervasiveness is when you don't keep those feelings and issues in their watertight compartments. It's when you don't talk back to those overly broad feelings. A leak in one area spreads through the whole ship.

You're an empty nester and feeling lonely about being at home. So you stop calling your friends and sacrifice those relationships, too. And, you stop going to your Tai Chi classes and you abandon your daily walks.

Did you know the Titanic was designed to stay afloat with multiple watertight compartments flooded? In fact, 25% of its compartments could be flooded and it could still float. When it sank, it's because almost 40% of its compartments were flooded.

To put that into perspective, that means you'd be "unsinkable" as long as six or more of the nine areas of your life aren't flooded. Do you have one activity that you do on a fairly regular basis that "fills" this compartment of your life?

If the "parenting and family life" compartment feels like it's "sprung a leak" right now, fill your other compartments. That will allow you some time to "patch that leak." Before you know it, that leaky compartment may fill up in a different way — with something new!

Write down one or more activities that help you to fill each of the following "compartments" of the ship that is your life:

Spiritual life: _____

Service: _____

Citizen: _____

Parenting/Family: _____

Work/Productivity: _____

Hobbies: _____

Just for Fun: _____

Health: _____

Relationships (Romance & Friendships): _____

_____

3. BE HAPPY

Chapter 18

Overspending & Overcoming Shopping Addiction

The Lesson of the Mandala

*It's usually quite hard to let go and move on, but once
you do, you'll feel free and realize it was the best
decision you've ever made.*
~Author Unknown

pushed and shoved then I pushed some more. When did my
closet get so full? I looked down at the two shopping bags of
clothes purchased on my latest spree. Maybe it was time to admit
I had a problem.

Like many women, I always loved to shop. In my teen years, I
was what my girlfriends and I affectionately called "a mall rat," a girl
who hung out at the mall every weekend, checking out the current
fashions while simultaneously checking out other teenagers of the
male persuasion. Fast-forward twenty-five years. After the death of
my mother, I once again found pleasure in walking the mall. No
longer bound by caregiving responsibilities, I could spend as much
time there as I pleased, have a pleasant lunch in the food court and
get a bit of exercise in a temperature-controlled environment. It was
the perfect activity. And now I even had something I didn't have as a
teenager — credit cards.

Armed with my plastic and fueled by the sugar and caffeine of a
tall mocha latte, I could shop for hours, returning home with incredible
bargains. I'd hold up a sweater for my husband to see. "Can you believe
this was only eight dollars?" I'd proclaim proudly. "And this one," I'd
say while lifting a pair of slacks, "cost only slightly more — and it has
a designer label!"

Oh, I was quite the shopper all right. It didn't matter to me that
my sweater drawer overflowed and caused me to annex the extras to
a storage container shoved under the bed. Nor did I mind when an

excess of accessories was required to be housed in a plastic box atop my dresser. It had been so long since I did anything special for myself, I rationalized. I deserved some new things.

Yet now I was forced to take a closer look at my situation. I poked around my overstuffed closet and pulled out a few of my more recent purchases: a poncho emblazoned with butterflies, two pair of leopard leggings, two blue blazers and several sets of T-shirts in duplicate colors. Clearly, I had gone from a bargain shopper to a shopping warrior whose battle cry was "one if on sale, two if on clearance!"

I slowly pulled a few more articles out of my closet and laid them on the floor in a careful circle, creating a sort of textile mandala. Long ago, when I still had time to read, I recalled reading about the Buddhist monks of Tibet who painstakingly created mandalas, a circular design created with colored sand, only to disassemble them upon their completion, signifying the impermanence of life. The letting go, they feel, is as important as the act of creation itself. It is only through the letting go, they believe, that growth and healing can take place. Yes, nothing is forever, I thought, looking back on my mother's long illness and her ultimate passing. It was time to let go.

I pulled each piece of clothing out of my closet and sorted them into several piles. Clothing with tags still attached would be returned to the store for a refund. Worn out clothing would go directly into the trash. Anything still in good condition but in a wrong size, style or color for me would be donated to an organization that helped women in need. The remainder would be returned to my closet. After that, I vowed, there would be no more shopping for a long, long time.

This act, which took all of about an hour, was exhilarating and freeing in a way I could have never imagined. Cleaning out my closet and drawers created a domino effect of benefits. Dressing each morning became a much simpler task since it was easier to both find and select outfits in a closet that had room to spare. Housecleaning became less of a chore once I no longer had to move boxes and bags of clothing to accomplish the task. Weekends were much freer, as well, once I wasn't spending so much time at the mall bargain hunting. No longer did I have to reconcile charge bills, file away receipts and run to the bank to transfer money for department store payments.

Now, with my newfound spare time, I make frequent trips to the library and catch up on my reading. I took up knitting again and committed to making two sweaters a year for a worldwide organization that distributes them to needy children. I renewed old friendships that had been put on hiatus during my caregiving days, and if I want to take a walk I lace up my sneakers and pound the pavement in the fresh air regardless of temperature. My life is varied and full again, all because I let go. It's true really, I think, what the Tibetan monks say. The real healing comes from the letting go.

— Monica A. Andermann —

Dr. Mike...

There are addictions where the solution comes in a black-or-white formula: abstinence. A heroin addict hits rock bottom. The treatment: inpatient rehab, 12-step meetings, and abstinence.

Then, there are the addictions where abstinence isn't possible. Shopping addicts still need to buy groceries. Food addicts still need to eat. If you're addicted to your phone but have a demanding job, you probably can't give that up entirely, either.

In the brain, what do cocaine, alcohol, poker, fatty foods, shopping, and even getting a "like" on Facebook have in common? They all give the brain something it likes: a little hit of dopamine. That feels good, and it keeps people coming back for more.

For some people, a little "retail therapy" once in a while may be just fine. You buy yourself a new sweater. You can afford it, and perhaps that's fine.

But if you can't stop thinking about shopping, have tried to cut back but can't, and have suffered major life consequences because of excessive shopping, it may be time to take a look at this behavior in a new way.

For Monica, shopping became her drug. As with other addictions, rationalizations became commonplace: *It had been so long since I did anything special for myself... I deserved some new things.*

Sometimes, that can be true. Maybe you *do* deserve something special. You *should* do something that makes you feel better. Remember when Monica renewed old friendships or took those trips to the library to catch up on reading? There are so many things we can do for ourselves that don't cost any money.

Monica did some incredible work in getting to know herself better. If excess shopping is on your mind, perhaps there are some questions to ask yourself: *Is this rationalization costing me relationships... or straining them? Am I racking up debt on my credit card? Could that eventually cost me my house or lead to bankruptcy?*

There's a precious moment—sometimes only a millisecond—between an impulse and an action. A simple strategy called mindfulness can seize this precious moment… so that it doesn't seize us. In today's smart phone, app-driven world, that precious moment is becoming shorter and shorter.

It used to take time to buy something. You had to get in your car or call a toll-free number. Now all you have to do is press a button on your phone. The credit card has already been stored, and your purchase arrives at your house days later.

And so, there's a brain-training strategy to help fix this. It's called mindfulness. Mindfulness is simply paying attention to the present moment. In that precious moment, stop and check in with yourself. Check in with your mind and body. Take a moment to just ask yourself: *What's going on with me right now?*

There are also great common-sense strategies that can help create a little distance from triggers. If you were a drug addict, you would need to get rid of any drugs you had hidden. It would include deleting your dealer's phone number.

If you can't stop shopping, you also need to create a bit of distance. That may include getting rid of credit cards. You may need to talk to a credit counselor who can help you create a plan. Paying in cash or debit cards may help you to increase accountability. Create a budget. Delete stored credit or debit card numbers from one-button apps so you can't just press a button in times of stress or sadness.

Eventually, you may even find one of the most rewarding parts of healing: purpose. Monica knitted sweaters and gave them to an organization that distributed them to needy children. And, she found peace and freedom in the simple act of letting go. What will you attract into your life when you stop clinging to all that excess stuff?

1. Change how you THINK

A pitfall thought pattern shopping addicts often face is **paralysis-analysis**. Some worries may be shopping related: *What if that sweater isn't here when I come back? Oh gosh… that would be awful! What if I can't find it online?! I better just buy it now.*

Or, **paralysis-analysis** can be the trigger of the shopping. Getting stuck in anxious worries can often lead people to cope by doing something that makes them feel better in the moment. **Paralysis-analysis** gets you stuck in one area of your life. You can't stop worrying about your weight gain… your financial problems… your loneliness…

You can't seem to take meaningful action and you feel stuck on this one problem. So, you take action in another area: you buy.

Here's an antidote: Remember that precious moment just before pressing the "buy" button? Imagine you're there now. Or, use this brain-training meditation the next time you find yourself in one of those moments.

Take a beat… and a breath.
What's going on with me in this moment?
Why am I about to click the Buy button?
Where is this need to buy coming from?

Notice your mind…
your thoughts and your feelings…
Notice your body…

Now, whatever you found here…
The stress or sadness…
First, just surround it with understanding and non-judgment
Allow that loving part of you to just surround it with compassion

Now, ask yourself…
What's a better way for me to get this need met?
See yourself choosing these healthier choices…
If you're stressed, see that bath or that walk you're about to take
If you're lonely, see that call to a friend you'll make after this meditation

And isn't it so nice to know…
that you can invite yourself into this peaceful place
whenever you'd like…

How did this meditation allow me to create more space between the impulse to buy and the act of buying?

_____

_____

_____

How did this meditation help me to turn off **paralysis-analysis**?

_____

_____

_____

2. Change how you ACT

Now, create some freedom from *stuff* and *things*. If there are any returnable items with tags still on them, that's a great place to start. Return those.

It's time for a little spring-cleaning. Get three boxes or just create piles. Label one *Keep*. Label one *Donate*. Label one *Throw Away*.

When going through your closet, it's helpful to consider if you actually need something. Will you actually wear this in the next year? If not, it's time to get rid of it.

If it's in wearable condition, donate it.

It it's an unwearable shoe from 1990 with holes, throw it away.

When you throw that box away, notice how good it feels to be that much lighter.

When you give that box to charity or someone who will use it, notice how nice it feels to not hold on… and to give to someone else.

When you look at your new closet that's no longer overflowing, make sure you notice how nice it feels to be free of all that excess stuff.

3. BE HAPPY

Chapter 19

Think,
Act & Be
Happy

Think Positive

Affirmations Changed My Life

An affirmation opens the door. It's a beginning
point on the path to change.
~Louise L. Hay

In 1998, I was miserable. I had a three-year-old son whom I adored, but his father was a different story altogether. I was in a miserable marriage and in poor health. I lived in a small town and worked a job I hated. We were so broke all the time that we were always one paycheck or financial disaster away from being homeless. It was not a good time.

Things had grown so bad that my husband and I slept in separate bedrooms. Every night, I retreated to my room and buried my head in a book or my journal. One day, after reading an article on the Internet about affirmations, I realized I was desperate enough to give them a try.

I'd always thought affirmations were silly. I associated them with the old Al Franken *Saturday Night Live* character, Stuart Smalley, who would gaze at himself in the mirror, saying aloud, "I'm good enough, I'm smart enough, and doggone it people like me." While that was a funny running gag on *SNL*, I didn't think I could bring myself to do it, because it just felt embarrassing.

Still, after reading the article about affirmations earlier that day and reflecting on my current misery, I realized I needed to do something—anything—to change my life. I threw caution to the wind and started making affirmations.

Unlike Stuart Smalley, I didn't say them out loud while gazing at myself in the mirror. Instead, I pulled out a spiral-bound notebook. I closed my eyes and envisioned the life I wanted for myself. I saw my son and me living with a man whom I truly loved in a supportive and honest relationship. I pictured us living in a comfortable home. I saw myself in a well-paying job that I loved that still allowed me plenty of time with my son. I pictured myself whole, happy, and filled with vibrant health. I imagined having a happy family and lots of friends, as well as engaging in activities that filled me with joy and purpose.

Once I had a picture in my mind of exactly how I wanted my life to look, I wrote ten statements that affirmed each of the things I visualized. Instead of writing them as statements of want, I wrote the affirmations as if I already had the things I envisioned. For example, I wrote, "I am grateful I have a job that intellectually, creatively, and financially fulfills me while allowing me to spend plenty of time with my son."

After I settled on ten affirmations, I wrote them by hand in my notebook. Every night, I wrote each affirmation ten times. Then, I closed my eyes and visualized the life I wanted. I ended by expressing thanks to the universe for giving me such a wonderful life.

I did this for months, filling two notebooks full of the same ten affirmations, written over and over every night as I sat alone in my room.

Slowly, life took over. Eventually, I only wrote my affirmations once a week, then once a month. Then, I forgot about them altogether. My life went on, and it changed drastically.

My husband and I separated and divorced, but we worked out an arrangement between the two of us to support what our son needed from both of his parents. I moved to a new town and started working a job in a field I loved: writing. The job paid extremely well, and I was allowed to telecommute several days a week so I had plenty of time to hang out with my son. I was thrilled.

At my new job, I met a wonderful man. After a few years, the two of us married. We both made good money, and I was no longer a paycheck away from financial ruin. My husband was also an amazing stepdad to my son, and he had a son who gave my child the sibling he'd always wanted. As I grew happier, my health improved significantly, as well.

In 2003, we moved into a lovely new home on a hillside with a beautiful view of the valley. Along with working from home and spending time with my son, I also had the time to engage in hobbies and volunteer activities that enriched my life. Through my activities, I made many new friendships. Life was good on our hill, and I was very happy.

One day, shortly after moving into our home, I was digging through a box when I came across two battered spiral notebooks. I opened them with interest, wondering what I had written. In their pages I found my ten affirmations, repeated over and over again.

As I read the affirmations I had written five years earlier, I was shocked. Every affirmation I'd so carefully repeated and visualized described precisely the way my life had turned out. Through affirmation and visualization, I had created exactly the life I wanted for myself.

With such a powerful example of how well affirmations and visualizations work, I now realize that Stuart Smalley was on to something, after all. Using these tools can set the wheels in motion to bring about lasting change in your life.

Today, I use affirmation and visualization as a regular tool, and it is one I am grateful to have. Occasionally I forget about the tools when life gets in the way. However, I always return to visualization and affirmation. Whenever I do, I see the visualized outcomes manifesting quickly as my mindset changes and I am spurred to action. I am eternally grateful.

— Karen Frazier —

Thoughts, Words and Actions

By doing the work to love ourselves more, I believe we
will love each other better.
~Laverne Cox

I sat across from my counselor Christina during my one-on-one session at the outpatient rehab. "You want me to do what?" I asked, incredulous. I had suffered from liver cirrhosis just two months before and had barely escaped alive. Determined to keep my newfound sobriety, I had checked myself into an outpatient rehab to learn about why I was an alcoholic and what demons from my past I could deal with. After spending seven years at the bottom of a vodka bottle, I was going to need all the help I could get.

"I want you to look in the mirror every morning and I want you to repeat your mantra for the day. I am going to give you these Post-its and every morning I want you to write something positive about yourself and say it in the mirror."

I hadn't looked in a mirror in years. Any time I was faced with one I averted my eyes and literally jumped out of the way. My eyes and skin were still yellowed by jaundice. My abdomen was immensely swollen from fluid and I endured daily questions about when I was due. My hair was falling out in clumps due to an iron deficiency, and I still couldn't climb stairs without running out of breath. I was crashing at my mother's house because I had nowhere else to go. I couldn't work. I was broke. My limbs were so skinny they knocked together at night, waking me up with bruises. She wanted me to do what?

"So after you write it down on your Post-it note, I want you to paste it in your journal so you can see it throughout the day. I will be checking it next week." I started to grumble but she held up her hand. "Just try it. It's an experiment."

I left her office with a stack of Post-it notes. I had promised myself that I was going to try whatever they suggested.

The next morning I stared at my Post-it note, pen in hand. "You are important" came into my head and I jotted it down. Now for the hard part.

I peeked around my bathroom door. The mirror ran pretty much the length of the entire bathroom, so there really was no other option than to face it once you entered. I closed my eyes and walked in, laughing at myself for being so ridiculous, but also recognizing that my heart hurt. I felt so sad that I had come to the point that just looking in the mirror was such a burden. Did I really hate the sight of myself that much?

I forced myself to open my eyes. There I was, skinny limbs, jutting belly, bird bone wrists… I kept looking and told myself, "You… are important… You are im… portant… You are important. You are important. You are important!" By the end I was shouting at myself, shaking my fist at my reflection. I hadn't survived this far to give in to my fear! I needed to face myself.

I proudly posted my proclamation into my journal. I continued to do so every day that week.

I gained sober time, was put on a diuretic for the bloating and slowly began gaining muscle. The Post-it notes gathered in my book. "You are beautiful." "Look at how far you have come." "You are intelligent." "Your feelings are valid." Soon I was looking at my face in the mirror every morning without flinching.

Another part of rehab that filled in quite a bit of the puzzle was PTSD therapy with a local group that offered services for survivors of sexual abuse. All of a sudden I had a name for the terror that I felt, and an opportunity to take control of that fear. The counselor handed me a ball of clay. "I want you to sculpt your future. You're an artist, right?" she asked. I nodded my head. "You have as much control over your future as you have over this ball of clay. Shape it." I sculpted a tiny book for my novel, a Ph.D. graduation cap for my education goals, a small skull for my future shop, a plane for travel and a TV because one day I'd like to have my own travel show.

"Your thoughts become words, and your words become actions," she said, observing what we were creating. "Positive thoughts become positive words and your positive words will become positive actions." I had been talking to myself like I was a piece of trash for decades. No wonder I was where I was.

The next morning I said to myself in the mirror, "I love you. We are going to get back on our feet. We are going to get a job. We are going to find an apartment. I. Love. You." Those thoughts became words and pretty soon after landing a full-time job at a hotel, I got off the wrong stop on the bus. I huffed and lugged my bag off the bus. I still wasn't at full strength and was incredibly annoyed at myself for the added ten-minute walk. I started to curse myself and then stopped. That kind of thinking wasn't going to get me anywhere. Sometimes the best things are found when we get lost. I passed by the street next to the donut shop with all the lovely Victorian row houses, the last ones in Kansas City. I had always wanted to live there, but they never seemed to have a vacancy. Of course, this was the first time I saw a "For Rent" sign, and pretty soon I was living there and paying for it myself.

Actively practicing positive thinking continued to yield results for me. The crippling anxiety that I had lived with for years subsided. I had finally learned how to control the fear that seemed inescapable.

I have been sober for more than two years now, without a single relapse. I have recovered as much as a person can from liver cirrhosis and now lead a normal life, albeit with a lot of doctor checkups and a few prescriptions. And I will never be able to drink again.

That little flicker of optimism has turned into a full-blown lifestyle. Without it, I certainly would not still be here. People ask, "How do you stay so upbeat?" It's not easy. Sometimes I come home and want to sell all my things, live in a yurt in the desert, wear fancy hats and never speak to anyone again. That's okay. I let the emotion roll over me, but I don't let it control my behavior. After a good cry, it's back to planning mode. Happiness is a conscious choice, one that I make every single day. It's a choice that anyone can make. Make it.

— Monique Gabrielle Salazar —

Dr. Mike...

The power of positive thinking is powerful, indeed.

As Monique learned, changing your thoughts may mean the difference between starting a new life and staying stuck in a life that means certain death. Even though affirmations felt a little silly at first, Karen learned that they had the power to help her create the future she always wanted.

If you were raised in a "pull yourself up by the bootstraps" sort of family, these optimistic and kind statements may even feel totally foreign to you. Or maybe you think positive thoughts are just downright crazy.

Remember when Monique's skin was still yellow from jaundice and her hair was still falling out in clumps? Imagine yourself in her shoes. Perhaps you can already relate. Maybe there's already something that bothers you: your weight, your age…

Imagine someone hands you a Post-it and tells you: write something positive about yourself… and then say it out loud in the mirror. You'd probably be thinking: *Are you crazy?*

Mental and physical diseases that affect so many of us are fueled by the negative, pessimistic, and downright horrific things we say to ourselves.

Monique knew what these statements felt like. Remember when she said, *I had been talking to myself like I was a piece of trash for decades. No wonder I was where I was.*

How do *you* talk to yourself? Here's an exercise that will help you train your brain. Stop for a moment and imagine that you're in the cartoon section of the Sunday paper with those thought bubbles appearing over your head. Now, imagine we can all read what you're saying to yourself throughout your day.

As awful as the following statements may be, I have found them to be very common self-talk found in people's "thought bubbles":

Can't you do anything right?
You look so old… so fat… so ugly!
What's wrong with you?
Are you just plain stupid?

I may not know you personally, but I know you picked up this book, and I know that *Chicken Soup for the Soul* readers tend to be loving, kind, and warm-hearted people... so I already *know* those words aren't the kind of things you'd say to a friend. So the question is: Can you talk to yourself with the same compassion, warmth, and understanding you give to others?

Perhaps you follow some version of the Golden Rule. You treat others with the same kindness as you would yourself. But to follow this rule, don't you have to assume that you're actually treating *yourself* with kindness?

If you are dealing with a difficult-to-treat illness, changing your self-talk may even improve the way you feel. Some of these conditions include digestive woes, chronic pain, and autoimmune conditions.

While medications are a part of difficult-to-treat conditions, cognitive behavioral therapy is often recommended. Why? Because the way you talk to yourself truly makes a difference.

In fact, pessimism can prevent *any* treatment from working. If you look for evidence of why you're *not* better, you're likely to find it. But guess what? The opposite is also true. In fact, the placebo effect is essentially an affirmation. You believe something is going to make you better. And so, it does — because you *believe* it.

Maybe your problem isn't a disease that causes pain or physical problems. You know exactly what needs to change in your life. You're one paycheck away from being broke like Karen was. You picked up this book to inspire you during an intensive treatment program — like the one Monique was in.

Maybe your problem is your job. Your relationship. Your finances.

Here's my strategy. If something's working for you, do more of *that*. If something's not working, change it. But often, a great place to start is to change your frame of mind.

Why? Thoughts create feelings. Feelings create actions. The sum of your actions has created your life as it stands today. This is you training your brain.

Or as Monique learned... *Your thoughts become words, and your words become actions.* That's what I loved most about Karen and Monique's stories. Both of these women showed how Post-it notes and affirmations have the power to help create incredible lives.

It's one thing to just sit around and think positive thoughts and affirmations. If you want them to work, you have to *connect* them with your daily actions.

Sometimes, these daily actions can be boring or tedious. It means waking up and showing up to work on time. It means sacrificing your weekend to study for the course you're taking that will help you get a better job one day. That's how affirmations become reality.

You may not even notice it happening, because you create this new life one day at a time. That was Karen's experience. There was a divorce, a move, and a new relationship. But even through those bumpy times, she was positive and specific with the universe about what she was going to create for herself.

Years later, she realized she had created the life she wanted.

So did Monique. With years of sobriety under her belt, she was now working. One of those "never available" great Victorians in Kansas City suddenly had a "For Rent" sign, and it became hers. If you stop to take a look and do your part, you may discover that the universe is always conspiring in your favor.

1. Change how you THINK

Monique had a battle cry: *I love you. We are going to get back on our feet. We are going to get a job. We are going to find an apartment. I. Love. You.*

What's your battle cry?

It's time to exterminate the pitfall thought pattern **pessimism** from your self-talk.

I want you to start by looking at the way you talk to a friend or a child. Perhaps this person needs a pep talk. She is about to go in for a big job interview. Or, he is about to make a big decision about a relationship and is looking for advice. Perhaps this person is feeling insecure about something.

Imagine you're in the funny section of the newspaper. You're a cartoon character. Write one example of a common thing you might say to a loved one…

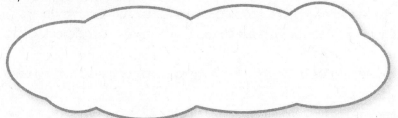

Now, let's look at how *you* talk to yourself. This time imagine it's you at a time in your life where you tend to be hard on yourself. Perhaps you're standing in front of a mirror in a bathing suit. Or, you're about to go into a big job interview — or out on a date. What is something you might commonly *think* to yourself….

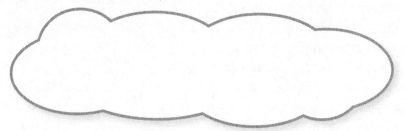

If you found that the way you talked to your loved one and the way you talked to yourself was equally supportive, warm, loving, and kind, that's wonderful! If you are more **pessimistic** when it comes to your self-talk, let's change that now.

Here's a guided self-love affirmation practice that can help turn **pessimism** into **optimism**:

- Take a moment in silence.
- Isn't it so nice to take this moment for yourself?
- Even taking this moment is a way of saying: *Yes, I deserve this. I'm worthy.*
- So you've already begun to change the way you're treating yourself, haven't you?
- Isn't that nice to know?

- Now, I want you to rewind the tape of your life….
- Perhaps taking a moment now to look at the roots of your **pessimism**.
- Maybe you hear some of your father's voice… and your mother's.
- Or children who were mean to you… or a mixture of different voices.

But in this meditation, imagine I'm giving you a pair of special X-ray glasses.

- *Imagine you're putting them on right now.*
- *These X-ray glasses allow you to see right through a person's defenses to his or her heart.*
- *You see… if someone was unkind to you or grew up teaching you negativity, it's only because somebody taught that to them… and hurt them.*
- *In this moment, these X-ray glasses provide you loving-kindness and compassion for this person.*
- *You see this person as a child being made fun of, being put down, or being taught* **pessimism.**
- *See yourself sending your love to this person.*
- *You wish they could have had it better… and then you would have had it better.*

Now, imagine you have a magic wand… and it heals this person's cause of **pessimism.** And like a ripple on a lake… you see that healing traveling forward in time.

- *You see that person being more positive or kind to you.*
- *Imagine all the healing that would take place….*
- *Wouldn't that be so nice?*
- *If only you had a real magic wand…*

- *But then you realize that you actually do have a magic wand.*
- *Because in each and every moment…*
- *In the present moment of your life*
- *You have the power to change how to talk to yourself.*
- *And that is the true magic.*

- *The X-ray glasses you're still wearing also allow you to see something else.*
- *Imagine they help you to see what's right with you.*
- *There's so much there, right?*
- *And now… armed with all of this new positivity.*
- *It's time to create a new battle cry for yourself.*

- *Imagine that you are going to stitch this battle cry over your mind and your body…*
- *And that this battle cry helps you to create an incredible future*
- *Because you already have so much right, don't you?*
- *And your future is going to be so bright.*

My new, positive battle cry is:

_____

_____

_____

2. Change how you ACT

Take a lesson from Karen. Write ten affirmations *as if you already had these good things in your life.*

Karen wrote: *I am grateful I have a job that intellectually, creatively, and financially fulfills me while allowing me to spend plenty of time with my son.*

She wrote this affirmation before it was actually true. Of course, this affirmation *became* her reality.

Now, write your affirmation in the same way. This life is *already* your reality. The universe and your subconscious are listening.

But now, connect this with actionable goals you will set for yourself. Next to each affirmation, write something that you will need to *do* a little differently today, a short time from now, and at some point in the future. These are the things you will do to make this affirmation become reality.

A goal you set for yourself *today* may be: *I'll get up fifteen minutes earlier to research jobs every day this week.*

A goal you set for yourself a *short time from now* may be: *I'll start sending out at least two résumés per week starting next month.*

A goal you set for yourself **at some point** may be: *I will ensure that this job allows me the flexibility to work from home to spend time with my son and practice yoga daily.*

This practice helps you to create the *glue* to turn an affirmation into your everyday life.

Your thoughts become words, and your words become actions.

This is how you train your brain…and change your life.

1. I'm grateful that I:

_____

*To make this affirmation my reality, my goal **today** is to:*

_____

*To make this affirmation my reality, my goal a **short time from now** is to:*

_____

*To make this affirmation my reality, my goal **at some point in the future** is to:*

_____

2. I'm grateful that I:

_____

*To make this affirmation my reality, my goal **today** is to:*

_____

*To make this affirmation my reality, my goal a **short time from now** is to:*

_____

*To make this affirmation my reality, my goal **at some point in the future** is to:*

_____

3. I'm grateful that I:

_____

*To make this affirmation my reality, my goal **today** is to:*

_____

*To make this affirmation my reality, my goal a **short time from now** is to:*

_____

*To make this affirmation my reality, my goal **at some point in the future** is to:*

_____

4. I'm grateful that I:

_____

*To make this affirmation my reality, my goal **today** is to:*

_____

*To make this affirmation my reality, my goal a **short time from now** is to:*

_____

*To make this affirmation my reality, my goal **at some point** in the future is to:*

_____

5. I'm grateful that I:

_____

*To make this affirmation my reality, my goal **today** is to:*

_____

*To make this affirmation my reality, my goal a **short time from now** is to:*

_____

*To make this affirmation my reality, my goal **at some point in the future** is to:*

_____

6. I'm grateful that I:

_____

*To make this affirmation my reality, my goal **today** is to:*

_____

*To make this affirmation my reality, my goal a **short time from now** is to:*

_____

*To make this affirmation my reality, my goal **at some point in the future** is to:*

_____

7. I'm grateful that I:

_____

*To make this affirmation my reality, my goal **today** is to:*

_____

*To make this affirmation my reality, my goal a **short time from now** is to:*

_____

*To make this affirmation my reality, my goal **at some point in the future** is to:*

_____

8. I'm grateful that I:

_____

*To make this affirmation my reality, my goal **today** is to:*

_____

*To make this affirmation my reality, my goal a **short time from now** is to:*

_____

*To make this affirmation my reality, my goal **at some point in the future** is to:*

_____

9. I'm grateful that I:

_____

*To make this affirmation my reality, my goal **today** is to:*

_____

*To make this affirmation my reality, my goal a **short time from now** is to:*

_____

*To make this affirmation my reality, my goal **at some point in the future** is to:*

_____

10. I'm grateful that I:

_____

*To make this affirmation my reality, my goal **today** is to:*

_____

*To make this affirmation my reality, my goal a **short time from now** is to:*

_____

*To make this affirmation my reality, my goal **at some point in the future** is to:*

_____

3. BE HAPPY

Chapter 20

Think,
Act & Be
Happy

Grieving and Recovery

The Uninvited Guest

Enjoy when you can, and endure when you must.
~Johann Wolfgang von Goethe

sit on the park bench eating cheesy popcorn and watching young children on the playground. I am enjoying the day, the sun on my face, and the smell of fresh grass.

Randomly I think, *I wish Samantha could run and play with them.*

And there it is, the cold hand in my cheesy popcorn, the presence taking up too much space on the park bench, blocking my sunshine. My Grief.

"Really?" I say. "I didn't invite you. Get your hand out of my cheesy corn." Instead, I end up having to scoot over, making more room for My Grief. Grief comes and goes when I least expect it. I'll be in my car, driving along listening to music and I'll catch it in the corner of my eye, kicking the back of my seat.

"Hey Heather."

"Aww crap, what are you doing here?"

"It's been a while. I thought I would stop in for a visit."

"Well, make sure you fasten your seatbelt and be quiet. My daughter's sleeping and I don't want you to wake her up."

"Can I change the station?"

"No."

"Can I play with the window?"

"No, you can just come along for the ride."

So we go on the ride together, fingernails thumping on the dashboard as a reminder of who decided to show up today. Yes, I am quite aware of your presence, you don't need to remind me.

Grief's appearance used to rattle me, send me into the bathroom crying hysterically. Render me useless for a day. Sometimes it still does, but as Grief has been established as a consistent visitor in our household, we have drawn up a contract. We have an agreement.

As the mom of two children, one who died at birth and one who has a progressive disease, I will grieve. I will grieve for many dreams that will not come to fruition. I will grieve for a life I thought would be different.

I will grieve at times. And I will not grieve at times. I will laugh at times. I will not laugh at times.

Grief can come into our house but is not allowed to stay. If allowed to stay, it would devour the corners of our house. It would suck up the oxygen in the room. It would consume me.

And that is not acceptable.

Grief tends to run within the Special Needs community I am a part of; I bump into him quite often, even visiting other families....

"How are you?"

"My daughter has pneumonia. She is in the hospital on a ventilator."

I look around and see Grief, sitting on the couch, smugly picking at dirty fingernails.

And I meet those who sadly keep very, very close company with this unwanted guest. Grief hangs over them like a shroud. It is hard to laugh. It is hard to love, because in copious amounts Grief tends to ooze; like a nasty septic wound... draining life from us.

But we still have to laugh, we still have to play, we still have to live... life carries on.

I cannot, at the end of my life say... well, it was long, hard and I was sad.

Surprisingly, our relationship is not based entirely on conflict. My interactions with Grief have allowed me to see myself raw, unprotected, and exposed. At times I feel that I have lost my skin... yes, here I am. Be careful, that's my beating heart you see there. Do not touch.

I am no longer afraid to approach others regarding their own tragedies. I bring up the tough conversations. How is your mother? I am sorry for your loss. I am so sorry your daughter is in the hospital. I hug, I cry, I listen. Not because I am an über-sensitive person but because I know Grief sometimes travels alone except when he travels with his favorites... Isolation and Loneliness.

Sometimes Grief shows up at a party... drinks my wine, eats my last bite of fudgy dessert. It's an annoyance really, but since Grief is not a constant life guest, I have learned to tolerate the time we spend together. Sometimes we even enjoy an introspective moment or two.

We have set the rules and sometimes they are followed. We cannot have a permanent impy, uninvited guest... we don't have the room... not in our lives, not in my heart... life is too short and despite the bad things that can happen... life is too sweet.

— Heather Schichtel —

How Running Helped Me Heal

*I've learned that finishing a marathon isn't just an
athletic achievement. It's a state of mind; a state of
mind that says anything is possible.*
~John Hanc

It was a week after my mom had died, and I didn't know how to go on with life. Instead of going to work or the grocery store, I covered myself with blankets, wishing that I, too, could disappear. I was twenty-eight years old, and my mom had been fifty-four. It felt like I had been robbed.

So when I received an email from a friend about a 5K benefiting pancreatic cancer research, I ignored it. It seemed too close to the heart, as pancreatic cancer was the disease that had taken my mother away from me. But something about my friend's words — "I can help organize the whole thing" — stuck with me. I felt obliged to agree, if only to accept her support.

Together, my friends and I walked in honor of my mom. I tried to ignore the shirts of other participants, many bearing pictures of the loved ones they had lost. They were a painful reminder that my mom was no longer there for me to vent about life's everyday annoyances, or to see me get married or have kids.

My friends and I grabbed lunch after, and I actually enjoyed myself. But I immediately felt guilty.

In the weeks to come, I managed to reenter the world of the living. I knew my mom would have wanted it that way. She was the type who never got defeated. In fact, when she was pregnant with me, the doctors had warned her that as a diabetic, she'd be risking her life to have me. "But I was going to have you, no matter what," Mom told me. It was this very spirit that helped me get by.

Besides, keeping myself busy was preferable to driving myself crazy with things like wondering what would have happened if I had had the chance to say goodbye. It haunted me that I had gone to work on her last day instead of taking time off to see her, although I knew she wasn't feeling well. But Mom had instilled a serious work ethic in me, discouraging me from ever taking a day off.

A year later, to my surprise, I signed up for the same 5K. It seemed like the right thing to do. I checked our team's website daily, feeling a twinge of pride each time a donation ticked up our total.

The majority of our team walked the 5K, but several members ran the 10K. When the race ended, I noticed the runners all had one thing in common: They were beaming. They made it look so rewarding — and effortless. I wanted in.

So I enrolled in a 10K two months later. Considering I could barely run a mile, it was ambitious. But my boyfriend and I devised a training plan so I wouldn't come in last. I followed it religiously and didn't let anything get in my way — not even a trip to San Francisco.

Running up and down the city's hills, I was flooded with memories. I had lived there after college and my mother had visited often. I passed Bloomingdale's, recalling the time she and I had gotten into a screaming brawl there, much to other shoppers' dismay. It had all started because my sister and I had a spat over the fact that I had been thirty minutes late meeting her somewhere. "Why can't you guys just get along?" Mom had asked. I turned on her, too.

I was about to beat myself up when I remembered what Mom had once said after her diagnosis. "I don't want you to feel guilty about anything." Her paper-thin hands had held me tightly. She knew I could be my own worst enemy, always eager to blame myself. A weight lifted from my shoulders. I ran with a surge of energy.

In the following months, I found myself laughing with friends again without feeling the remnants of guilt. And I was able to sleep without having nightmares about my mom's final moments. Life felt lighter.

When race day arrived, I gave it my all — not for myself, but for my mom — and for all she had taught me and continued to teach me. As I ran, whenever I felt like slowing down, I pictured her cheering me on, as she had done at all of my soccer games and recitals as a kid.

Crossing the finish line, I was filled with her love and a sense of peace. So much so that shortly thereafter I signed up for a half marathon.

— Kristin Julie Viola —

Dr. Mike...

I t doesn't matter if you lose a child, a parent, a friend, or a pet. Every kind of loss can break your heart.

As hard as we try, our brains can't make sense of the nonsensical. We argue with our new reality.

The person who loses someone suddenly, in an accident, thinks: *I never got to say goodbye.*

The person who loses someone to illness thinks: *I wish she didn't have to suffer slowly like this.*

Any way you cut it, it's devastating.

Like snowflakes, people are different in the way they grieve. Some are quiet. Some are loud. Some tell everyone they're fine, and one day — they realize they're not. Others tell everyone they're not okay, and one day — they realize they will be.

Perhaps your story is similar to Heather's in some way. You've lost a child. Or, maybe it's been a long time since your loss.

You could be having a perfectly fine day — like Heather's nice day at the park. Perhaps you're sitting *on the park bench eating cheesy popcorn and watching young children on the playground.*

Then, out of nowhere grief hits you like a ton of bricks.

I wish Samantha could run and play with them.

Can you relate to Heather's out-of-the-blue grief?

Is your story similar to Kristin's? Have you, too, lost a parent? Did your loss just happen?

When Kristin got that e-mail about that 5K benefiting pancreatic cancer research, she ignored it. In the beginning, she only accepted because she "felt obliged to agree, if only to accept her support."

Speaking of races, perhaps you've read up on the five stages of grief. You thought grief would be like some long, terrible kind of race. In your mind, you thought there'd be a starting line. Then, you'd pass through denial, anger, bargaining, and depression.

One day, you'd cross over that finish line with your hands up in the air and find yourself in a blissful land called "acceptance." Then, the "grief" would all be over… or so you thought.

Except that "grief" returns to pay you a visit. It's that "uninvited guest," as Heather calls it. And, you realize that the five stages aren't a race at all. There is no finish line.

Grief shows up uninvited when you least expect it. A wave of sadness hits you on a Tuesday afternoon while you're sitting at a stop light.

But it also leaves you alone most of the time now, and you get to smile and laugh, too. You live a full life. I believe our loved ones look down and smile when we smile. What do you believe?

Finding a way to remember and honor your loved one can be an incredible part of the healing process. Kristin did that by finishing that 5K — and then registering for a half-marathon. She was honoring her mom while helping others at the same time.

For you, it could be a charity. Or, it could be something as simple as framing a favorite photo of you and your loved one. Perhaps it will remind you of one of your favorite stories about you and the person or pet you miss so much. Tell it to people.

If there are tears involved in telling your story, that's okay. There will probably be laughs along the way, too.

There's something I call "the sweet spot" of grief. It lies somewhere between dwelling in it 24/7 and avoiding it at all costs. You don't want to spend eight hours a day going through your old photos, because that would prevent you from living a full life. But you also don't want to be that person who takes down every photo and tells everyone to never say your loved one's name again.

At the end of the day, also remember that *you* are the true expert on you. Even though I've given you my two cents, there's no right or wrong way to grieve. You're a snowflake. You're unique in the way you grieve, because the relationship *you* had with the person or animal you loved was special.

Make space in your heart for this process. One day, one visit, and five kilometers at a time.

1. Change how you THINK

If you have suffered a loss, the pitfall thought pattern **permanence** can make it feel like those awful, gray clouds that are hanging over you won't ever pass. This debilitating grief will paralyze you forever.

You many be thinking:

How can I possibly move on? How can I make it through another day? Will I ever feel normal again?

In the beginning, lean on others. Take it moment by moment. Get out of bed. Comb your hair. Put food in your mouth. Call your friend. Take a shower. Repeat.

Today's hurricane may become next year's passing storm. Heather had that uninvited guest, Grief, pay her a visit years after her child passed. Yet, I'd guess the storm that hit her in the park was less intense than the hurricane she endured right after she lost her daughter.

When *your* "uninvited guest" shows up in a few years, those dark clouds probably won't be a category-4 hurricane that rips everything from its path.

Maybe that hurricane will be downgraded to a category-3 hurricane in a few weeks. In a month, perhaps it will wax and wane. Some days will probably feel like you're still caught in a terrible hurricane. A few hours later, perhaps it feels like it's being downgraded to a category 2 or 1. You may even find a moment or two where the sun peeks out. That's normal.

When grief stops by for a visit in the future, perhaps the visits will be more and more short-lived — like they probably are for Heather now. Of course, it would also be perfectly normal to have a few visits that last longer than others.

If it's been a few months since your loss and those dark days are still lasting a few weeks or more, talk to a mental health professional to get screened for depression. Then, you and your healthcare provider can decide what additional support or resources you may need.

Here's a tool you can use right here and now. When it comes to the way you think about grief, **permanence** is an illusion that makes loss feel even worse than it already is. You probably already know from your experience that **permanence** isn't true, don't you?

Let me help you deal with **permanence** with a little brain-training exercise. Think back to a more minor loss in your life that was hard at the time — but got better over time. Perhaps it was the loss of a job or the end of a relationship.

Do you remember how **permanence** made it feel like *this will never pass?*

How does thinking back on this minor loss help you remember that things do get a little better with time?

_____

_____

_____

When it comes to loss, this doesn't mean the pain is going to just go away. It doesn't mean you will ever forget your loved one. It does help you to remember that today's unrelenting hurricane may one day feel like a storm that ebbs and flows.

Be on the lookout for the day when you see the first little ray of sun peeking out at you.

2. Change how you ACT

Have you heard the story of the man caught in a terrible storm? The town was ordered to evacuate, but one man refused to do so.

As the flood waters poured through the town, a friendly neighbor drove by and kindly offered him a seat in his car.

The man declined. "God will save me."

The waters continued to flood his home. He had to move to the second floor. A boat came by to rescue him.

He declined again. "God will save me."

The waters rose again. Now, he was on the roof. A police helicopter threw a ladder down.

He declined for the third time. "God will save me."

The man drowned.

When he got to heaven, he asked God: "Why didn't you save me?"

God replied, "Why didn't I save you? I sent you a car, a boat, and a helicopter!"

When it comes to loss, we need to take the *ladder* that is offered to us. Sometimes that *ladder* is offered to us in the form of something incredibly simple. A friend calls and offers to help you do something productive — something like taking you to the grocery store.

Perhaps you can just do something pleasurable for an afternoon — like take a warm bath or take yourself to see a funny movie. Sometimes we have to reach for the first rung on our own *ladder*.

Maybe you'll get an e-mail from a friend inviting you to register for a 5K to help fund cancer research — which fills your life with *purpose*.

You may still be sad, but perhaps the rungs on this ladder can help you find a smile or two as well.

When it comes to loss and grief, it's important to make room for multiple emotions at the same time. You're allowed to be sad and experience other emotions at the same time. If this was a quiz and the question was:

How are you feeling?

…then perhaps the answers to choose from would be:

a) heartbroken
b) sad
c) happy to see my friend who makes me laugh
d) all of the above

It's okay to choose D. By climbing your *ladder*, you may find that simple activities make room for positive emotions to exist in your life again, too.

Every activity you choose will be you climbing your way out of what can feel like a very dark and deep hole. Just keep putting one foot on the next rung of that ladder… and climb… one day at a time.

As days become weeks, your heart will continue to heal. Eventually, you will be ready to climb higher on the *ladder*. Instead of just doing something that's productive or pleasurable, you could do something that gives you purpose or power.

Climbing the *ladder* can be a wonderful way to help nurture a healing heart.

In the beginning, you'll keep the activities really simple.

Start by doing something today that adds a little *productivity* to your day. Buy groceries. Do the dishes.

Then, consider an activity that adds *pleasure* to your day. Maybe that's something you could do for yourself tomorrow. Do you like to take warm baths? Is there a favorite restaurant you love going to with your friends?

What's something that adds *peace* to your day? Do you miss your yoga class? Your meditation practice? Your place of worship? Write down an activity or two.

Do the same for *power*, *passion*, *pride*, and *purpose*.

When you're ready, add a new activity, or reinstate an old one to your daily life. Notice how engaging in all these activities changes your thoughts. Do you see how you're changing the way you feel?

Eventually, you may notice that you're doing things from the *ladder* all the time. You volunteer at a summer camp for kids who have suffered a loss. This adds *purpose* to your life. You feel *productive* every single day as you get your chores done. You add *power* to your life as you face your fears by taking that public speaking class on Tuesdays.

Meditation class is on Thursdays; that's your weekly dose of *peace*. Your *passion* is horses, and you get to ride every other week. You are filled with *pride* every time you look at all you've accomplished at work. You make sure to take care of yourself, and there's some pleasure, too — that pedicure with your best friend once in a while adds some *pleasure* to your weekend.

Write one activity in each category that will become your *Ladder*. Then, start to climb that ladder as you feel ready. Every day, do one activity from this list. This will help to pull you out of that deep well of grief that — in the beginning — can feel as though it may drown you. List one or two activities in each category that will help you experience positive emotions with your sadness.

7. Purpose: _____

_____

6. Pride: _____

_____

5. Passion: _____

_____

4. Power: _____

_____

3. Peace: _____

_____

2. Pleasure: _____

_____

1. Productivity: _____

_____

3. BE HAPPY

Chapter 21

Think,
Act & Be
Happy

Keep Your
Love Alive

Wake-Up Call

*Which is the true nightmare, the horrific dream that
you have in your sleep or the dissatisfied reality that
awaits you when you awake?*
~Justin Alcala

That unique blended scent of funeral flowers overwhelmed me as I walked slowly toward the gleaming oak casket. My husband was dead and I had to say my final farewell.

Mercifully I woke just then, my tears flowing. It was only a dream, I told myself, and yet the scene lingered with me.

I quickly patted the bed beside me and I panicked upon finding it empty. Then I remembered that my husband had gone into work early.

I reached for my phone. "Barry, are you okay?" I asked, relieved when he answered his office phone.

"Of course. I'm fine," he said, sounding pleased that I asked, probably because lately I'd been irritable more often than not.

"What's wrong?" he asked.

"Nothing. Nothing at all," I said. After hesitating, I said, "I love you."

"I love you too," he said.

I said goodbye, knowing that I needed to share more than I could on a brief phone call. I hoped he would be willing to listen when he came home, though I didn't really deserve it. We had been going through a challenging time in our marriage for the past two years. We'd moved to a new state where the work my husband had hoped for hadn't materialized. We had two newly adopted, older children with (understandable) emotional problems that were not only overwhelming for them to deal with, but for our whole family. Even though we ended up returning to Indiana and a secure job for my husband, I fell apart.

I hadn't recovered from the years of worrying about money, dreading the mail and phone calls because of bills. I resented my husband for it and I didn't know how to change my attitude. I tried prayer. I tried reading books. I tried talking with friends. It was all to no avail.

I became self-centered: I lost weight, went back to college to finish up my degree, and ignored my husband. By then our daughter was in college and our son was just finishing up his homeschooling. I made a new set of friends, and went out with them nearly every weekend. It was as if I were a teenager again.

My husband lovingly continued to support my choices. He worked overtime to pay for my college classes, while I found part-time work to buy my books. He cooked on the nights I had to study for exams. He drove me in bad weather to lunches with my friends and came back to pick me up afterwards.

The nightmare I'd just had opened my eyes to all the good things about my husband. I was deeply ashamed of my behavior.

I owed this man so much more than an apology, and I quickly got busy, thankful I had a rare day off. First I cleaned the house thoroughly. Time was always short due to my schooling and the subsequent teaching job I took, so I hadn't done more than the basics such as the dishes and laundry in a long time. Now I swept under the cushions and placed the pillows at a jaunty angle I knew he'd appreciate. I filled the air with a lovely apple-scented spray.

I went shopping and bought a new dress that I thought he'd like. Then I stopped by the salon where I used to get my hair done. "Do you have time to flat-iron this mess?" I begged, pointing at my unruly hair. In fifteen minutes I was on my way, smiling at my smooth hair in the mirror.

There was still time to buy the things for his favorite dinner (fried chicken, mashed potatoes, green beans and rolls) and stock up on his preferred snacks, something else I hadn't bothered to do in a really long time.

When everything was ready, I waited anxiously by the door. Finally I saw his Nissan pull in. I barely waited for him to get in the door before holding his face in my hands and kissing him.

"Look at you," he said, touching my hair.

"This is for you." I handed him a blue envelope. The card contained a note apologizing for the bitterness in my heart, for the things (real and imagined) that I hadn't forgiven him for. For complaining and nagging. For exaggerating every bad thing. For downplaying the good.

When he read it, we both broke down in tears and I clung to him the way I had wanted to when I woke that morning after my nightmare. I felt as if I were myself for the first time in a long time.

We talked, really talked, over dinner, and it felt as if no ground had ever been lost in our marriage. I never wanted to take him for granted again, and I told him so.

If I ever think I am beginning to take him for granted nowadays, I stop, close my eyes and think about that dream, that nightmare, and I imagine what would happen if it came true. It changes my attitude every time.

— Drema Sizemore Drudge —

To Celebrate

There is no satisfaction without a struggle first.
~Marty Liquori

"We need to talk," my husband Michael stated as he woke me up.

Even though I was in a hazy state, the tone of his voice and words indicated something serious. Normally, he would sneak into our bed after his restaurant shift, letting his presence be known by the combined smells of cigarettes and alcohol. That night he didn't and it terrified me.

Our marriage was not the best during that time. We were like two ships passing. Our work schedules conflicted — my shift days and his nights. The phone became our sole connection as we called to check in with each other. He was working as the assistant manager of a restaurant, making a great salary with some perks, namely alcohol. The restaurant closed but the staff would stay and drink — and head out to other bars. To him, home meant sleeping it off and arguing with me about his habits. No, it was not the marriage we envisioned, but it was what we had — a faint connection to each other.

So there we sat on a tiny concrete balcony. He lit a cigarette and began to speak. He was being transferred. The promised general manager's position he coveted was given to the boss's relative. He knew his drinking was heavy and he was tired of fighting.

"It may be time to quit my job. What should I do?" he asked.

An immediate sense of relief washed over me; we were okay. I gave him the only answer I had. "What ever you feel is right." He tendered his resignation the next day. He cleared the house of alcohol that night. He quit smoking the next week.

Things got worse before they got better. He worked a handful of jobs, each a disappointment. It was hard on him, every interview leading to quizzical looks when they noted his management experience. They could not comprehend why someone would leave a high-paying career to work elsewhere. Eventually, he was hired at a lawn company. He left early each morning to pick up his list of houses. He was too good at it. The harder he worked the more houses they assigned. To make matters worse, the company equipment and truck were always malfunctioning. Every shift became a battle. Whenever I suggested that he quit, his pride prevailed: "I will do whatever it takes to support this family."

I finally received the dreaded call. He had broken down emotionally and couldn't do it anymore. He was found at the side of the road crying and heaving. The lawn company was called to pick up their vehicle; he would not be driving it again. The next week was spent in a haze of antidepressants and worry. I vividly remember taking a long walk together and doing most of the talking. He held my hand but remained silent and stared off into the distance. I was terrified that he was lost, racked with guilt that I had not seen this coming. Was it us? Was it me? "You are the only thing keeping me going," he reassured me.

Truthfully, I do not know how it happened; I just remember standing at the store financing the treadmill. He decided to run. He was taken aback at first; it was harder than he thought. Every day he would struggle against those taunting red lights on the machine. Outwardly, I smirked at his sweaty face as he huffed and puffed, but deep down I was thankful. The fire of ambition was back in his eyes. His running gradually improved, and the treadmill became a friend not a foe. He started running outside, stepping into his new running gear to head out the door. Soon, "I have to run first" became a familiar phrase to our friends and family. It was a euphoria I was not privy to, no matter how he would try to explain it. It was freedom. The doctor agreed, and saw no need to continue his antidepressants.

On the work front we received the news that Michael had been one of the few applicants selected for a government-sponsored apprenticeship program. It allowed him to be paid weekly while going to school for retraining. In celebration, he signed up for his first 5K race; it became a new addiction. He wanted to run a marathon. It was a lofty goal, as the 5K run was painful and slow, but his mind was set. We became regular faces on the running circuit as he built his endurance on smaller runs. A small collection of finisher medals and bib numbers were hanging in our home. Our conversations were peppered with technical running terms and training regimes. I didn't mind any of it. His smile was back.

The day of his first marathon arrived. If I could only explain to you the electricity you feel when you stand among competing runners on race day. It hums in the air as you watch people engaging in their pre-race rituals. Michael was shaking his legs with nervous energy, constantly checking his watch while we waited for my in-laws and his sisters to show up. We walked around holding hands; we were happier now than ever. Over the course of the year we managed to move into a new home and get pregnant. I was seven months along.

The family clan arrived and we all stood at the starting gate and saw him off. We sat on the bleachers and waited, taking turns getting coffee, cheering on the runners. At the three-hour mark, we left the bleachers and weaved among the crowd to the finish line. Poised with our cameras, we fidgeted. Like a mirage, I finally spotted him in the distance running at a slow clip, his face in anguish. He had a slight limp. Relief flooded me as we cheered him on. He spotted us as he stumbled through the finishing gate. Corralled by race volunteers he was given water and ushered forward into the runner's pen.

It seemed like eternity, while I fought through the masses of people to see him on the other side. He had done it. I was so proud. He found us and waved. I ran forward as he opened his arms, and reached for me over the half fence. Tears streamed down his face and mine, and he began sobbing. "I love you. I could never have done this without you," he whispered in my ear through the tears.

Three weeks later we had a baby girl. To celebrate he decided to start training for his first triathlon.

— Carla O'Brien —

Dr. Mike...

Love is like a tennis match. The problems start when one or both people in a relationship start playing a singles match when they should be playing doubles. To win the game of love, you have to remember it's you and your partner. Your opponent isn't your partner. It's the world.

That means that when one of you wins, you both win. If one of you is scrubbing dishes so the other one can study, that's a win-win situation. The dishes get done today, and that exam will eventually lead to a better life for the family tomorrow.

At some point in their marriage, Drema started playing that singles match of tennis. It's common in relationships. When it happens, you can feel that "you versus me" energy. Communication breaks down. Distance grows. Intimacy becomes less frequent.

As Drema said, resentments had grown over the years. Life wasn't easy for Drema and her husband. There were disappointments. A job that didn't materialize. Bill collectors started calling.

There was the added stress of going back to school. Drema and her husband had two newly adopted children.

Luckily, Drema's subconscious was taking care of her. That nightmare she had was a true wake-up call.

When all those things left unsaid finally bubbled up to the surface, she had to let it out. She needed to say some things to her husband. Drema told us, *The card contained a note apologizing for the bitterness in my heart, for the things (real and imagined) that I hadn't forgiven him for.*

With those words, Drema and her husband were on the same team again. She became his partner again. Drema was like a tennis player walking across the court. With that letter, Drema and her husband became a team again.

1. Change how you THINK

Sometimes, the stress of daily life can be overwhelming. It's like a dam that can only hold so much water. A crack starts to form. Sometimes, it can even feel like the dam may break.

I'm sure Drema felt like that dam when her husband's job didn't materialize after they moved to a new state. Every time a bill collector called, that crack got a little bit bigger. When you're a new mom and have mouths to feed, it can feel overwhelming.

Perhaps you've been in Drema's shoes. Or maybe you feel like there's a small crack because of a bad financial decision your significant other made. When that's true, resentments grow.

There's also a pitfall thought pattern that tends to creep in. It's **psychic** thinking.

This pitfall thought pattern works in two ways. First, we expect our partners to be **psychic** and read *our* minds… because we haven't actually told them!

Or, we can act like *we* are the **psychic** ones. Even though partners haven't verbalized something, we think we know why they're doing something.

Let's look at how **psychic** thinking got Drema and her husband into trouble. During these stressful times, Drema said she tried prayer, reading books, and talking to friends, but she didn't know how to change her attitude. And so, she "ignored" her husband. She distanced herself from him.

It's interesting that Drema tried talking to friends about the way she felt. However, the only way her husband would truly know how she felt was to talk *directly* to him. After all, he's not **psychic**!

Perhaps Drema acted like a **psychic** herself. As they were going through these tough times, did she make assumptions about her husband's behavior?

He must not love me. Anyone who cared about his family wouldn't act like this.

So many of us make these assumptions — even though our significant other hasn't verbalized these things.

The antidote to **psychic** thinking is incredibly simple: open-hearted communication.

This requires you to put down the defensiveness and open your heart. You have to expose your Achilles' heel and tell the person why certain actions trigger you to respond in certain ways that may be negative. It requires that you speak in loving, caring, and positive language. This isn't easy when years of resentments have built up.

Drema solved her **psychic** thinking with that letter that brought her and her husband to tears. It brought her and her husband closer to each other than they had ever been before.

To overcome **psychic** thinking, it may be helpful for *you* to start by writing your own letter. There will be things you want to *say* and questions you want to *ask*.

Perhaps this letter will be something you give to your significant other. Or, perhaps this will just be an exercise that will help you to have a conversation tomorrow night at dinner.

When writing this letter, there are a few simple guidelines that can help it be more effective, especially to make sure that you're not still assuming that your partner is **psychic:**

1. Start with something kind.
Example: *Thank you for the fifteen incredible years of marriage. When I met you, I felt like I was all alone in this world. You made it seem like I wasn't.*

2. Transform accusations that start with "you" into vulnerable statements that begin with "I."
Example: *You took that job and bankrupted us! How could you do that to us? You're a terrible husband and father!* BECOMES *I've been feeling really anxious about money.*

3. Then, dig deeper if there's something there.
Example: *...and this reminds me of all the financial turmoil I went through as a child. I don't want us to end up like my dad. I also am really scared my panic attacks are going to come back. I've been having trouble eating lately, because my stomach has been so sick worrying about all this.*

4. Help solve the problem by asking for what you want in positive and specific language.

Example: *Would you be willing to see our accountant with me next week so we can make a decision on whether or not we can afford to keep the house — or if we need to sell it? I think it would help me sleep better at night.*

For questions you want to *ask* — because you are not a **psychic:**

Transform questions that feel like accusations into open-hearted invitations. Example: *Do you even love me anymore? Why don't you ever want to spend time with me?* BECOMES *I've really been missing our intimacy and those dinners we used to have together. Would you have dinner with me at our first-date spot on Friday?*

There's a line in the John Mayer song "Say" that sums it up nicely: *Even if your hands are shaking… Do it with a heart wide open… Say what you need to say.* Now try writing your open-hearted letter of love:

Dear _____,

_____

_____

_____

_____

_____

_____

_____

Love, _____

Keep Your Love Alive |

2. Change how you ACT

Real-world relationships come with real-world problems. Jobs, health problems, disability, children, money, addiction... You name it. If you want to see a "perfect" relationship, watch a fairy tale. Perfection doesn't exist in the real world.

Carla and Michael had a lot of serious, real-world problems that put a strain on their relationship. But even when the going gets rough, happy endings can be possible... even in the real world. Carla and Michael had one.

Sometimes, you need to start by examining your thoughts and changing what you say — like Drema did. Other times, you need to start by changing your actions. Or as they say: put your money where your mouth is.

That's what Michael's treadmill was all about. The action of getting on that treadmill every day was Michael's way of communicating to Carla (and himself): *I'm ready to make a change.*

It's one thing for an alcoholic to say, *I'm sorry. I'll change.* It's quite another for that alcoholic to stop drinking and attend ninety Alcoholics Anonymous meetings in ninety days.

When making a meaningful change in your relationship, it may be helpful for you to identify your partner's primary love language. Also, know what *your* primary love language is. This is the central principle of Gary Chapman's timeless book *The Five Love Languages.*

How does *your partner* experience love? And, how do you experience love? Is it through gifts, time spent together, the words you say, acts of service, or touch?

You and your partner may have the same primary love language. Or, you may have different love languages.

By knowing what languages you both speak, you can choose actions that will help both of you to feel truly loved. You'll become bilingual in the language of love. If you don't know your partner's primary love language, take a guess.

Then, ask your partner to fill out this same page below (you can take a picture of this page with your phone and send it as an exercise or make a photocopy). Compare notes to see if you both were right, and have a talk about it.

Then, identify one *action* you could give to your partner that will "speak" his or her language… and ask for one *action* that would be your partner's "speaking" your language.

My primary love language is (circle one):

gifts
time spent together
words
acts of service
touch

One action that my partner could do more of for me — to "speak my language" — is to:

_____

My partner's primary love language is (circle one):

gifts
time spent together
words
acts of service
touch

One action that I could do more of for my partner, so that I am speaking his or her language, may be:

_____

3. BE HAPPY

Chapter 22

Think,
Act & Be
Happy

Say Goodbye
to Bad Habits

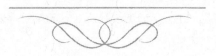

It Helps to Have a Friend

A true friend reaches for your hand
and touches your heart.
~Author Unknown

"Mm, good coffee," said my next door neighbor, Virginia, pushing aside the folded laundry on my couch. "What kind? And what'd you do to your finger?"

"You noticed," I said gingerly holding my cup between my thumb and third finger. "Chocolate Raspberry and I bit my nail and cuticle back too far."

"You're a nail biter?" she asked, dismissing the name of my favorite flavored coffee.

"Yeah," I admitted. "It's my life-long, childhood habit."

"When do you do it?" she asked, leaning over the coffee table and eyeballing me.

I straightened a little. "When do I do what? Make flavored coffee? Only when you come over. Bill doesn't like it. He says it is women's coffee."

"Your nails, silly," she said, laughing. "When do you bite your nails?"

I shrugged. "How do I know? All the time, I guess. If I don't bite them, I pick them off. It really only hurts when I get them too short or get an infection."

Virginia gasped. "You got an infection from biting your nails?"

"Uh-huh," I said, "It happens when my wounded little fingers go swimming in dirty dishwater." I tried to be nonchalant, but Virginia wouldn't turn loose.

"I'll help you quit," she volunteered.

"It's a lost cause," I countered. "I've tried to quit all my life. When I was a little girl my aunt offered me five dollars to quit, but I couldn't."

"Well, for the next two weeks I'm going to come over every morning and give you a manicure," she announced. "Together we're going to kick your habit!"

"Every morning?" I said in disbelief. "What do you think you're going to manicure, the ends of my fingers?"

"You'll see," she said. "I won't stay long, just long enough to do your nails."

The next morning, Virginia was at my kitchen door with a tray full of manicuring equipment. The sun streamed in the breakfast nook window as she spread my hands out flat on the table. She surveyed the damage and set right to work.

"First we have to file off the rough places and trim the snags," she said.

There wasn't much to file but she filed and filed. Then she gently pushed back my cuticles and trimmed off snags.

"Ow!" I said when she pushed on a tender spot. My fingers weren't overjoyed with the attention, but I was intrigued that she would spend so much time on such awful-looking hands. Finally she opened a small bottle of clear nail polish and carefully polished each stub as if it were a magnificently long nail.

"There!" she said triumphantly. "See you tomorrow." She quickly loaded up her tray and left.

I sat there a long time looking at my shiny stubs. No one had ever spent that much time caring for them before, especially not me.

That afternoon I attacked a long put-off project. I spread fabric on the floor and took out the pattern for my new dress. As I worked to place the pattern pieces just right before cutting, I felt my bottom teeth rub against a fingernail. I quickly separated the two. Within a minute I felt it again.

"I'll ruin the polish," I wailed.

By the third time, I realized my hand had a mind of its own, bypassing my brain.

The next morning Virginia came again. She took a cotton ball and some polish remover and took off yesterday's polish. The nicks smarted, but I didn't complain. Again she filed and filed, pushed back cuticles, painted stubs, and was gone.

Later in the day, when I was working on my grocery list, I discovered my left hand in my mouth. I quickly retrieved it and sat on it while I completed the list.

Every day for a week Virginia came over and did a complete manicure. She filed so much I feared my nails would never grow, but they looked and felt so much better because the surrounding tissue was no longer inflamed.

Gradually, as I became aware of where my hands were, I could keep them in my lap or wherever else my brain directed them. No longer did they subconsciously go to my mouth. My nails had become my focal point because Virginia cared about them. And I was learning to care, too.

At the end of two weeks there was a smooth band of white around the tip of each nail.

"We're going to switch to twice a week now," Virginia said. She laughed. "I'll have to see if I can break my new habit of Chocolate Raspberry coffee."

The last time Virginia came to do my nails, she brought a bottle of shocking pink polish. She polished and I "oohed and ahhed" as I displayed a set of long, polished nails. Then she pronounced me "graduated."

So was I no longer tempted by a crunchy nail treat? Hardly! I found that every three or four months I had to reinforce my decision and new habit. Virginia suggested that I temporarily cover the evidence of any fingernail attack with a press-on nail, refocus on where my hands were, and start manicuring again.

I found myself frequently whispering, "Thank you, Lord, for a friend who cared enough to help me break my nail-biting habit." Otherwise, I might never have tried.

—Pauline Youd—

Ready to Listen

What I need is someone who will
make me do what I can.
~Ralph Waldo Emerson

Today, I weigh nearly 150 pounds less than I did three years ago, and the weight loss began with a compliment: "You look great."

I was the mother of two adopted special needs children when I decided to go back to college. Our daughter was beginning college herself, our son doing well after years of struggling, when something inside me whispered, "It's time." I hadn't made myself a priority for over a decade. I had no idea that not only would I finish my degree and go on to grad school, but I would also lose 150 pounds in the process!

My weight had climbed as my self-confidence sank under the strain of being the mother of two wonderful yet challenged children. Often I didn't feel as if I had the answers, and I worried I was failing at everything. Before long, I was 180 pounds over my ideal weight, and I felt food was the only bright spot in my life. The troubles with our children had caused my beloved husband and me often to feel disconnected from one another.

One day after I returned to college, I dressed in a suit for an appointment with the head of the English department to discuss my senior research project, and the professor not only noticed, but also commented upon it. I'm sure it was quite a change from the stretchy jeans and T-shirts I habitually wore to class. "You look great," he said, and I realized then that I wasn't invisible. That day I went home and purged my wardrobe of the most hated pieces of "fat" clothing. I vowed to rebuild it slowly with only clothes I would be proud to be seen wearing. If this professor I so respected was letting me know the way to get ahead in my career was to look professional, I would listen.

"I don't look great," I thought when he said that, looking down, "but I bet I could." I had already let him challenge my mind with books, so I decided to allow that compliment to challenge me to attain my physical best. I had never been thin, and I could blame it on genetics. I didn't exactly look out of place in family photos. But I was ready for the challenge. I had used his advice to improve my writing and my critical thinking skills, and I saw the connection between developing my brain and my body for the first time.

I began to exercise, slowly at first. I did Denise Austin videos (twenty minutes each) every morning. I took walks when the weather was nice. I once again tried low-carb eating, which quickly took care of my cravings, and virtually eliminated my need for nightly mindless eating fests. I began to read or write instead of watching television, and bit by bit, the weight came off. I went to a nutritionist when I felt I was backsliding a bit, just to be sure I stayed the course. I also entered and won a weight loss competition at work; having my picture put in the local paper for the win was a blast for a former chunky. I felt fantastic!

I committed more and more time to exercise. I would like to lose another thirty pounds, but I have kept my weight within a ten-pound range for the past year and a half, and I can't imagine I could ever feel better than I do right now. I am a size 12-14, and I feel alive and hopeful, as if I could do anything. Most days I exercise for two hours — an hour in the morning, and a relaxing walk in the evening, or I lift weights while watching TV with my husband. I have discovered I adore exercise, and I might even enter a race at some point. Who knew?

I still eat low-carb when my weight begins to creep up, but mostly I listen to my body and eat what it wants, while striving to focus on healthier foods such as whole grains and fresh produce. I still struggle to fit in vegetables, as my taste buds don't always agree with my body on that one! I also try to get three servings of dairy a day, as well as eight or more glasses of water. Sometimes we try to reinvent the wheel when the wheel's rolling just fine — the conventional wisdom about eating less and moving more really works!

At my son's graduation party, I publicly ate two pieces of ice cream cake without a trace of guilt. If I really want it, I eat it. Life is long, and losing weight and keeping it off will be an ongoing project. That's the only way to approach it.

For the first time in my life, I feel attractive. I am able to look back, too, and see the love and care I put into raising my children. Maybe I didn't have all the answers, but they know I love them, and they are striving for their goals, too, as they see me go towards mine. Losing weight is only the first of many goals — right now I am writing my first novel. If I can lose weight, I can do anything! My husband, while delighted that his wife now gets wolf whistles, has made it clear he will love me whatever my size. We have been able to reconnect as my self-confidence has returned.

As for that professor who gave me the confidence to begin my weight loss — while I did the work, he gave me the courage to begin. He had no way of knowing that those three small words spoken on a random Wednesday morning would transform a life.

— Drema Sizemore Drudge —

Dr. Mike...

Do you have a bad habit? Bad habits come in all shapes and sizes. There are classic habits — like Pauline's nail biting. There are habits that can kill you — like smoking.

Then, there are those habits that are like sheep in wolves' clothing. They don't *seem* all that bad. You pop a soda open at every meal. Or, you get in the habit of not moving enough — like Drema.

No matter which category your habit falls into, it most certainly is affected by stress. Pauline and Drema understood that.

When Pauline "attacked a long put-off project," her stress levels went up. When that happened, she found the nail biting starting again. Suddenly, that finger had found its way back into her mouth.

Drema's stress was fairly constant. She had adopted two special needs children and was going back to college. Any working parent knows what it's like to be stressed. Drema's stress fueled her mindless-eating habit and her sedentary-lifestyle habit.

In the brain, there are healthy and unhealthy ways to deal with stress. When you're stressed, the feel-good, stress-relieving chemical serotonin goes down in the brain. Biting your nails or eating lots of sugar or flour does help manage serotonin levels — but in an unhealthy way. You can even become addicted.

For others, habits are tied to the brain's main feel-good "upper" — dopamine. Cigarettes, cocaine, gambling, alcohol, fried foods, video games, and that light on your cell phone indicating a social media "like" all give your brain a little hit of dopamine. That's why you can become addicted to anything from cigarettes to cell phones.

When it comes to training your brain, there's a powerful strategy that helped Pauline and Drema to be successful. They focused on the *healthy* habits that made them happy as they removed the *unhealthy* ones. The clinical term for this strategy is called *replacement therapy*.

Need a stress-relieving, serotonin boost? Swap in crocheting as you're swapping out nail biting. Swap in spiralized zucchini as you're swapping out pasta. Swap in walking and swap out sitting. Now, you're boosting serotonin in a healthy way.

Replacement therapy works for dopamine, too. If you need a little hit of reward or feel-good pleasure, you can swap in coffee as you're swapping out cigarettes. Swap in sprints on the treadmill as you're swapping out video games. Swap in actual time with friends as you're swapping out hours spent glued to social media.

In some way, I guess I'm telling you to go get high — but on all the activities and foods that are good for you. It will help you say goodbye to all those bad habits.

When you choose that healthy behavior over and over again, you're training your brain. Pathways are formed in the brain. After a month or two, you have new, healthy habits that have replaced the old, unhealthy ones.

For Pauline, manicures, flavored coffee, and friendship helped her say goodbye to nail biting.

For Drema, it was Denise Austin workout videos, walking, and lower-carb eating that helped her say goodbye to mindless eating and her sedentary lifestyle.

For you, it might be crocheting, crafting, or karate. Weave, glue gun, or high kick your way to a healthier, happier life.

1. Change how you THINK

If you have a bad habit, you also may struggle with the pitfall thought pattern **pessimistic** thinking. In fact, many times **pessimistic** thinking may be part of the reason why you picked up the bad habit in the first place!

For Pauline, perhaps those **pessimistic** thoughts sounded something like *I can't kick this bad habit.* (When it comes to training your brain, can't is one of those four-letter words we're going to banish.) Of course, feeling like you're powerless over a habit can lead to all sorts of anxiety.

Pessimistic thinking dragged Drema down, too.

Often I didn't feel as if I had the answers, and I worried I was failing at everything.

For you, **pessimistic** thinking may even have you contemplating those catastrophic, worst-case scenarios: *Why is John five minutes late?*

Maybe he got in a car accident!

Lack of self-worth, hopelessness, and worst-case-scenario fears all fuel bad habits. Soda cans get opened, cigarettes get smoked, nails get bitten, and unhealthy foods get mindlessly eaten.

In the short term, bad habits may help you feel a little better. But, they're just Band-Aids. In the long run, these bad habits rob you of your vitality. Remember when Drema got to be 180 pounds over her ideal weight? *I felt food was the only bright spot in my life.*

Using a bad habit to manage your stress is like making a deal with the devil. It comes with a very high cost.

The antidote to **pessimism**?

Like a child talking back to a parent, I want *you* to talk back to these naysaying thoughts. Exclaim, "You're not the boss of me!"

Consider the alternative, *optimistic* explanations before going down rabbit holes of far-fetched scenarios worthy of a true crime story on *Dateline.*

In other words: Don't confuse the *probable* with the *possible.*

In the example above, John getting in a horrific car accident is the *possible.* It's also *possible* that you could get struck by lightning… three times in three days in a row.

It's *possible* you could go to Vegas and win a $100,000 jackpot on your first spin… and then another one on your second. Horrific car accident, lightning strike, Vegas fortune are all *possible* scenarios.

A better formula for happiness is to train your brain to focus its energy on the *probable.*

Still want to buy that Lotto ticket when the jackpot is over $100 million? So be it. (I just hope that Lotto ticket isn't your version of a retirement plan; that would still make you someone who's focusing on the *possible* — not the *probable.* Better to set up an IRA or 401(k) — *probable*-based ways of saving for retirement.)

A *probable*-based mindset will help you to feel more relaxed and less stressed. That will make it easier for you to let go of bad habits rooted in nervous energy.

A *probable*-based mindset also helps you to consider all the ways you will be successful in eventually letting the bad habit go completely — as you replace it with healthier rituals each and every day.

This exercise will help you to feel more at ease. It will help you get rid of those **pessimistic** thoughts that fuel bad habits.

- One type of **pessimistic** thinking is when you tell yourself I *can't*. Think of something you've told yourself you can't do — and how this led to anxiety — and how this fueled a bad habit. For example, Pauline may have thought, *I can't kick this bad habit… and my nails are probably going to get infected and fall off… I'm so embarrassed… and no one will ever want to be seen with me…* which, of course, fuels *more* nail biting).

- Another type of **pessimistic** thinking is when you go down rabbit holes of worst-case-scenario, catastrophic thinking. You may think *Why is John five minutes late? Maybe he got in a car accident…* which, of course, can fuel bad habits like mindless eating or smoking.

Now, think of a **pessimistic** thought that focused on the negative, possible outcomes — and fueled your bad habit.

When I considered the *possible*, I was afraid of:

_____

But if I had stopped to consider the *probable*, I would have thought:

_____

It's also helpful to stop and consider all the times your life has already been filled with situations that have worked out. Isn't it nice to focus on that? You may even find that the more energy you give this, the more your life will be filled with positivity. Now that you have taken this moment to shift your thinking, you'll find that your mind will naturally adjust itself in the future as well.

2. Change how you ACT

Now that you've talked back to those thoughts that may have contributed to your bad habits, let's put the power of replacement therapy to work for you in your life.

Pauline and Drema both used the power of behavioral replacement therapy. They focused on what they were *adding* to their lives — not what they were taking *away*.

Think about activities that could add *peace* or *pleasure* to your life.

If your bad habit is stress related, you'll want to add one or more activities that add *peace*. That will boost your serotonin levels. When serotonin goes up, stress goes down.

If your bad habit is about pleasure, you'll want to add one or more activities that add *pleasure* to your life. That will boost your dopamine levels. When dopamine goes up, you get that boost of excitement and reward your brain wanted.

Of course, we all need serotonin *and* dopamine to feel great. So you might as well add an activity that fills you with *peace* — like meditation or drinking tea — and one that fills you with *pleasure* — like that kickboxing class set to loud music or learning how to cook a healthy new recipe. Think of one activity that would add each of the following to your life…

Activities or healthy foods that fill me with *peace* are:

_____

Activities or healthy foods that add *pleasure* to my life are:

_____

Every time you are tempted to have a reunion with a bad habit, say hello to one of these healthy ones instead. By training your brain this way, these new routines will become your new, instinctual go-to rituals.

3. BE HAPPY

Chapter 23

Find Love Again

Life on the Monkey Bars

*Getting over a painful experience is much like crossing
monkey bars. You have to let go at some point
in order to move forward.*
~Author Unknown

I was sitting on the landing at the top of the stairs, my heart pounding. I didn't know how I was going to make the next rent payment and the bills were piling up. I was ready to give up, but then I thought about the little girl sleeping soundly in the room next to me. I couldn't leave her. Not now. Not ever. I thought about her own spirit and a memory came back to me.

"Don't let go Mommy, hang on tight," yelled my daughter as I hoisted her on my shoulders to help her travel through the bars one by one. After the third round through the course, I felt a sudden numbing pain in my neck, so I decided it was finally time to teach my little five-year-old how to use the monkey bars on her own.

"No Mommy, no, I'm scared," she cried.

"You're scared because you don't know how to fall," I told her. Her little forehead wrinkled and her tiny brows came together in the way they always did when she thought Mommy was off her rocker just a little bit.

I continued, "If you learn how to fall, then you'll realize it wasn't so bad, so you won't be so scared to go through it. Look, let me show you." I jumped up on one of the bars and felt all of my 175 pounds pulling me towards the ground. I didn't realize how much more difficult it was to hang on with all the weight I was carrying, but I made an attempt to demonstrate. My fingers slipped off the bar, and I landed on my feet with a slight crouch to maintain my balance, arms extended in front of me.

"Let me try!" she shrilled with the eagerness of a five-year-old.

"You're smaller than I am, so I'm gonna keep my arms out in case you need to grab them on the way down," I assured her.

"No, Mommy! I want to do it on my own," she said with a pout, crossing her arms and stamping her foot.

She climbed the rungs and reached for the first bar. "Go ahead," I prompted, "throw your heart into it and your body will follow."

"I'm gonna fall… I'm gonna… Mommy… hold me!" she cried. I wanted to run to her, but I didn't move a muscle. I could feel the piercing stares of a group of mommies who were watching.

"You can do it. Let go if you have to and try to land on your feet."

Her hand slipped and she landed with a thud. She looked at me as if waiting to see what I was going to say. I heard some of the moms gasp and could only guess that their stares had now turned into glares. My thoughts raced: Was I a bad mother for letting her do that? Did they think it was child abuse? Was I going to be reported to CPS? Would they feel the same if she were a boy?

"Great job!" I cheered. "Was it that bad?"

"No, Mommy," she said with excitement as she dusted the wood chips off her backside.

"That's fantastic, sweetheart," I said. "And now that you know how to fall and pick yourself up, get back up again and start moving forward by swinging from one arm to the other. You just have to keep going."

"Okay, Mommy, but go away this time and let me try it on my own."

I resisted the urge to help once more and she swung herself with great fervor, her little hands moved from one bar to the next. She made it halfway when she called out, "Look, Mom! Look! Watch me… I'm gonna fall."

She beamed and I ran to her and swung her around.

"I did it! I did it!" she cried.

"You sure did, sweetheart! I'm so proud of you! You showed so much courage."

The memory was just what I needed. I stopped crying, got up from that landing at the top of the stairs and went to bed. Life hadn't turned out the way I planned. I had thrown my whole heart into a marriage that left me questioning my own self-worth and abilities. I had to embrace the challenge that life had given me, allow myself to fall, dust myself off, get back on that bar and keep going.

Tomorrow would be another day to try again... to put one hand in front of the other and keep moving forward.

—Jax Cortez—

Never Too Old

For 'mid old friends, tried and true,
Once more we our youth renewed.
~Author Unknown

My heart was racing as I put down the phone. What was I thinking? A male friend at my age? I scarcely knew what to say when my grandson asked me, "Grandma, do you have a boyfriend?" Yet, I could not deny that Ted made me feel special again. Talking to him on the phone stirred up feelings that I thought were dead. We had gone to high school together and then went very separate ways. Though we had never been close, a common bond of grief now brought us together with a new understanding of mature friendship.

We had both lost our mates.

We e-mailed each other almost every day. Eventually, gifts, cards, and flowers began to arrive. Then one day he showed up at my door and asked me out.

What would my children think? What would my friends say? My beloved husband of forty-eight years had passed away four years earlier. Though I loved him with every fiber of my being, I could not bring him back. It was time to let go. The past is lovely, filled with tender memories, but it is a desolate place to live.

I tearfully removed my wedding rings and put them away. It was not a one-time process. The action was repeated off and on for two years before I finally was able to be at peace with it.

"I have a decision to make," I'd explained to my children. "I can go on crying my life away or I can step out of my comfort zone and take a chance on living and possibly loving again."

Their immediate response had been, "Go for it! You have a right to be happy. Dad wouldn't want you to live in pain."

Another friend had said, "It is impossible to go forward if you are constantly looking back."

Even armed with that affirmation, the process of courting at seventy is a little like hunting with a dog that has lost his sense of smell. Ted had rented one of those hearse-sized, four-door trucks standing high off the ground. He apologized for the obvious overkill of the size of the vehicle, but it was all that was available from the local car rental. He gallantly opened the door and watched in painful silence as I struggled to make the leap inside. He flailed his arms at my clumsy attempt to get lift off, not knowing quite where to put his hands to boost me in.

Once inside we sat quietly trying to regain our dignity.

As we drove down the freeway to the nearest big city, where we planned to dine in style, I began to ponder the wisdom of riding in a vehicle with a guy who mentioned that he was considering cataract surgery. It was no comfort that he was still wearing the bright yellow sunglasses that covered most of his face, even though it was dark outside. I discreetly suggested that we might be just as well served by dining at a restaurant close by.

He readily agreed, though it meant that the place would be full of locals, all curious to see who the widow woman was with, who he was related to, and why he was in town. Ted put up with all the gawking and probing with good-natured humor. I guess he thought no one could really see him behind those glasses and by the time they had him figured out he would be out of town. To his credit, he must have decided that I was worth the scrutiny, because he was back the next day and every day until he had to fly home.

We discussed many important topics, such as long-term health care plans, retirement funds, children, grandchildren, religion, politics — and fiber. We decided that love is not exclusive. It has many facets. It expands to fill the expectations put upon it and rather than diminish the past, embraces it.

He likes documentaries. I like feature films. He likes fish. I like steak. I am the land. He is the sea. There is much to learn, much to process, and much to gain. We have only begun this new journey, but this I can tell you: Love at any age is sweet.

— Kay Thomann —

Dr. Mike...

Do you relate to Jax's story? Are you ready to dust yourself off after a relationship or marriage that didn't work out?

Or have you already opened a second chapter—like Kay?

Perhaps it's scary to think about starting this process all over again. Whether you're newly single, widowed, or just hesitant to take that first step, there are a few things to keep in mind when it comes to this incredible journey we call love.

They say a lot of things about love. It's patient. It's kind. It lifts you up where you belong.

When most people think of love, they see a fresh-faced couple in their twenties and a picture-perfect wedding. Yet that's just *one* of the many ways that love can appear.

Like the best things in life, love is complex. Don't pigeonhole love. Sometimes love will leave you dusty-bottomed—like Jax's daughter falling off the monkey bars. Her daughter learned from her mistake.

In that moment, Jax realized she could be like her daughter. The monkey bars were a metaphor for her love life. Jax's daughter was her inspiration. Instead of beating herself up over her past, what would her life be like if she just learned from her fall and then got back up? Remember those Sammy Cahn lyrics most famously sung by Frank Sinatra? *Love is lovelier the second time around, just as wonderful with both feet on the ground.*

Too often, we spend years lying on the ground. Sometimes, it's almost like we're rolling around in the dirt instead of dusting ourselves off.

It's healthy to avoid jumping right into a relationship the month after a long marriage has ended. But after a reasonable amount of time has passed, it's time to "get back on that horse."

If you don't, you can start to feel insecure, unworthy, and even guilty. If you spend too much time off that horse, it may even feel overwhelming to get back on. That's normal. I'll help you to train your brain to make it feel easier.

When it comes to love, remember that ups and downs are the

nature of the beast. One day, you're on top of the world. The next, you reach for that rung but fall to the ground. Love requires you to accept this as part of the potentially-rewarding deal.

Your part of the bargain: take the risk that you could potentially get hurt, do things that make you uncomfortable, and potentially get your heart broken. The cost of entry is high, but so is the jackpot. If love were a lottery, it would be a Powerball.

Love can change your whole life. Are you willing to roll the dice? Or, would you rather play it safe? Get in the game, or stay on the sidelines. The choice is yours.

If you decide to go on this journey, you will learn so many things about yourself. Love can be the greatest teacher you will ever know. Your partner-to-be will likely trigger unresolved issues in you.

Good news: you'll have the opportunity to "finish" your "unfinished business." Abandonment, daddy issues, fear of intimacy, and all those other psych 101 classics.

If a relationship doesn't work out, you learn what you *don't* want in a relationship. Sometimes, that is a really important lesson.

It's a lesson that Jax learned. Instead of holding onto anger, release it. Thank your ex for that lesson. Every relationship we are in teaches us what we *want* and what we *don't* want. Heed that lesson, and go on to create a better, deeper relationship the next time around.

Kay learned something, too. She had to break free from those love-blocking beliefs.

A love-blocking belief usually is some version of this. *I'm too ___ for love.* In Kay's case, it was "old."

Do you have a love-blocking belief? How would you fill in that sentence?

Guess what. You're *never* too old for love. Love isn't ageist. Love isn't sexist or sizeist, either.

In fact, love does not discriminate against *any* group. Love is truly an "equal opportunity." Your age, race, religion, gender, appearance, or sexual orientation *does not matter* to love.

If the only people worthy of love were rich, straight, twenty-four-year-olds who looked like models, we'd have a *lot* of single people out there. If you happen to be all those things, that's wonderful. You deserve love. If you're not that lucky twenty-four-year-old, no matter, you deserve love, too, and you will find it.

You see, real love is truly universal.

Perhaps you have fears about what *other people* may say. Kay had them.

What would my children think? What would my friends say?

Perhaps Kay's children did have a tough time at first, but I'd guess they quickly came around when they realized how happy she was. People who truly love you just want you to be happy. And you *will* be happy, and a better version of yourself, too. Because in addition to helping you resolve some of those old issues, your new love will help to bring out the very best in you. That *new you* will make all the other people in your life happy, too!

Ted made Kay feel special again, and *all* human beings deserve to feel that — whether you're twenty-seven or seventy-seven. And Jax's next husband (he's out there) will make her feel that way, too.

So dust yourself off, reach for that next bar, open that next chapter, and go write your happy ending.

1. Change how you THINK

If it's time to "get back on that horse," then it's also time to banish the pitfall thought pattern **paralysis-analysis**.

The essence of this type of thinking stews in negative thoughts.

What if I create a dating profile and nobody messages me — and then *I just feel worse about myself? I might as well not even try.*

What if I tell him I have feelings for him... and he laughs in my face? Am I being crazy? I'll just continue to be his best friend — for the next ten years without saying anything... *while this continues to prevent me from being able to have feelings for anyone else.*

This type of churning blocks positive action, creating a state of paralysis. In this moment, you're like Jax's daughter on the monkey bars. Fear holds you back.

Don't let go Mommy, hang on tight... No Mommy, no, I'm scared.

Only you're not a little boy or girl anymore, are you? You are your own parent to your own inner child. It's up to you to train that brain of yours to open itself up to trying again.

Are you going to clutch the monkey bars in fear—refusing to reach for the next bar? Or, will you take a risk? Will you reach for that next bar—even if you fall?

There was certainly some **paralysis-analysis** Kay had to work through: *My heart was racing as I put down the phone. What was I thinking? A male friend at my age? What would my children think? What would my friends say? My beloved husband of forty-eight years had passed away four years earlier. Though I loved him with every fiber of my being, I could not bring him back. It was time to let go.*

And there it is. That moment. Kay was ready to take that leap of faith. She had to reach for the next rung on the monkey bars. Will you?

Feel that moment when you're suspended in mid-air, not knowing if your hand is going to connect with the next bar. Oh, the rush. The adrenaline! Lean into it. Don't avoid it. It's called love, and it could change your entire life.

Here's a brain-training exercise to help you extinguish **paralysis-analysis**. Kay thought, *What would my children think? What would my friends say?* That was Kay's thought. What's yours? Perhaps you have your eye on someone. Or, perhaps you're scared to get back in the game at all. Maybe you've never been in love, and the whole idea of dating scares you. No matter which boat you're in, you can train your brain to invite more love into your life.

The first step in this exercise is to say the thought out loud. Your second step is to write it down. When we acknowledge **paralysis-analysis** and its irrational and momentum-blocking thoughts, it helps to take the air out of its sails. This exercise helps your brain see that these thoughts may be too extreme or a bit out of touch with reality.

You see, **paralysis-analysis** is busy chewing on all the would-be's, the what-if's, the what-could-go-wrong's. They spin them around and around in your head like a washing machine that's stuck in the "on" position.

My **paralysis-analysis** thought that blocks love and keeps me stuck is:

_____

_____

_____

2. Change how you ACT

As you already know, paralysis and analysis go hand in hand. You chew on those naysaying thoughts, and then it becomes hard to move forward. The longer you delay taking that first step, the more those negative what-if's start to pile up… and so on and so forth.

Thus, the most potent antidote to **paralysis-analysis** is action. This will help you to extinguish that thought you wrote in the section above.

I want you to imagine that you are on the monkey bars of love. Wherever you are on that playground, it's now time for you to reach for that next rung. You don't have to get to the end of the bars today. You just have to figure out what that next rung looks like for *you*.

If you've never been in a relationship, maybe that means creating an online dating profile.

If you're newly single, maybe that means going on that blind date your best friend has been trying to set you up on for years.

If you're a widow and have been keeping your new relationship a secret, maybe that means telling your best friend about it.

This *action* is the antidote to **paralysis-analysis**, because you're no longer stuck.

It will help you gather *contrary evidence* from your own life experience. This will prove to yourself that the love-blocking thought you wrote in the section above isn't true.

It's time to take action to invite love into your life.

The *action* that will take me to the next rung on my own "monkey bars" of love is to:

_____

_____

_____

Once you have taken this action, circle back to that **paralysis-analysis**, love-blocking thought you wrote in the section above. How did taking this *action* help you to prove that this love-blocking thought wasn't true?

_____

_____

_____

Whether your action resulted in your next love, or it just helped you break out of your paralysis, what was the positive outcome of your attempt?

_____

_____

_____

3. BE HAPPY

Afterword
Look What You've Accomplished

H ow did you like your tour of everything your incredible brain can do for you? We harnessed the power of real-life personal Chicken Soup for the Soul stories and common-sense rational brain training. You learned how to address the problem areas in your life, by changing how you think about things, and then by changing your actions.

You read about the **seven common pitfall thought patterns** and how to strip them from your own thinking. You said goodbye to: **Paralysis-analysis**, **Permanence**, **Personalization**, **Pervasiveness**, **Pessimism**, **Polarization**, and thinking you're **Psychic**. And then, after you analyzed your thoughts and banished those negative ways of viewing your life, we trained your brain to act in your own best interest.

Look back at the questions you answered throughout the book. You'll see your voyage of self-discovery as you confronted your pitfall thoughts head on and came up with productive solutions that really worked. Step by step, you taught your brain how to use cognitive behavioral therapy (CBT) to solve your own problems. You learned how to use the stories of other people like you, combined with simple steps to retrain your brain and guided journaling to change the way you think and act. You found your path to happiness.

Go back and re-read the chapters you need the most. Study what you wrote and feel free to edit those journal entries… because you're already a different person. You're the next version of yourself.

Let's recap how you trained your brain to think, act, and be happy:

In Chapter 1, you learned some tips that work for overcoming depression and for internalizing the knowledge that it doesn't have to be a permanent condition.

In Chapter 2, we explained how you can train your brain to recognize all the blessings in your life, and how that gratitude can help you become more optimistic.

Chapter 3 showed you how to put stressful things in perspective, with some easy-to-implement tips that will help bring you back to a place of calm.

That place of calm may help you as you learn tips that work for weight loss in Chapter 4, including how to train your brain to recognize when you're eating for the wrong reasons.

In Chapter 5, you learned how to lovingly impose structure and limits on your children, finding that sweet spot between being too permissive and too authoritarian.

You or someone you love may be living with disabilities or chronic illness, and Chapter 6 showed you how to abandon pessimism, choose hope, and focus on the positive.

Abandoning despair and healing from abuse means remembering not to take it personally, and Chapter 7 taught you how to shed that past and find your way forward.

You learned how to reduce your stress levels and abandon an unrealistic, unhealthy goal in Chapter 8, when you realized that you don't have to be perfect

After you gave yourself that break, you learned one of the most important life skills there is in Chapter 9—how to use the power of forgiveness to liberate yourself from past hurts.

Shedding those feelings of pessimism and permanence is key to moving forward, and you read about that in Chapter 10, where we talked about thriving after cancer.

One key to happiness is to realize that bad things don't have to be permanent, so Chapter 11 was about moving on and reclaiming your life after hardships and disappointments.

In Chapter 12, you learned easy-to-implement tips for overcoming insomnia that will help you sink into restful, restorative sleep every night, and stay that way till morning.

If you're like most people, you or someone close to you is living in a blended family, and in Chapter 13 you learned strategies that work for creating a happy stepfamily.

If you're lucky, you'll be in the difficult, but rewarding, position of caring for elderly parents one day. You learned how to care for yourself at the same time in Chapter 14.

Most of us have at least one silly fear, or a full-blown phobia, and in Chapter 15 you learned how to take ten baby steps to vanquish that anxiety, slowly but surely.

You learned how to take steps toward making healthy choices for your body in Chapter 16, where you realized you are making these choices for *all* the people you love.

And in Chapter 17, you learned how to enjoy that empty nest even when all those people you love have flown off to pursue their adult lives, the ones you wanted for them.

Chapter 18 taught you how to appreciate less stuff and liberate yourself from too much spending, and even how to overcome that shopping addiction.

And in Chapter 19, you learned how to train your brain to use the power of positive thinking by using affirmations to turn pessimism into optimism.

Grieving can feel like a deep, black hole and in Chapter 20 you learned how to climb the ladder to recovery step by step by making a plan for emerging into your new life.

In Chapter 21, you learned how to keep the love alive, by not assuming the other person knows what you're thinking, and by deliberately and openly communicating.

If you're one of the 100% of us who have a bad habit or two, you learned how to vanquish that behavior in Chapter 22, by replacing it with a different — healthy — one.

And finally, in Chapter 23, you learned how to open yourself up to the possibility of finding love again after a failed relationship or the loss of your (first) soul mate.

Change doesn't happen overnight, but every little step makes a difference, and you CAN train your brain to use the tips in this book. Each chapter offered you an opportunity to address one key area of your life, and to learn how to THINK differently, ACT in your best interests, and BE HAPPY.

Your very powerful and flexible brain is built to make these changes happen for you, to create a loving, productive life full of people, activities, and things that make you happy. Because, as Thomas Edison said, "If we all did the things we are capable of doing, we would literally astound ourselves."

You should be very proud of yourself. You changed your thoughts. You changed your actions. Now, stay happy.

Meet Our Contributors

Monica A. Andermann lives and writes on Long Island where she shares a home with her husband and their little tabby, Samson. Her work has been included in such publications as *Woman's World*, *The Secret Place* and *Guideposts* as well as many other *Chicken Soup for the Soul* titles.

Elizabeth Atwater's intense love for books and storytelling as a very young child naturally developed into a love of writing. She has yet to suffer from the dreaded writer's block. Give her a little extra time and solitude, and the words will flow from her mind like a happily singing brook on a mountainside.

Barbara Burris studied creative writing at University of Wisconsin-Madison. She loves to read, paint and take endless photographs of the countryside around her. She is currently at work on her mother-in-law's biography and a series of autobiographical essays about cottage life.

Barbara Carpenter maintains the blog becblog.com, and a site where episodes of an on-going drama appear: bectales.com. This is her fifth contribution to the *Chicken Soup for the Soul* series. She is passionate about her two children, four grandchildren, one great-grandson and her husband of fifty-two years. Life is good.

Jax Cortez is a former schoolteacher with a master's degree in Education turned freelance writer, blogger, and indie author. She is happily married to her crime-fighting husband and adores her rambunctious little girl. She enjoys writing stories of empowerment and practicing the self-defense system of Krav Maga.

Gwen Daye is a wife, homemaker, dog rescuer, and parent of two teenagers, and is so excited to have her third piece published in the *Chicken Soup for the Soul* series!

Beth DiCola self-published *Homeseekers: Flight to the Mountain* under her maiden name, S.B. Broshar. She is sixty-eight years old and discovering a different life through writing. She is currently working on the continuing story in her second novel and is a member of a local writers' group. E-mail her at diuncola@gmail.com.

David Dow is a stroke survivor, speaker, and co-author of *Healing the Broken Brain*. He's a nonprofit founder dedicated to helping other stroke survivors. His life story of healing and recovery has been featured in *People* magazine and on *The Doctors*. David makes his home in North Carolina.

Drema Sizemore Drudge is a Spalding University MFA graduate. She is an agented author who primarily writes fiction about art. Drema and her husband Barry live in Indiana. Read more about her at dremadrudge.com.

Melissa Ford is the author of the award-winning website Stirrup Queens (www.stirrup-queens.com), as well as the novel *Life from Scratch*. Melissa completed her MFA at the University of Massachusetts. She lives in Washington, DC, with her writer husband, Joshua, and their twins.

Shannon Francklin lives in Atlanta, GA with her husband Michael and Kira. She is a full-time mother and enjoys her soccer mom life. Shannon and Michael are grateful to God and Dr. Andrew Toledo, her IVF doctor, for giving them Kira. Shannon would like to thank her wonderful friend Caroline Updyke for writing this story.

Karen Frazier is a freelance writer and author. Her books cover multiple topics, including spirituality, health and nutrition, and cooking. She is married and has a college-age son, teenaged stepson, four dogs, and a cat. She lives in the Pacific Northwest with her husband.

Jennifer Gauthier is currently studying Social Services at Laurentian University. She plans to one day work with children and teenagers. Jennifer could not have made it this far without the help of her mother Lynn, Janyk, Anne, Helene and her grandmothers: Gillette and Rachelle. E-mail her at jengauthier@hotmail.com.

Jenna Glatzer is the bestselling author or ghostwriter of more than twenty-five books. She is Céline Dion's authorized biographer and the author of a Marilyn Monroe biography authorized by her estate. Jenna has the most wonderful eight-year-old daughter. Learn more at www.jennaglatzer.com.

Judythe Guarnera connects with people through her volunteer work as a mediator and through her writing. Her first novel, *Twenty-Nine Sneezes*, is in the final editing stage. She has been published in a variety of venues, including a previous Chicken Soup for the Soul anthology.

Cara Holman is thankful that her cancer diagnosis three years ago led her to join a writing group, rekindling her writing aspirations. She lives in Portland, Oregon with her husband and the youngest of their three children. Her writings have appeared online, in an anthology and on her blog: http://caraholman.wordpress.com.

Deanna Ingalls teaches kindergarten in Alabama. She would like to thank her husband for encouraging her to follow her dreams and her three children for being the inspiration for her writing. This is her second story published in the *Chicken Soup for the Soul* series. E-mail her at teachingauthor@gmail.com.

April Knight is proud to be a contributor to the *Chicken Soup for the Soul* series. She is currently writing romance novels for people over fifty. April spends her days riding horses and her nights writing mystery novels. She also writes a newspaper column and novels under her tribal name Crying Wind Hummingbird.

Kathleen Kohler writes stories about the ups and downs of family life for numerous magazines and anthologies. She and her husband live in the Pacific Northwest, and have three children and seven grandchildren. Visit www.kathleenkohler.com to read more of her articles or enter her latest drawing.

Jennifer Lawler is a writer in the Midwest, focusing on martial arts and empowerment issues. Her website is www.jenniferlawler.com.

Cindy Martin has a BRE degree, is a writer and speaker and the mother of two special needs children. She enjoys traveling, being with her family and acreage living. Cindy is founder of Step by Step Consulting, designed to help families of special needs children. Learn more at www.lifemeetsreality.com.

Toni L. Martin is a programmer-analyst by day and a group leader for the Florida Writers Association by night. Both are sedentary jobs. Her personal trainer, a 10-pound Italian Greyhound, does his best to keep her in shape in her spare time.

Lauren Nevins holds a BA in Psychology from Stony Brook University and a Masters in Social Work from Adelphi University. Lauren enjoys spending time with her family and dreams of one day publishing her memoirs. Lauren can be reached via e-mail at lenswriter@yahoo.com.

Carla O'Brien has not attempted the sport of running. Her days are spent chasing a crawling baby and a toddler with sticky hands. She enjoys meeting new people and working as a hotel guest service agent. You will still find her, with the girls, cheering Dad on from the sidelines.

Lou Prudhomme is a teacher, writer, grief counselor, and volunteer chaplain with a Bachelor of Arts and a master's degree from the University of Minnesota Duluth. She is the mother of four and grandmother to fifteen, with homes in Minnesota and Florida. No day is ever long enough to do all that she loves to do.

Johanna Richardson lost her mother, stepdad, mother-in-law and grandmother-in-law to dementia. She received her master's degree from the University of San Francisco. Johanna adores being with her husband and family. She loves reading, music, film, traveling and serving as Peer Volunteer for the national Alzheimer's Association.

Monique Gabrielle Salazar holds a degree in Political Science and is an active member of the Kansas City arts community. She owns a suit accessories business that provides unique and one-of-a-kind stylish pieces. She enjoys making music, performing, painting, sculpting and above all, writing. E-mail her at mgswrites@gmail.com.

Isaac Saul is a political reporter and columnist at the positive news website *A Plus*. He was born just north of Philadelphia and went to school at the University of Pittsburgh. He is a national champion ultimate Frisbee player, an avid traveler, and a political junkie. You can find him on Twitter @Ike_Saul.

Heather Schichtel is a freelance writer and special needs advocate. All of the inspiration for the story in this book came from her sweet daughter who is missed every day. She thanks her husband, family and an incredible group of friends for constant love and support. You can follow Heather at www.samsmom-heathers.blogspot.com.

Gina Tate is a stay-at-home mom of three. She enjoys cooking, learning new healthy recipes, sipping coffee with friends, and being active with her kids. Gina graduated from Bible college at Faith School of Theology in Charleston, ME and enjoys teaching from the Bible to kids, teens, and adults.

Kay Thomann is a newlywed. She and her new husband enjoy summers in Alaska and winters in Iowa, with intermittent trips south.

She continues to write stories to entertain and inspire her readers and is grateful to have been published in *Chicken Soup for the Soul: From Lemons to Lemonade*.

Marla H. Thurman lives in Signal Mountain, Tennessee, with her dogs Oreo and Sleeper. She is currently working on draft four of her memoirs. Her dream is that one day her favorite author, Pat Conroy, will ask for her autograph.

Marilyn Turk received her B.A. degree in journalism from LSU and has been published in *Guideposts*, *The Upper Room*, *Clubhouse Jr.*, *Coastal Christian Family*, and *Chicken Soup for the Soul*. She and husband Chuck enjoy fishing and playing tennis. She is writing a Christian historical novel. Learn more at Pathwayheart.com.

In 2006, **Aimée L. Urban** was named a top 40 business professional under 40 and one of PA's Best 50 Women in Business in 2007. She serves on the Workforce Investment Board and is a past president of the American Business Women's Association. Aimée's greatest passions in life are her husband, two children and three dogs. E-mail her at aimée.urban@adeccona.com.

Denise Valuk lives and writes in San Antonio, TX, while homeschooling her three boys. Her writing experiences include *Guideposts*, *Mysterious Ways* and *Chicken Soup for the Soul: Touched by an Angel*. Denise spends her free time hiking through Texas with her boys. Contact her through her website at www.denisevaluk.com.

Kristin Viola is a Los Angeles-based writer who has contributed to the *Los Angeles Times*, Zagat, *Angeleno* and other publications. Aside from running, she loves traveling, reading and a good glass of wine. E-mail her at kjviola@gmail.com.

Valerie Whisenand, writing as Valerie Hansen, is the author of many Christian novels. When she moved to the Ozarks, she found her calling as well as a beautiful atmosphere filled with loving, caring people. She's been married to her high school sweetheart for a gazillion years! E-mail her at val@valeriehansen.com.

Laura Wisniewski is a registered nurse, motivational speaker, and freelance writer. She is a training specialist for a large healthcare system on the west coast of Florida. Her hobbies include biking, kayaking, sailing and grandparenting. E-mail her at laura@nursingvoice.com.

Dallas Woodburn has written fiction and nonfiction for a variety of publications including the *Nashville Review*, the *Los Angeles Times*, and *Louisiana Literature*. Her short story collection was a finalist for the Flannery O'Connor Award for Short Fiction. Connect with her at writeonbooks.org and daybydaymasterpiece.com.

Susan Kimmel Wright lives in a western Pennsylvania farmhouse with her husband and an ever-changing assortment of animals and adult children. She has authored three children's mystery novels and has had many stories published in the *Chicken Soup for the Soul* series. E-mail her at wereallwright@gmail.com.

Pauline Youd is the author of children's Bible story books, magazine articles, and devotions for both adults and children. Her hobbies include musical comedy theater. Pauline tutors reading and writing, and teaches Sunday school. She lives in California with her husband, Bill, and one very fluffy cat.

All bios were current as of the time the stories were originally published by Chicken Soup for the Soul.

Meet Our Authors
Amy Newmark &
Dr. Mike Dow

Amy Newmark is the bestselling author, editor-in-chief, and publisher of the *Chicken Soup for the Soul* book series. Since 2008, she has published more than 150 new books, most of them national bestsellers in the U.S. and Canada, more than doubling the number of Chicken Soup for the Soul titles in print today. She is also the author of *Simply Happy*, a crash course in Chicken Soup for the Soul advice and wisdom that is filled with easy-to-implement, practical tips for enjoying a better life.

Amy is credited with revitalizing the Chicken Soup for the Soul brand, which has been a publishing industry phenomenon since the first book came out in 1993. By compiling inspirational and aspirational true stories curated from ordinary people who have had extraordinary experiences, Amy has kept the twenty-five-year-old Chicken Soup for

the Soul brand fresh and relevant.

Amy graduated *magna cum laude* from Harvard University where she majored in Portuguese and minored in French. She then embarked on a three-decade career as a Wall Street analyst, a hedge fund manager, and a corporate executive in the technology field. She is a Chartered Financial Analyst.

Her return to literary pursuits was inevitable, as her honors thesis in college involved traveling throughout Brazil's impoverished northeast region, collecting stories from regular people. She is delighted to have come full circle in her writing career — from collecting stories "from the people" in Brazil as a twenty-year-old to, three decades later, collecting stories "from the people" for Chicken Soup for the Soul.

When Amy and her husband Bill, the CEO of Chicken Soup for the Soul, are not working, they are visiting their four grown children and their first grandchild.

Follow Amy on Twitter @amynewmark. Listen to her free podcast, Chicken Soup for the Soul with Amy Newmark on Apple Podcasts, Google Play, the Podcasts app on iPhone, or by using your favorite podcast app on other devices.

Dr. Mike Dow, Psy.D., Ph.D., is a New York Times bestselling author and America's go-to therapist. His books have been published in several different languages and are bestsellers in Europe and Asia.

As a brain health, addiction, and relationship expert, Dr. Mike has hosted shows on TLC, VH1, E!, Investigation Discovery, and Logo. He is part of Dr. Oz's core team of experts, a recurring guest cohost on *The Doctors*, and has made regular appearances on *Today*, *Rachael Ray*, *Wendy Williams*, *Meredith Vieira*, *Ricki Lake*, *Nancy Grace*, and *Dr. Drew on Call*. You've also seen him as a therapist on *Life With La Toya* and *Ben and Lauren: Happily Ever After*.

Inspired by his brother who suffered a massive stroke when he was ten years old, Dr. Mike made it his personal mission to help people heal their brains. He co-wrote a book with his brother, *Healing the Broken Brain*, which has been called "Stroke Recovery 101."

Dr. Mike's other books include *Diet Rehab*, *The Brain Fog Fix*, *Heal*

Your Drained Brain, and *Your Subconscious Brain Can Change Your Life*.

His own "aha moment" was when he realized that helping others could be his full-time job instead of an extracurricular activity. Dr. Mike began his career working with adolescent survivors of abuse for the Los Angeles Department of Mental Health.

Dr. Mike has an M.S. in Marriage and Family Therapy, a Doctorate (Psy.D.) in Psychology, and a second Doctorate (Ph.D.) in Clinical Sexology. He also has post-doctoral education in neurofeedback, psychopharmacology, and clinical hypnosis. He is a graduate of USC where he was a Presidential Scholar.

You'll usually see him walking two very cute rescue dogs around Los Angeles. When his partner Dr. Chris isn't on the night shift in the emergency room, he's there, too. Dr. Mike hangs out a lot on Facebook and Instagram @drmikedow.

Sharing Happiness, Inspiration, and Hope

Real people sharing real stories, every day, all over the world. In 2007, *USA Today* named *Chicken Soup for the Soul* one of the five most memorable books in the last quarter-century. With over 100 million books sold to date in the U.S. and Canada alone, more than 250 titles in print, and translations into nearly fifty languages, "chicken soup for the soul®" is one of the world's best-known phrases.

Today, twenty-five years after we first began sharing happiness, inspiration and hope through our books, we continue to delight our readers with new titles, but have also evolved beyond the bookstore with super premium pet food, television shows, podcasts, positive journalism from aplus.com, movies and TV shows on the Popcornflix app, and licensed products, all revolving around true stories, as we continue "changing the world one story at a time®." Thanks for reading!

Changing your life one story at a time®
www.chickensoup.com